STUDIES ON ETHNIC GROUPS IN CHINA

STEVAN HARRELL, Editor

Lijiang

Stories

SHAMANS, TAXI DRIVERS,

AND RUNAWAY BRIDES IN

REFORM-ERA CHINA

EMILY CHAO

A China Program Book

UNIVERSITY OF WASHINGTON PRESS

Seattle and London

cv

This book is supported in part by the China Studies Program, a division of the Henry M. Jackson School of International Studies at the University of Washington. Additional support is provided by the Donald R. Ellegood International Publications Endowment.

© 2012 by the University of Washington Press
Printed and bound in the United States of America
Designed by Richard Hendel
Composed in Quadraat and Aller types
Quadraat type design by Fred Smeijers
Aller typeface designed by Dalton Maag Ltd
16 15 14 13 12 5 4 3 2 1

University of Washington Press
PO Box 50096, Seattle, WA 98145, USA
www.washington.edu/uwpress

Library of Congress Cataloging-in-Publication Data
Chao, Emily.
Lijiang stories : shamans, taxi drivers, and runaway brides in reform-era China / by Emily Chao.
p. cm.—(Studies on ethnic groups in china)
Includes bibliographical references and index.
ISBN 978-0-295-99222-8 (cloth : alk. paper)
ISBN 978-0-295-99223-5 (pbk : alk. paper)
1. Naxi (Chinese people)—China—Lijiang Shi—
Government relations. 2. Naxi (Chinese people)—
China—Lijiang Shi—Economic conditions. 3. Naxi
(Chinese people)—China—Lijiang Shi—Social life and
customs. 4. Post-communisim—China—Lijiang Shi.
5. Lijiang Shi (China)—Ethnic relations. 6. Lijiang Shi
(China)—Social conditions. I. Title.
DS731.N39C43 2012   305.895'4—dc23   2012018966

FOR PHIL

CONTENTS

FOREWORD

As China gets more and more connected with the rest of the world, and absorbs and adapts more and more of today's popular culture, it remains a multiethnic and multinational country. But its ways of being multiethnic have changed greatly in the three decades and more since the beginning of the Reform Era in 1980. As differences between ethnic groups in their everyday economic and cultural practices recede, as everybody learns the standard Chinese language, as members of minority groups increasingly pursue secondary and higher education and take professional and technical jobs, at the same time China's ethnic diversity is celebrated as never before, in the form of specific cultural practices standardized, packaged, staged, and sold for tourists and others in a consumer economy.

For more than two thirds of those three decades of transformation, Emily Chao has been working in one particularly interesting corner of the Chinese map, observing and analyzing the changing contours of multiethnicity in Lijiang, Yunnan. Lijiang is where the indigenous Naxi people have been adapting to various sorts of interaction with states ruled from China since the Ming Dynasty, and where they have continued to adapt, initially, to the transformation from collective to individual and from planned to market economy; then to a major earthquake; and in the most recent decade and a half, to the incursions of Chinese and global mass culture in the form of media, tourism, and economic growth.

Out of the changing patterns of ethnic interaction and representation, Professor Chao has fashioned stories. And the first thing to notice about this delightful book is how good, how compelling the stories are. The Maoist shaman, the reluctant bride-snatcher, the ritual huckster, and the purportedly stinky cabbie are characters out of an ethnic *Decameron* or *Canterbury Tales*, who happen to play their roles in late twentieth- and early twenty-first-century Lijiang but would seem as implausible but still very real as they would have in medieval Tuscany or South England.

But beyond their entertainment value, there are lessons to be learned from these stories. First, like ethnicity itself, ethnic culture is, as Chao says, "a discursive creation." Naxi culture has not only been refashioned for tourists, including real fashionistas, but it has also been re-interpreted on a more scholarly level. Such things as Dongba ritual and bride-snatching, which Chao demonstrates to have been phenomena of particular times and places, have become in the current discourse emblems of the Naxi *minzu*, or "nationality," as a whole. In doing so, they perhaps reinforce the idea of the existence of that *minzu* as an objective fact, when it too is a creation of a historically situated discourse of nation-building, itself changing in form as one Beijing-centric civilizing project has replaced another over the years.

Second, whatever limits exist to the commercialization of culture, busting through them seems, like almost everything else in today's China, to be a matter of price. A musician of Han origin takes a musical genre originally from Fujian and promotes it as Naxi culture, something that Naxi people resent until it starts bringing them national renown and increases in touristic income. If you don't like it, you can complain, and of course people do. But at the same time, busting through the limits doesn't eliminate them altogether, and when Naxi women perhaps gain a little too much economic autonomy by driving late-night cabs, they end up stigmatized with "fox-stench," something borrowed from Chinese folklore.

Third, even as Mao Zedong's thoughts are safely rendered irrelevant by today's booming market economy and alarming socioeconomic inequality and his image reduced to a few iconic, ironic statues and memorabilia of what were probably not actually the good old days, his dictum about "making the past serve the present" has never been truer or more useful. It may be impossible to "rescue history from the *minzu*," to paraphrase Prasenjit Duara, but Chao's stories and her analysis make it very clear just how the politics of *minzu* captured the history of the nation.

So, to the reader, enjoy these stories, revel in them, marvel at their complexity, their unexpected twists, and the way they tangle the past and the present into a knot of paradox. But more than that, gain from these stories a vivid example of just how complex the reality of ethnic group, nation, multiethnic state, and global culture has become in our current century, and how ethnography, born out of a colonial project to document the exotic, still helps us view and understand a world in which the faraway seems less and less exotic and more like a different-colored version of home.

STEVAN HARRELL
July 2012

ACKNOWLEDGMENTS

Writing a book is both a solitary and a collective project. There are many people who contributed to this work, either through their own inspirational scholarship and teaching or through reading, commenting, and discussing sections of this manuscript.

I wish to thank Aihwa Ong, Sherry Ortner, and the late Norma Diamond, all teachers who read and commented on earlier versions of this work. China colleagues in other institutions—Ann Anagnost, Melissa Brown, Myron Cohen, Nicole Constable, Laurel Kendall, Charlene Makley, Chas McKhann, Beth Notar, Tim Oakes, Louisa Schein—deserve my appreciation for helpful conversations and feedback on papers that have made their way into this book. Sydney White, whose research stay in Lijiang partially overlapped with mine, deserves profuse thanks for her humor, navigational assistance, and scholarly insight.

My research would not have been possible without the guidance and support of colleagues at the Yunnan Academy of Social Sciences (Yunnan Shehui Kexueyuan)—He Yaohua, Guo Dalie, the late He Zhiwu, and particularly Yang Fuquan. I thank them for many informative conversations and for introducing me to Naxi Studies. I also wish to thank Zhao Yintang for sharing her research on Naxi women and for conversations about gender in Lijiang's Old Town.

I am grateful to *Cultural Anthropology* and *Modern China* for permitting me to reproduce versions of articles first published in their journals. I additionally thank the Institute for East Asian Studies at the University of California, Berkeley, for allowing me to include a portion of an article originally published in *Negotiating Ethnicities in China and Taiwan*. The Harvard-Yenching Library generously granted permission to use an image from the *Road to Heaven* (Hazhipi), a Naxi scroll originally collected by Joseph Rock, for the book's cover.

I am greatly indebted to my fine colleagues at the Dongba Cultural Research Institute (Dongba Wenhua Yanjiusuo), who shared their knowledge and views with me over the years. I am grateful to the late He Wanbao, Li Jingsheng, He Fayuan, Zhao Shihong, Li Lifen, Wang Shiying, He Qingyuan, Li Ying, He Liming, He Pingzhen, He Baoling, and the late Xi Yuhua. In addition to their willingness to answer an endless number of questions, they introduced me to their relatives and shared their research and scholarly insights with me over the course of some twenty years. Li Ying, Xi Yuhua, and Li Lifen deserve particular gratitude for accompanying me on excursions at different times, often under difficult conditions, while Li Ying provided assistance with Naxi pinyin translations for this book and Li Lifen offered essential intellectual and practical support during the final stages of my research. I also thank He Chunyi, Li Shaojun, He Liangqing, and "Xiao He" for accompanying me during other periods of fieldwork. In East Wind and Pagoda Hill villages, He Yuquan and He Shiwen provided generous hospitality and invaluable local knowledge that made my fieldwork possible. I cannot thank them enough. Xuan Haitao, Xuan Songtao, and Xuan Xiaowen hosted many dinners in their Beimenpo home and shared valuable insights about changes in Lijiang. I thank Zhou Yongfu and Mu Zhen for their hospitality and support in Kunming.

I owe a depth of gratitude to the *dongba* masters at the Dongba Cultural Research Institute (who have all passed away)—He Kaichiang, He Jigui, and He Shicheng—for generously sharing their humor, stories, and alternative interpretations of events over many evening meals at the institute.

Stevan Harrell generously provided me with detailed comments on the entire manuscript. I greatly appreciate his informed suggestions and support of this project. At the University of Washington Press, Lorri Hagman's persistence and enthusiasm for this book were key to its conception. Laura Iwasaki and Marilyn Trueblood provided valuable editorial assistance.

The Committee on Scholarly Communication with China (formerly the Committee on Scholarly Communication with the People's Republic of China) and the Wenner-Gren Foundation generously funded my initial field research in the early 1990s. I am also indebted to the University of California, Berkeley, for providing me with a postdoctoral fellowship that enabled me to rethink my original research. Pitzer College granted me generous sabbaticals, as well as supplied funding for research and writing, which have been invaluable.

For their support as friends and colleagues, I thank Aileen Alfandary, Bao Jiemin, Susan Blum, Stephanie Bower, Grace Chen, Angelina Chin, Cynthia Humes, Marilyn Chapin Massey, Norma Rodriguez, and Arthur Rosenbaum. The completion of this book would not have been possible without the extraordinary encouragement and dedication of my wonderful colleagues Audrey Bilger and Zayn Kassam, who read and commented on multiple drafts of the entire manuscript.

I am grateful to family members—Hsiaotse Chao and Paohsuan Chao—for their assistance with questions of translation and their encouragement. I wish to thank my son, Max, for his sense of humor, which has always put things in perspective, and for living with a distracted parent for more than a year. I am immeasurably grateful to Phil Haft, my husband, who has been my greatest critic and advocate, for reading virtually every word I have written.

Finally, I wish to express my deep appreciation to the people of East Wind and Pagoda Hill villages and Lijiang Town for generously sharing their stories and views of the bewildering changes that have shaped their lives over the course of the past twenty-one years.

Lijiang Stories

FIG. I.1 Statue of two peasants facing a statue of Mao

I n the early 1990s, two important landmarks in Lijiang Town[1] faced each other across a large plaza bisected by the town's main road. One was an iconic statue of Chairman Mao, some forty-five feet high and set atop an imposing twenty-five-foot pedestal. Mao stood with his arm raised, his hand reaching outward and his fingers pointing toward the sky. The second landmark was a pair of statues: a peasant couple, the woman (in a Naxi sheepskin cape embroidered with stars) holding a bowl of grain and the man (with a wool hat characteristic of those worn in the mountains) with arms extended as if in greeting. Local lore was that these figures represented Lijiang's "common people" (laobaixing), who were begging Mao for more grain. According to the story told about the statues, Mao's response, indicated by the fingers on his upraised hand, was "You get only five liang" (a little more than half a pound).

By 2005, Mao's attention was no longer directed toward the peasants because those statues had been removed. Once a small market town catering to the numerous ethnic groups of northern Yunnan, Lijiang is the capital of Lijiang Autonomous Naxi County. Since the late 1990s, it has been transformed into a major site of national and international tourism. Town residents quipped that Mao's hand was raised to hail a taxi, but that he was too far from the curb to get one to notice him. Some residents joked that with the plaza crowded and bustling with people and the constant din of taxis honking their horns, now even the taxi-hailing Mao was trying to get out of town. Other residents appeared to disagree, however, saying that the pigeons roosting on top of his statue demonstrate that Mao, too, had become entrepreneurial and was raising birds for profit.

Unlike many towns and cities across China, in Lijiang Town—where there had been an underground Communist Party and the 1949 revolution was celebrated by crowds lining both sides of the streets—Mao's statue has not yet been removed. Imaginings of his subjectivity are still relevant to popular speculation, even if only for purposes of levity. A faded symbol of social collectivity, in the 1990s, his presence gave rise to critiques of austerity and hunger during the Maoist era. But in 2005, divergent views about Lijiang's new economy were expressed through alleged speculation about Mao's supposed pleasure or displeasure at what Lijiang had become.

By 2011, Mao's statue was not so anachronistic. Images of Mao in shops and souvenir stores could occasionally be found along with Cultural Revolution posters. Unlike their appearance in the late 1980s and early 1990s, when they were considered part of a second Mao cult,[2] these images are either used to attract tourists or represent the state campaign to promote "Red Culture" (Hong Wenhua): the songs, symbols, and ideology of the Maoist era intended to foster social stability, loyalty, and devotion to the Communist Party on the eve of its ninetieth birthday.

At dusk, the entrance to Lijiang's Old Town[3] becomes a narrow gauntlet of bars and nightclubs lined with hostesses dressed in tight-fitting silk gowns, or qipao, or perhaps exquisite fur hats and colorful ethnic attire, stationed next to male barkers. Under a nightclub's magenta spotlight, a young woman wearing Tibetan clothing sang about the delight of Tibetan girls assigned to wash the clothes of People's Liberation Army (PLA) soldiers. As she mimicked the gesture of washing laundry, her hips daintily swayed in rhythm with her song. In a neighboring bar, a robust young man, his bare chest revealed under a loosely worn, fur-trimmed Tibetan jacket, belted out a song about his gratitude to "the Communist Party without which there would be no new China." Red Culture could also be found at one of the few state-run stores, where towers of caked Pu'er tea framed by Cultural Revolution posters were incongruously displayed next to a small silver statue of the god of wealth (cai shen) holding a silver ingot.[4] The image seemed to symbolize a postsocialist Lijiang (from 1996 onward) in which there is no contradiction between the state's revival of Red Culture—its defense against the social instability created by decades of market reform—and its explicit faith in the "market economy" (shichang jingji) and celebration of wealth.

HISTORICAL SETTING

Drawing on fieldwork conducted between 1990 and 2011, this book focuses on how, amid the contradictions of the market economy, Lijiang residents have reimagined their culture and history. Lijiang City and the autonomous county are populated primarily by the Naxi, one of China's fifty-five minority

FIG. 1.3 Red Culture and the god of wealth

ethnic groups (*shaoshu minzu*). The Naxi are a Tibeto-Burman–speaking ethnic group with a written history dating from the Tang dynasty (618–907).

In the sense that my research is based on fieldwork conducted in two Naxi villages and Lijiang's Old Town, it is about the lives of people who categorize themselves, among other ways, as Naxi. I have strong reservations about further reifying the ethnic category "Naxi," for while some of its aspects are representative and popularly embraced, others are imagined and problematic. The following chapters, therefore, seek to depict—through the contextualization of narratives, events, and practices—the ways in which the complex interplay of state discourse and local agency has shaped gender, class, and ethnic identity.

CATEGORIZING THE ETHNIC

The Chinese state undertook its first post-1949 ethnic classification project (*minzu shibie*) in the 1950s, but it was not until the early 1980s that the state began heavily investing in the collection, editing, and translation into Chinese of the folk cultural materials of ethnic groups (*minzu*) (China White Paper 1999). Scholarly institutions and ethnic groups across China were enlisted to engage in projects of self-definition and promote their identities as "ethnic." Explanations for this intensification of ethnic expression tend to emphasize either the agency of the ethnic groups or the role of state orchestration.[5] While I am not seeking to discount the role of local agency in projects of ethnic definition, my analysis places emphasis on the discursive fields that reached beyond the ethnic groups themselves as critical to an understanding of this phenomenon.

This representation of ethnic categories coincided with the state's renarration of national identity, from the beginning of the reform era (roughly from the 1980s) and in terms of China being a multiethnic nation. Various authors have explained that representations of the putative "primitivity" and "backwardness" of China's ethnic minorities were key to the identification of the Han majority as occupying the space of Chinese modernity (Gladney 1994; Schein 2000). This reading is compatible with my understanding of the construction of ethnic categories in relation to one another—that is, that the representation of any ethnic group takes into account its implicit differentiation from other ethnic groups and, most significantly, its implicit differentiation from the politically dominant Han majority.

My approach assumes that ethnic categories are discursive creations rather than reflections of organic realities. In China, while ethnic categories may be partly understood as representations of groups, they are simultaneously a means of hierarchically ordering those groups within the Chinese state. Erik Mueggler writes that Western studies of ethnicity have focused largely either on delineating "cultural and linguistic differences among ethnic groups" or on "the process by which ethnic difference is created in dialogue with the Chinese state" and the marking of minorities as "exotic others" (2001, 19). Taking a slightly different approach, Mueggler questions the distinctiveness of the Han by pointing out how "Chinese culture" has been informed by interaction with non-Han peoples (Mueggler 2001; see also Rawski 1996). This refusal to emphasize ethnicity is attractive because it foregrounds the movement of people and assumes a "flexible field of cultural practice" (Mueggler 2001, 19).[6] It temporalizes rather than ethnicizes the study of China's citizens and allows for a more complex understanding of diversity within China.

A long-standing bias in the field of China studies assumes that the study of China and the study of the Han are one and the same. The emphasis on the reality of ethnic categories and the categorization of ethnic groups (as not being Han) created a discursive and scholarly absence of minorities from the study and teaching about China in the West.[7] This inattention to minority groups was bad history because it neglected to consider the movement of groups and the permeability of culture. By assuming the reality of ethnic categories, historians and anthropologists obscured the creation of those categories as an exercise of state power. Hence, rather than focusing on the Naxi ethnic group, the focus here will be on the process of creating difference in Lijiang.

In particular, this book examines perceptions of boundaries and boundary construction as a means of understanding how biopolitical categorization shaped both local perceptions and local practices. At a discursive level, the creation of the category "Naxi" led to a representation of internal stratification that mirrored the state's stratification of all ethnic groups. The Naxi scholars, intellectuals, and politicians who defined the characteristics of the Naxi ethnic group imagined cultural difference as geographically based, that is, as situated in Lijiang Town, in the Lijiang basin, and in the surrounding mountain districts. My research on the category "Naxi" required working at these different field sites as a means of examining the basis for these representations and studying the local understanding of difference in these areas.

Even though all categories are in some sense constructed, cobbled together out of invented and historical elements, the elaboration of ethnic categories in the 1980s created distinct populations who could be governed and mobilized as an economic resource for the larger, national, western development project. In order to understand this project, it is necessary to understand the politics of population categorization—what Foucault refers to as "biopolitics"—and the major changes that took place during the reform era.

BIOPOLITICAL CLASSIFICATIONS

Ann Anagnost's analysis of "quality" (suzhi), used with reference to body and population quality, provides important insights into the rise of biopolitics in China's reform era. According to Anagnost, China's movement from a planned to a market economy represented a reorganization of value in terms of the "biopolitical realm" in which human life became "a new frontier for capital accumulation" (2004, 189). The nation was divided into population categories: the rural (backward, uncivilized, low quality) and the urban (modern, civilized, high quality) (Anagnost 1997, 121; 2004, 189, 190). Foucault's concept of biopower, a technology of power used by states and nations to control population that was essential to the rise of modern capitalism, enables us to understand ethnic categorizations.

China's shift to a market-driven economy was characterized by the discursive construction of populations according to "quality." The application of the idea of quality with respect to population dates to the economic reforms that began in 1976 (Anagnost 2004), and ideas about population quality as an explanation for rural poverty first appeared in the 1980s (Anagnost 2001, 190). Anagnost makes a connection between the denigration of rural migrants as "low quality" and their exploitation as underpaid sources for capital accumulation in the market economy. While her analysis focuses on the categorization of the rural population, her insights are highly relevant to understanding the consequences of ethnic categorization.

The 1980s' state-sponsored revival of ethnicity was enacted in the same national arena in which discussion about population quality loomed large and might be understood as a parallel and overlapping project. According to Farquhar, Foucault's understanding of power includes "the 'regulatory' power of states over populations (including the practices that produce subpopulations such as racial groups)" (2005, 304). In the Chinese context, it was the production of ethnic groups that enabled a form of regulatory control. The minority groups lived largely in rural areas. Newly essentialized according to ethnic attributes, they could be seen as distinct populations with qualities unlike those of the broader population. And while ethnic groups, or at least their elites, defined their ethnicity in laudatory terms, state and popular discourse depicted them with the same value-laden terminology applied to the rural population: they were imagined as backward, uncivilized, primitive, and of a low cultural level. Both forms of essentialist discourse (rural/urban and ethnic/nonethnic) were biopolitical because they assigned value or the lack of value to bodies and populations (collectivities of bodies)—significant characterizations that in subsequent years were enlisted to naturalize economic, political, and social inequality.

Biopolitical categorization fostered popular perceptions that the rural body and the rural population could not transcend their devaluation as "rural" despite their relocation to urban sites or their attempts to narrate modern identities (H. Yan 2003; Pun 2003; Jacka 2005). Similarly, state-promoted projects of ethnic essentialization may be understood as the coding of a new type of value (and absence of value) in ethnic bodies and populations.[8] The reform era's value coding enacted and rigidified a form of stratification based on ethnic difference. Having been identified as a distinct kind of population, members of ethnic groups were governed under special educational, reproductive, and economic policies.

Ethnic groups embraced the reform-era celebration of multiethnic identity and readily participated in state-financed projects of ethnic self-definition. The essentialization of Naxi culture by Naxi intellectuals, politicians, and other elites was a means of creating prestige and enhancing the political stature of the Naxi minority. In pursuing such projects, the Naxi were not unique. Disaggregated from the national population, ethnic minority intellectuals or elites throughout China engaged in producing what Stevan Harrell refers to as ethnographies of "ethnic assertion" in which they sought to displace "sinocentric culturalism" and promote ethnic groups (2001, 151). Through the lens of biopolitical discourse, ethnic groups might be understood as seeking to champion themselves as "populations of quality," and, in this respect, their projects may be understood as seeking to recode value. It is not my intention to detract from those interpretations that seek to make local agency more visible (Litzinger 2000; Schein 2000). Rather, my focus is on the way in which ethnicity, economic difference, and gender were constituted in concert in a postsocialist arena in which categorization according to population and imaginings of quality reigned.

POSTSOCIALISM

Changes in Lijiang have to be understood in the context of national level shifts in economic policies. In the wake of the 1989 Tiananmen protests, the state accelerated efforts to promote market-based privatization (Rofel 2007, 8; H. Wang 2004, 21). Early in the reform era, in 1978–84, the income gap between rural and urban residents decreased, but there was growing inequality within rural areas (Rofel 2007, 8). Post-1984 urban reform and market expansion began to widen the economic gap between urban and rural populations (H. Wang 2004, 12, 17). Rather than attributing the urban-rural gap to market expansion, the government explained it in terms of the differential quality of populations.[9]

The period following either 1989 or the early 1990s has been referred to as postsocialist China (Rofel 2007; H. Wang 2004; Zhang and Ong 2008; L. Zhang 2001). Postsocialism is often marked by Deng Xiaoping's southern tour in 1992, which led to the creation of special economic zones. Then, at the Fourteenth Party Congress in 1992, the Chinese Communist Party recognized the "conceptual framework of 'the market' as a mechanism of government" (Hoffman 2004, 168). Li Zhang and Aihwa Ong trace the emergence of biopolitics to the postsocialist 1990s, which "sought to universalize individual responsibility and initiative" (2008, 14). While reforms associated with postsocialist China began to be instituted in the early 1990s, the effect of these reforms varied geographically. It was not until the late 1990s, in the aftermath of two significant events—the Lijiang earthquake of 1996 and the Asian financial crisis of 1997—that postsocialism was under way in Lijiang.

Lijiang's economy substantially changed after the earthquake. Extensive media attention conveyed to a national audience images of an earthquake-torn Lijiang in desperate need of assistance. Lijiang's rebuilding eerily corresponds to what Naomi Klein has termed "disaster capitalism," in which catastrophic events are used as "opportunities for transforming old economic regimes into neoliberal ones" (Ortner 2011, 3). Persuaded by promises of poverty alleviation, prosperity, and modernity, local officials and inhabitants embraced a model of tourism development that would expand and rely on a private-sector economy instead of state-operated entities and public employment.

At a global level, the Asian financial crisis of late 1997 could be described as another disaster (Klein 2007).[10] The decreased demand for Chinese products gave new urgency to the state's promotion of increased domestic consumption as a means of fostering economic recovery (Pun 2003, 473). China had suffered from the overproduction of goods in the second half of the 1990s, leading to the mobilization of Chinese citizens for the purpose of stimulating economic growth through consumer spending (Pun 2003, 473). The national promotion of tourism and domestic travel to newly developed tourist sites would provide opportunities for this domestic consumer spending. In 1999, the State Council encouraged Chinese urbanites to travel with incentives such as "golden days"—additional paid holidays intended to encourage domestic travel. Tourism in Lijiang after the mid-1990s developed in tandem with the state's promotion of domestic consumption and tourism. The promotion of ethnic tourism in order to bolster domestic consumption was but the second phase in the creation (through new forms of documentation and projects of ethnic display) of ethnic categories, a human resource that could be exploited for capital accumulation (see Swain 1990; Schein 2000; Notar 2006; Oakes 2007).

Lijiang came to be marketed as a site of national antiquity and ethnic difference. In 1997, it was designated a World Heritage Site by the United Nations Educational, Scientific and Cultural Organization (UNESCO), and Lijiang Town's economy was reoriented to focus on tourism development. This entailed the widespread closing of state-sector factories and substantial expanding of the private-sector economy, changes informed by neoliberal ideas that identify market expansion as central to prosperity. The new emphasis on tourism was understood locally as part of a shift to a market economy. Lijiang was only one of several areas in China's western, largely minority-occupied, interior targeted for this development. Tourism development was locally, and perhaps nationally, understood as a means of alleviating poverty and fostering economic development and prosperity, but it may also be understood in a slightly different way.

Tourism mobilized minority populations, which had been newly essentialized in terms of ethnic qualities, as "a new frontier for capital accumulation"

(Anagnost 2004, 189). The attraction of Lijiang and other minority areas developed for tourism was enabled by the showcasing of ethnic difference and its development into forms of consumption. In the context of ethnicized tourist sites, ethnic populations and bodies appear to have "quality" insofar as they attract tourists, but this quality was comparable only to that of the migrant workers and laborers who toiled in urban factories. Neither rural migrant nor ethnic bodies were considered to be of high quality, that is, possessing quality in terms of state or popular national discourse. As discussed in chapter 3, populations from more allegedly "backward" areas were imagined to be *more* ethnically authentic. While ethnic representations valorized ethnic authenticity, ethnic groups were not credited with having high quality, nor were they seen as potential prime movers in economic development. Differentiations of quality were clearly articulated in the promotion of the Campaign to Open Up the West (Xibu Dakaifa), which encouraged national migration to the western interior in order to foster economic development. This campaign emphasized the "backwardness" of the ethnic groups who largely populated the interior and how they would benefit from this migration by learning from the "advanced" Han (Goodman 2004; Oakes 2007, 240).

Despite the ethnocentrism of development discourse, local governments—and the Lijiang government in particular—have embraced tourism and ethnocommodification in the conviction that it will alleviate poverty and lead to prosperity. As discussed in chapters 4 and 5, this conviction has remained firm even when the beneficiaries were not local residents.

At the discursive level, the promotion of ethnicity did not imbue the Naxi population with quality. Instead, the tourism project resulted in conferring quality on visitors from China's urban centers: just as the consumption of goods has increasingly marked the modern subject, tourism and ethnoconsumption enable urbanites to craft cosmopolitan identities in the context of China's global ascension (see Chio 2010). Tourism has expanded the local economy, but, for the most part, those who have profited most significantly from Lijiang's commodity economy (*shiping jingji*) have been not the local people themselves but outsiders who have opened businesses in Lijiang that capitalize on tourism. And it has mostly escaped notice that Lijiang's economic transformation has had negative repercussions for its rural residents.

The following chapters construct an episodic history of Lijiang from 1990 through 2011. The focus on events and stories helps track the discourses and changes that have shaped the lives of Lijiang residents over two decades: from the early days of the reform era to the reign of neoliberalism in the twenty-first century.

ORGANIZATION OF THE BOOK

Chapter 1, "The Maoist Shaman and the Madman," examines the crisis created by biopolitical discourse, in which individual citizens were considered responsible for their own welfare. It describes the dilemma faced by residents of East Wind Village, a village in the Lijiang basin, in dealing with a fellow villager who had gone mad. This madman's declining welfare resonated with tensions created by the rise of a value system at odds with the declining moral community of the village. This case, which took place in the early 1990s, highlights the growth of economic inequality among rural households and the lack of rural structures for providing assistance to disadvantaged villagers. A shamanic ritual held in East Wind Village to cure the madman revealed tensions between a shaman (*sanba*) who sought to reimagine socialism and some villagers who perceived the state as impotent on the eve of the postsocialist era.

Chapter 2, "*Dongba* Culture and the Authenticization of Marginality," examines "the ethnic" as a category of population and biopolitics in action. It traces the ongoing project, from its beginning in 1981, of imagining the Naxi as a group with a distinct ethnic value hierarchically differentiated from other ethnic groups. *Dongba* culture (*dongba wenhua*) was created through a transcoding of the forms of economic and gender inequality. For the Naxi elites who articulated *dongba* culture, Han structures of prestige (the legacy of imperial expansion) and reform-era discourse informed what could be favorably essentialized as ethnic. By locating Naxi authenticity at a remove from themselves, Naxi elites revealed the hegemony of biopolitical distinctions that, despite the national celebration of diversity, marked ethnic bodies and populations as low quality, backward, and associated with the past.

Chapter 3, "Ethnicizing Myth, Bride Abduction, and Elopement," illustrates what is at stake in biopolitical invention. Once Naxi culture became equated with the culture of the *dongba*, *dongba* religious texts were equated with Naxi history and culture. This chapter questions whether bride abduction, which is described in an important *dongba* text, was a standard practice in all Naxi-occupied areas. Research conducted in 1990–92 on marriage in three different sites—Lijiang Town, a basin village, and a mountain village—revealed that bride abduction and elopement were regionally variant marriage strategies used by impoverished households. But rather than being understood as contingent strategies of the economically marginal, abduction and elopement were naturalized in the postsocialist era as the proclivities of ethnic bodies and populations.

Chapter 4, "Biopolitics: Fox Stench, Gender Boundaries, and the Moral Economy of Postsocialism," chronicles the economic transformation of Lijiang Town as a result of tourism development, based on research conducted in the late 1990s. It describes how two discourses of body quality—the quality of the postsocialist female body and of the rural migrant body—converged in depictions of female taxi drivers. Stories about body odor, kidnapping, aberrant sexual reproduction, and murder demonstrate how urbanites mobilized the discourse of essential difference in a misguided critique of upwardly mobile female taxi drivers who seemingly embodied changes brought about by capitalist privatization.

Chapter 5, "Marketing Difference: Dog Meat, Court Cases, and Ethnopreneurs," builds on the preceding chapter's discussion of the targeting of ethnic destinations for consumption and tourist development. Lijiang's appeal as a site of ethnic tourism in the twenty-first century reflects both the success of differentiating ethnic groups as exoticized populations and the mobilization of the "ethnic" for capital accumulation by state and local governments. This chapter illustrates how local residents are expected to sacrifice in the name of market expansion and the way in which local government and entrepreneurial interests are fused in the postsocialist economy.

The Conclusion considers how new models of value have shaped subjectivity and understandings of history in East Wind Village. It questions whether the development of new sites of antiquity, enmeshed in national strategies for economic expansion, will actually improve the lives of the largely ethnic populations enlisted in these projects.

FIG. I.4 Aerial view of Dayanzhen

FIG. 1.5 A streamside residence

FIG. 1.2 Mao's statue

FIG. 1.6 Lijiang's new city

THE MAOIST SHAMAN AND THE MADMAN

On a cool summer afternoon in 1991, a shaman (*sanba*) arrived in a dusty, mud-brick Naxi village to cure a farmer who had gone mad. During the ritual that followed, the shaman called on Chairman Mao, Zhou Enlai, and Deng Xiaoping to assist her in driving out demons, while she instructed the madman to brace up, learn from Lei Feng, and work for the greater good of his country. The shaman chanted: "The madman is one of the wretched masses. Arise if you don't want to be enslaved! Let our flesh and blood build the next Great Wall." She incorporated political slogans and phrases from the Chinese national anthem into her ritual incantations. She wore a shoulder bag adorned with a Red Guard armband and marched around the madman's courtyard as if she were going into battle. The shaman bowed to the gods and burned incense, but she also invoked the "gods" and the experiences of the Chinese revolution—all in an attempt to save the madman.

This extraordinary ritual was held in East Wind Village in southwest China.[1] The shaman grafted national discourse onto local ritual structure in a context in which there had once been a clear division between the state and the shamanic. Her performance revealed both the penetration of state power and the agency of the shaman in creating a syncretic form of ritual practice that momentarily blurred national and local epistemologies. During the ritual, the shaman's conjurings created a site for the reinscription of ritual meaning and the opening of new contingencies and ambivalences. The village audience immediately debated the merits of the ritual and ultimately assessed it to be a failure. However, whether a ritual is socially judged a success or a failure should not be the primary criterion for its examination; of greater interest is understanding why a given ritual was or was not socially persuasive.

Anthropological analysis has largely privileged rituals that are routinely performed and dramatize shared meanings and visions of reality. Failed rituals, those not associated with the successful reassertion or transformation of social order, are often relegated to the analyst's dustbin. Examining failed ritual redirects the analytic gaze toward local processes of legitimation and authentication, and simultaneously avoids accepting merely temporary arrangements of power as part of a timeless cultural essence. Although shifting the analytic focus from ritual to ritualization avoids the reification of ritual by attending to processes, it is still informed by the functionalist celebration of normative practice. Understanding the failure of ritual draws us into the complex arena of conflict and contingency where social dynamics enable new identities or create marginal ones.

Failed ritual in this case may be understood through a series of contextualizations that revealed ambivalence among East Wind villagers about national identity, ritual discourse, class, and symbols of power in the 1990s. The shaman's ritual brought out contradictions between Naxi historical experiences and a sense of shared national Chinese identity. The performance created a context in which different understandings of ritual among villagers and the lack of a singular all-encompassing belief system became apparent. And, finally, the shaman's use of Maoist symbols of power led villagers to rethink their objections to the very economic inequalities that had mobilized them to hold the ritual in the first place.

NAXI

There are approximately 250,000 Naxi residing in Lijiang Autonomous Naxi Prefecture in Yunnan.[2] East Wind Village is located in the Lijiang basin, about an hour and a half by bicycle from Lijiang Town, the cultural and marketing center of Lijiang Prefecture.

The village, built under the shadow of Wood Ear Mountain, faces a flat plain of dry farmland on which villagers grow wheat, corn, and beans. The village is composed of a number of walled courtyards connected by a maze of narrow dirt alleys. Each courtyard has one or two buildings made of red-mud bricks covered with pine fronds or gray ceramic tiles. Villagers use these buildings as living quarters and for raising pigs and chickens for household consumption. Only about a third of the village's eighty-four households have a draft animal, and most of these animals are collectively owned by close patrilineal kin whose courtyards tend to cluster together. East Wind Village has some of the poorest land in the Lijiang basin. Unlike that of neighboring villages, its land does not allow for rice cultivation. Water shortages are not uncommon. Families are allotted two-thirds of an acre (four *mu*) of land per person, in contrast to the one-third to half of an acre (two to three *mu*) per person allotted to basin villages with superior land. Except for the seasonal gathering of wild "matsutake mushrooms" (*songrong*) and "wood ear" (*muer*) from Wood Ear Mountain, the residents of East Wind Village are primarily subsistence agriculturalists.

Poor agricultural yields continued to hinder economic growth and prosperity into the 1990s. Only a handful of families had direct access to cash, either from the pensions of retired family members or from the salaries of employed family members who resided outside the village. Before the Chinese revolution in 1949, a single landlord family owned the choicest land in East Wind Village. Two other lineages owned the remaining village land. With the exception of one Han family, all the contemporary residents of the village claim to be descendants of these three Naxi lineages. Small, family-based farms were prevalent in East Wind Village before 1949, as they were in 1991.

Early in the 1990s, villagers conceived of recent history as divided into "pre- and post-liberation" eras.[3] At this time, the vast majority of East Wind Village residents supported the socialist state and had negative views of the pre-1949 era, which they associated with memories of hardship and poverty. Nevertheless, they did not have fond memories of collectivized farming and the political strife of the Maoist era. Many complained about the lack of freedom resulting from controlled work routines, and many recalled the collective era as one of frequent hunger. Production team authorities on collective farms—under pressure to represent their teams as successful—exaggerated actual grain yields, and as a result the village had barely enough grain for its own survival. Many villagers perceived collective-era "cadres" (*ganbu*), a term that refers to all officials in postrevolutionary China, as favoring their own immediate families in work assignments and work point allocations. Surprisingly, even the relatives of collective officials were critical of the officials' behavior. The resentment one detects in these accounts suggests that the collective era was characterized by strained kinship ties.

The most salient distinctions between villagers during the Maoist era were expressed in the idiom of class. Class labels, mandated by the Agrarian Reform Law of 1950, were assigned by local cadres. There was an element of arbitrariness to these labels because, particularly in minority areas such as Lijiang Prefecture, there were often only slight economic distinctions among villagers. Yet, in an attempt to conform to national directives, local officials dutifully assigned class labels. Cadres and members of the Red Guard organized class struggle sessions in which the masses publicly criticized neighbors identified by these labels as having exploitative class backgrounds. In East Wind Village, the most prosperous household was assigned the label of "landlord" (dizhu). The vast majority of villagers were classified as "poor peasants" (pinnong) who farmed small plots of land and hired themselves out as agricultural workers to make ends meet. A handful of villagers were "middle peasants" (zhongnong), meaning they were small subsistence farmers, or "rich peasants" (funong). The male descendants of the sole landlord family left the village, and the female descendants married into poor-peasant families. Although it is common knowledge that middle-peasant and rich-peasant families in East Wind Village incurred severe criticism from their neighbors—some were beaten and had their property confiscated—these families were loath to discuss this era. Many of the villagers enthusiastically supported the Communist Party during the Maoist era, but they seemed cynical, if not embarrassed, about this in the early 1990s. However, two village elders remained proud of their pasts as early recruits to the Communist Party; they had worked in the underground movement, wielded some political power during the Maoist era, and by the early 1990s were "cadres who had taken early retirement" (lixiu ganbu). Then again, survival during the Maoist era for many of the older villagers meant passively conforming to the rhetoric of the time. Many older women who could not speak Chinese or understand the ideological content of political recitations talked about using songs as mnemonic devices so that they could reproduce the required political responses.

While decollectivization and the household responsibility system (chengbao), both instituted in 1980, marked a significant improvement in the standard of living in East Wind Village as a whole, they also brought about new economic inequalities between individual households. Decollectivization dismantled the collectives, which had been in existence since 1957, and instituted a system of village-based government. In concert with this, the House-hold Responsibility System allotted land to individual households, which then became independent economic units. Village residents unanimously preferred the Household Responsibility System to the system of "collective agriculture" (jiti). More than half of the buildings in East Wind Village had been built after decollectivization. By the 1990s, villagers had enough to eat and many families boasted of being able to eat meat at least once a week. Vil-lagers highly valued the freedom to organize their own work routines. During the 1980s, rapidly changing standards of living in both the town and the basin made most villagers optimistic about the future. In the early 1990s, villagers would gather curiously at the few households with television sets and young people proudly sported fashionable clothing bought from stores in town. Some of the younger men planted fruit trees, and others planned to build a fish pond. Most villagers, however, continued to rely primarily on the farm-ing of grain and beans, as they had done before 1949, and by the early 1990s, many villagers had begun to doubt the state's promises that exemplary house-holds would serve as models ushering in prosperity for all. A few exemplary households continued to thrive into the 1990s, but the village remained far from prosperous.

DIVINATORY DISCOURSE AND THE MAGIC OF MAO

As the shaman entered the madman's courtyard, a rapt crowd of villagers gathered to watch her arrange offerings for the ritual. The villagers had high expectations of the shaman. Someone in an adjacent Naxi village had recom-mended her after she "cured" a local woman who had been unable to bear children.

A woman in her early forties, the shaman wore a Heqing Bai minority headdress, a Red Guard shoulder bag slung over an ordinary blue cotton shirt, apron-covered trousers, and the ubiquitous army-green tennis shoes. The shaman was not Naxi but of the Bai nationality. This was immediately ap-parent from the headdress, which identified her as from Heqing, about thirty miles (fifty km) from Lijiang Town; it is standard for rural Bai women to wear the headdress of their area. She conducted the ritual in Yunnanese, the lingua franca of the Lijiang basin area as well as of Heqing. What villagers found peculiar about her appearance was the Red Guard shoulder bag, a Cultural

Revolution relic rarely seen in the post-Mao-era Lijiang countryside. Villagers claimed that the shaman was originally a poor peasant who had once been a Red Guard and Communist Party official with a high enough rank to have attended political conferences as far away as Kunming, the provincial capital.

The shaman first burned incense and prepared colored flags, which she positioned according to compass points associated with fire, water, metal, and wood. She placed an assortment of offerings in cups and bowls in the center of the courtyard next to a live chicken. The shaman's actions—burning incense and bowing to the gods of the East, West, North, South, and Center—constituted *chu ba zei*, the standard procedure for beginning rituals in Lijiang Prefecture. Some Naxi families worship the gods by performing *chu ba zei* on the first and fifteenth of each month.

The shaman then began to sing: "I came to save the madman because I pity him! The madman is one of the wretched masses! We invite Mao Zhuxi [Chairman Mao], Zhou Enlai, and Deng Xiaoping to come and save the madman!" By invoking these names, she replaced a local ritual structure composed of the gods of heaven, mountain, and earth with a nationalized ritual structure presided over by this deified postrevolutionary trinity.

The shaman raised some wine cups toward the sky and poured water as if offering it to an invisible entity, and then she scattered rice in four directions as offerings to the gods. Addressing the madman, she began singing from the Chinese national anthem: "Arise if you don't want to be enslaved! Let our flesh and blood be used to build the next Great Wall!" She interrupted the anthem to begin singing verses from an anti-Japanese war hymn, during which she dramatized a mock decapitation: "We'll wield our knife toward the demons and cut off a demon's head! One-two, one-two-three, one-two-three-four!" She marched as if in battle, singing this strange medley interspersed with quotes from *Quotations from Chairman Mao Tse-tung* (Mao 1969), sung to the tune "Do-Re-Mi" from the *Sound of Music*, and exhortations to "emulate Lei Feng" (*xuexi Lei Feng*).

Her words were all too familiar; these songs once performed in schools and during political meetings evoked memories from the not-so-distant past and aroused vague feelings of patriotism and determination to carry out political campaigns or tasks of heavy labor. During the Cultural Revolution (1966–76), loudspeakers roused the villagers every morning with the inevitable revolutionary songs or the exercise count one-two-three-four (*yi-er-san-si*), which echoed through the village. Quotations from Chairman Mao, recited like daily mantras, spoke of what many villagers who had been true believers once considered the very meaning of life.[4] "Emulate Lei Feng!"—repeated every decade or so—exhorted the masses to learn and model their behavior on the personal sacrifices of that paragon of Communist righteousness. First in the 1960s, and then numerous times thereafter, the state promoted Lei Feng, a PLA soldier and tireless worker, as a model of socialist sacrifice. Lei Feng had rescued a bus filled with children by propping up a falling telephone pole, which eventually crushed and killed him. His diaries, often miraculously discovered in different places at the same time during Learn from Lei Feng campaigns, were narratives of sacrifice and tireless enthusiasm for serving the people. Versions of these diaries were the mainstay of political study sessions for years (Farquhar 1996). Lei Feng was both an embodiment of the Communist spirit (Spence 1990, 727) and a virtuous exemplar narrativized in the fashion of imperial and pre-1949 worthies (Ebrey 1981, 382).[5]

The strange juxtaposition of shamanic activity and revolutionary text made many of the young people whisper and giggle nervously. Shamanism belonged to the realm of prerevolutionary local practices that remained outside state control and was antithetical to the political slogans that articulated the voice of the state. Despite this apparent incoherence, many of the older people watched attentively; the performance even transfixed some of them. The shaman appeared to use song and slogan as mnemonic devices with which to conjure strong attitudes and emotions from specific historical memories. In doing this, she sought to mobilize the madman and the audience by appropriating the fierce determination of the past for battle in a new context of demon quelling.

After the shaman threw the increasingly dazed chicken in various directions, telling the madman to fetch it each time, the ritual began to wind down. A cool breeze was blowing, but the shaman's clothes were wet with perspiration as she alternately sang and trembled. More than an hour later, the shaman fed the chicken some rice and said, "Now they've eaten their fill and drunk until they are no longer thirsty, and so we ask that the demons go away and allow the madman to recover." Then she instructed the madman to bow in the direction of the village graveyard. The ritual closed with the host, some relatives, the madman, and the shaman walking to the graveyard to send off the demons. Once there, the group killed and feasted on the chicken.

Later, the relatives of the madman graciously thanked the shaman and sent her on her way with ten duck eggs. Relatives of the madman described the duck eggs as a gift or a token of the host family's gratitude.

Within moments of her departure, the village was abuzz with criticism of the ritual and the shaman. Before the shaman's arrival, the villagers had generally felt that one or more demons were afflicting the madman. After the ritual, however, and in spite of the shaman's demon-quelling efforts, the madman did not appear either substantially improved or particularly mad but was quiet and withdrawn. Most villagers felt that the shaman had not cured the madman, although some were hopeful that he might improve with time. By the next day, public opinion had moved toward a negative evaluation of the ritual itself. Some villagers called the shaman a "cheat" (pianzi), who had only come to East Wind Village seeking material gain. An older man complained, "She said Mao, Zhou, and Deng sent her to save the madman; she didn't know the names of the gods and didn't know how to sing shaman songs," and he imitated the high, melodic tune shamans sang. Many of the older villagers rejected the shaman's performance because her words, songs, and appearance were simply inconsistent with their cultural categories and shared memories of shamans and shamanic rituals. Before 1949, shamans in the Lijiang basin were men who wore cloth turbans, wielded drums or swords, and sang secret shamanic songs in a high melodic whisper.[6] This shaman, many villagers pointed out, was a woman—wearing an ethnic-minority headdress and toting a Red Guard bag—who sang revolutionary songs and spouted political slogans.

Most of the villagers under the age of forty had never seen a shaman perform, and their knowledge of shamanism was based on older villagers' memories of the performances of a shaman who had lived in the village before 1949. Their rejection of this shaman was based not so much on skepticism about her authenticity as on disapproval of what they saw as her promotion of the Maoist era. For many of the young people, the shaman's Red Guard shoulder bag and strident rhetoric suggested a reinvocation of values they had once subscribed to and had since rejected. But did the rejection of the trinity of Mao, Zhou, and Deng also suggest a perception of state powerlessness in comparison to local gods and folk cosmology? If so, can this be contextualized in terms of the declining role of the state since decollectivization in the Lijiang countryside? Given that villagers in the 1990s had gone through yet another Learn from Lei Feng campaign, what did their rejection of the recent reincarnation of Lei Feng as demon queller imply? One young man protested, "How can studying Lei Feng help? That has nothing to do with it." His response, which was echoed by other villagers, flatly rejected the shaman's implication that the madman's illness could be attributed to his ideological shortcomings. Perhaps this is why most villagers were sarcastic about the shaman's use of quotations from Chairman Mao and the model of Lei Feng. Neither the initial village support for the ritual nor the occasionally recognizable ritual actions performed by the shaman could override what the villagers perceived as anachronistic ritual incantations.

INTERPRETING SHAMANIC BRICOLAGE

Through her ritual agency, the shaman attempted to wed shamanic discourse to state discourse in order to restore the madman's mental health. The former called upon divine intervention, while the latter prescribed ideological adherence and personal sacrifice. The shaman did not invite the gods usually summoned by Naxi shamans; rather, she deified the state figures of Mao, Zhou, and Deng while celestializing the discourse of the Party and state. Her quotations from Mao and exhortations to emulate Lei Feng suggested that healing can be partially achieved by the divine intervention of the state but will also require the agency of the patient. Although the shaman initially diagnosed demons in the patient's family, she then personalized the problem by attributing the patient's madness to a demon inhabiting his body.

By repeatedly instructing the madman to learn from Lei Feng, this shaman implied that the madman and his condition might improve if he modeled himself after that revolutionary exemplar, an approach unlike rituals in some other villages that did not suggest that the afflicted was individually responsible or that sickness could be linked to ideological shortcomings. By focusing on the afflicted individual, this shaman desocialized and de-familialized illness and misfortune: she portrayed the madman's illness as an individual's problem as opposed to a problem of the extended family or village community. In this sense, the ritual's epistemology mirrored state discourse since the end of the collective era.

Social tensions had been rising in the post-Mao era as a result of incipient class formation and the growth of economic inequality in the countryside.

State discourse sought to quell these tensions by promoting community etiquette and village harmony (Anagnost 1985, 69). Pursuing this goal through a series of campaigns such as the Civilized Village Campaign, Five Speak Four Beautiful, the Civilized Household Campaign, and others, the state emphasized what it called "socialist morality," which focused on the development of moral character and fixed responsibility at the level of "individual consciousness" (Anagnost 1985, 71). Anagnost suggests that the reorganization of agriculture during decollectivization required new forms of ideological work in order to mute tensions emerging out of class antagonisms (ibid., 65). Similarly, in the shaman's ritual, the individual's proper ideological disposition and selfless sacrifice for the state reemerged as a remedy for the madman.

Yet the shaman was not suggesting that the madman's affliction could be cured solely by personal reform, because her ritual acts—which included a sacrifice and the propitiation of new gods—still required the intervention or patronage of deities or perceived powers, as well as her own intervention. Hence, the shaman's conjurings were a syncretic assemblage drawing on elements of both pre-1949 healing rituals and more contemporary constructions of personhood.

The ritual text, which might have appeared to the villagers to be a combination of incongruous images, gave coherence to the shaman's performance. The principal songs the shaman used were the national anthem and "The Knife Marching Song" (Dadao jingxingqu), an anti-Japanese song from the Sino-Japanese War (1937–45), which she interspersed with punchy quotations from Chairman Mao, the slogan "Learn from Lei Feng," and the catchy marching count. While the song evoked the visual image of battling and beheading demons—images congruous with ritual demon quelling—it also summoned a historically powerful memory of resistance and the context that inspired the imagining of Chinese nationhood. Catastrophes often fuel the strong sentiments that solidify a vision of nationhood (Anderson 1983, 158). Anderson suggests that, for the Chinese, the catastrophe that sparked the envisioning of Chinese nationhood was Japan's massive invasion in 1937 (ibid.; also see Johnson 1962, 1–14). "The Knife Marching Song," composed to rally the nation to fend off the Japanese, inspired a determination and sense of identity linked to the conception of Chinese nationhood. The national anthem, also composed during this era, evokes similar sentiments of nationalism.[7]

The shaman's use of song in her curing ritual was not arbitrary but allusive: the anti-Japanese marching song and the national anthem served to evoke the powerful moment when a new social body and a modern national identity emerged. The shaman's use of national imagery may be interpreted as an act of territorial resignification. In place of the heaven, earth, and mountain gods that govern a cosmological order, the shaman remapped ritual action and the moral community on an imagined national landscape. If the shaman's performance relocated the madman in a moral community enlarged to national proportions, it simultaneously became a site for the revaluation of the magical power required to mediate the restoration of that moral community's order. The magical power required to preside over a "national" cosmos was ritually reconfigured in the national trinity of the deified Mao, Zhou, and the then not-so-dead Deng.

In such a reconfiguration, local ritual structure becomes the basis for the incorporation of reimagined national sources of power. New national deities are, in turn, freighted with state discourse and epistemology, which may be deployed in the ritual arena they have entered. The shaman's exhortations to study Lei Feng offered a critique of local conceptions of misfortune, which solely blamed demons for the madman's predicament, and suggested her complicity with state discourse by assigning responsibility to the madman for lacking self-discipline. But the concept of self-discipline also spoke of a tactic of control necessitated by a more complex social body. This tactic echoed what Foucault describes as biopower, a discourse of the self-disciplining self necessitated by the emergence of the modern European state (1980, 140, 141), and agrees with the more self-conscious model of personhood promoted by the postrevolutionary Chinese state. The shaman's ritual may be understood as Lévi-Strauss's bricolage, a "concoction of symbols" (Lévi-Strauss 1966; Comaroff 1985) already laden with significance from the conflicting realms of the state and the shamanic. Had her ritual been successful, it might have brought about a transformed cosmological order infused with state power. The failure of the ritual, in the sense that it was not socially persuasive, directs us to analyze the various forces that inspired doubt among the residents of East Wind Village. The processes of legitimization and authentification encompass local dynamics, experiences of structural change, the significance of ritual practice, and interpretations of new forms of power.

While we may understand the shaman's convictions by analyzing the songs she selected, we cannot assume these songs had the same meaning for the village audience. As Gayatri Spivak has suggested, we should scrutinize moments of historical "transition" and pluralize them as moments of confrontation (1988, 3). In this case, rather than assuming that Japan's invasion caused people across the vast mass of China to simultaneously imagine themselves as part of the modern Chinese nation, we should consider plural experiences of this historical moment. Using this strategy, we may situate the villagers' sentiments by examining their response to the shaman's use of the national anthem and the anti-Japanese "The Knife Marching Song."

East Wind Village residents did not appear to have been inspired by the shaman's use of song. There is no doubt that "The Knife Marching Song" evokes patriotism and nationalism in an audience that includes the Naxi, but this hymn also references an alternative historical mesmory. During the war with Japan, many Naxi men cut off their right index fingers or committed suicide in order to avoid conscription by the Nationalists.[8] It is not uncommon in rural Naxi villages to find elderly men with their right index fingers missing. Many conscripted Naxi soldiers escaped and returned to Lijiang to die by their own hand rather than in a foreign land away from their families. While the shaman was probably unaware of this history, the villagers were familiar with Nationalist treatment of Naxi during the Sino-Japanese War.[9] In Lijiang, Naxi conscripts were bound with ropes around their necks and arms and then led off like prisoners by rifle-toting soldiers (Joseph Rock, quoted in Sutton 1974, 273). The Naxi resistance to conscription during the Republican era (1911–49) is painfully recounted in "Lawei ger,"[10] a popular Naxi folk song (Yang 1986). Hence, what Anderson has generalized for the Chinese as a "transition" to membership in an imagined nation was for many Naxi a confrontation with the Republican Chinese over the very question of allegiance and shared national identity. For those East Wind Village residents whose ancestors had committed suicide in order to avoid conscription, and for other villagers who identified with them, the shaman's evocative hymn must have summoned conflicting sentiments: national pride juxtaposed to a painful historical memory of the imposition of a national identity that many of the Naxi did not share. This painful memory may have contributed to the villagers' rejection of both the shaman's national cosmological narrative and, ultimately, her cure for the madman.

Without hesitation, contemporary Naxi acknowledge themselves as a part of the Chinese nation; however, this was not always the case. At various historical moments, the Naxi have resisted both national and imperial identities, as demonstrated by their resistance to conscription during the anti-Japanese and anti-Communist war efforts, as well as by the Naxi women who committed suicide rather than participate in Chinese-instituted marriage practices beginning in 1723 during the Qing dynasty (1644–1911) and in the Republican era (1911–1949) (Rock 1939; Jackson 1971; Chao 1990; Chao 1995).

If the villagers' ambivalence about national identity caused them to doubt the shaman's ritual, discontinuity in beliefs about ritual practice magnified the problem. An examination of historical layers of conflicting ritual practice reveals that there was no singular shared belief system among the residents of East Wind Village.

SITUATING RITUAL PRACTICE

Religious practice in pre-1949 Lijiang and East Wind Village included elements of Tibetan Buddhism, Chinese Buddhism, Daoism, the *dongba* religion, shamanism, and a variety of heterodox religious sects. An understanding of this diversity requires some discussion of the history of regional religious practices and Chinese territorial expansion into what is now southwest China.

Naxi territory borders Kham, a historical region on the southeastern Tibetan plateau, and the religious practices of Naxi in these border regions reflect the legacy of Tibetan Buddhist influences. The Mu family, ancient rulers of the Naxi, adopted Tibetan Buddhism in the 1600s and were patrons of Tibetan Buddhist temples located in Naxi territory. Daoist, Confucian, and Chinese Buddhist influences in Naxi religious practice derive from the Chinese expansion into the southwest during the Ming dynasty (1368–1644). The building of Chinese-style temples in Lijiang basin dates from this period, as does the official institution of the *tusi* system, a form of indirect government in which *tusi*, indigenous chiefs, ruled on behalf of the dynastic state. Under this system, the state attempted to convert indigenous rulers to Chinese ritual practice and simultaneously incorporate local gods into a Chinese cosmological structure. The state achieved this by bestowing new identities on local gods. For instance, it gave Sanduo—who was formerly worshipped as a sacred mountain god and was a god of local Naxi and Bai shamans—the title of "protector-general" of the empire. By giving local gods the stamp of state legitimacy, the state blended a local system of belief into its own. Moreover, it restricted the power of local gods by embedding them within an imperial cosmological hierarchy in a lower position than more powerful state-promoted deities.

With the end of the *tusi* system and the institution of direct Chinese rule in 1723, Chinese magistrates promoted Chinese-style rituals, particularly marriages and burial practices, among the Naxi population at large. In prerevolutionary East Wind Village, religious practice showed the signs of a successful Chinese project of ritual promotion. During the Republican era, the Naxi practiced Chinese-style life-cycle ceremonies, which were identified as Naxi ritual practices. Three Chinese-style temples housed deities who were part of a Chinese ritual pantheon: Guanyin Temple (Guanyin Miao); the Temple to Three Gods (standard Chinese [Mandarin] San Shen Miao [dedicated to Confucius, Lao Jun and Cai shenyi]; Hay Ghee Mei in Naxi); and the Temple to the Dragon King (Longwang Miao). The Guanyin Temple and the Temple to Three Gods were built by East Wind Village elites in the 1800s, during the Qing dynasty, and in the Republican era they served as schools where village children prepared for provincial examinations. The temple-building projects of elites, aimed at fostering their power and prestige, were compatible with the state project of creating a unified system of belief. The gods worshipped in these East Wind Village temples were also worshipped throughout Yunnan, which suggests that some standardization in beliefs had been achieved in the late imperial era.

More locally distinctive elements of East Wind Village ritual practice were evident in the annual Heaven Worship Ceremony (Meebiuq) for the Naxi god of heaven; Sanduo Jie, a holiday for worshipping the Naxi god Sanduo; Topiu, a harvest festival of Yi origin during which ancestors were worshipped; and Huobajie, the Yunnanese torch festival, of Yi origin, during which ghosts are driven out. The celebration of these rituals involved the entire village and reinforced a shared belief system that narrativized the origin of the Naxi people and provided a means of reproducing community well-being.

In Naxi and regional Han and Bai ritual before 1949, it was common to treat historical figures as deities. Confucius and Guan Yu were worshipped as gods throughout Yunnan by the Han, Bai, and Naxi. The Naxi and Bai god Sanduo was interpreted as both historical figure and deity. Powerful historical figures were thought to possess magical power or efficacy (ling), which supplicants could harness for themselves through acts of ritual propitiation. In other words, ritual formulas allowed for both the local manipulation of deities for personal benefit and the expansion of the supernatural realm through the deification of historical figures.

Before 1949, the Naxi, Han, Bai, Lisu, and Tibetan ethnic groups each had healers who may be glossed as shamans. People called upon these practitioners to cure illness, retrieve souls, perform divinations, and exorcize intractable spirits, usually ghosts or demons.

The Naxi had two types of ritual practitioners who were often referred to as shamans: dongba, often translated as "priest," and sanba, translated as "shaman." Dongba differed from sanba in that they acquired their skills through apprenticeships that required them to learn the pictographic texts chanted in structured rituals. Dongba usually inherited their professions and were always male. The role of sanba, open to both men and women, was not learned or chosen but came about after a traumatic illness opened up a channel of communication with a spirit or god. Aside from purification and propitiation of the gods, sanba do not follow standard or predictable sequences in their rituals. Neither role was prestigious, and it was often taken on by poor farmers seeking to supplement their livelihoods. East Wind Village had once been the home village of legendary dongba, but in the 1940s, the only ritual practitioner in residence was a sanba.

After the revolution, the state discouraged ritual practice in Naxi territory, as it did throughout China, and persecuted religious practitioners. In Lijiang Town during the Maoist era, government officials forced Buddhist monks and celibate female devotees to marry (sometimes each other) and publicly executed the leaders of religious sects.[11] In East Wind Village, temples were stripped of icons and made to serve as schools, and public ritual practice ceased altogether. Since then, numerous campaigns have sought to eradicate such practitioners as magical healers, shamans, sorcerers, geomancers, and exorcists. The state accused dongba and sanba of spreading feudal superstition and consigned them to the ranks of former landlords and rich peasants as objects of local denunciation. Nevertheless, the ban on ritual practitioners did not put an end to all ritual practice because sanba continued to hold clandestine rituals in private households in remote mountain villages. In East

Wind Village, however, as throughout the basin, the few remaining *dongba* and *sanba* abandoned their ritual roles during the Maoist era, as political rituals of class struggle replaced villagewide ritual practice. While some individual families continued to worship ancestors or their "house gods" (*si*), these practices were family based and no longer tied to a system of belief shared by the community.

For some villagers, Maoist-era political rituals took on a religious tenor. During the Cultural Revolution, Mao was worshipped as a god; his picture replaced ancestral tablets in some East Wind Village homes, and marriages were performed in front of his picture, with wedding parties reciting his quotations in unison. Mao's image was so sacred that pasting his picture on old buildings was thought to protect them from destruction. Other symbols of the state also made their way into the village's popular imagination during the Maoist era. Before 1949, Men Shen, a pair of gods usually depicted riding wild animals, were usually pasted on both sides of a household's entrance for protection against evil spirits. In post-1949 East Wind Village, new protectors replaced Men Shen: a PLA officer and a navy officer, each mounted on horseback. During this time, throughout China and for many in East Wind Village, Mao became truly godlike. For other villagers, however, ritualized recitations of Mao quotations or the singing of revolutionary songs spoke not so much of depth of belief as a strategy for survival.

The post-Mao era brought a relaxed implementation of the state's antireligion policy. The Chinese state redefined harvest and life-cycle rituals as "customs" (*fengsu xiguan*) rather than religious practices. As a result, throughout rural China, many residents eagerly resumed the practice of life-cycle rituals, which became important villagewide affairs. Yet, in East Wind Village, the shift in state policy was also greeted with confusion and caution about what constituted permissible religious activity. State policy, dating from the post-Mao era, tolerated the practice of "religion" (*zongjiao*)—narrowly defined to include Buddhism, Daoism, Islam, and Christianity—while strictly prohibiting practitioners of magic or purveyors of "feudal superstition" (*fengjian mixin*). But the category "religion" is the product of state-created differentiations as opposed to distinctions existing among common people.[12]

The post-Mao-era redefinition of practices formerly viewed as religion and customs was further complicated by the state's new stance on ethnic identity. In the 1980s, the state began to encourage expressions of ethnic identity among ethnic minorities, a policy that had reverberations for religious belief in East Wind Village. During the Maoist era, *dongba* practices fell under the rubric of feudal superstition. In the early 1980s, with the state actually funding institutes to record and study folk culture, Naxi leaders rehabilitated *dongba* religious practices (*dongba jiao*) and renamed them "*dongba* culture" (Chao 1996).[13] Naxi leaders have also officially equated *dongba* culture with the history and culture of the Naxi people. He Wanbao, a semiretired Communist Party official and native son of East Wind Village, spearheaded the transformation of *dongba* ritual practices into a key symbol of Naxi ethnic identity.

In the late 1980s, He Wanbao's *dongba* culture caused confusion in East Wind Village. He, who had been residing in the provincial capital, began spending more time at his old family home in East Wind Village and at the Dongba Cultural Research Institute (Dongba wenhua yanjiusuo) in Lijiang, which he had founded.[14] His promotion of *dongba* as Naxi scholars and his own interest in learning *dongba* practices appeared to signal an official Communist Party authorization of prerevolutionary ritual practice. In the 1990s, many middle-aged villagers, who had associated *dongba* with feudal superstition less than a decade earlier, began to take an interest in newly defined "Naxi cultural practices." Some young people with no experience of the old rituals reconsidered their views that these practices were backward, while the rebellious youth of the village continued to be skeptical. But most of the middle-aged and older villagers treated He with considerable respect and deference. He had been the highest-ranking Communist Party official in Lijiang Prefecture after the revolution, had orchestrated the transition to a socialist government in Lijiang, and had ordered the suppression and execution of religious cult leaders who resisted the state. But in 1957, provincial leaders denounced He for ethnic nationalism and he was exiled from Lijiang; he did not return until he was rehabilitated in 1978.

Rehabilitation meant that political labels such as "ethnic nationalist" and "rightist" were rescinded and people were reinstated to their former positions, sometimes posthumously. The denunciation of He and other ethnic leaders had been part of a larger shift in state policy away from embracing elements of ethnic difference and toward creating a Maoist-era national identity that sought to homogenize all internal difference. This ideal of internal homogeneity changed in the 1980s, with a new representation of China as an ethnically diverse nation open to trade and diplomatic relations with countries it regarded as imperialist enemies during the Maoist era. He Wanbao was quick to embrace the state's celebration of ethnic difference in the 1980s.

In the 1990s, he was again one of the most powerful and beloved leaders in Naxi territory. When he came to East Wind Village, the older men frequently wandered into his courtyard to reminisce about *dongba*, ritual practices they had witnessed, and the old society. He's presence conferred legitimacy on ritual practices that were viewed as "traditional." Moreover, through his influence, the older men of the village were recognized as sources of knowledge themselves, elevating them over young people who "knew nothing." Despite ambivalence about traditional ritual, the entire village attended when He invited *dongba* from the Dongba Cultural Research Institute to perform his nephew's marriage ceremony, which included *siku*, the Naxi ritual that invites the bride's *si*, a life force associated with productive increase or fertility and connected to her family's house god, into the groom's family.

There was no singular or unified belief system in East Wind Village on the eve of the shaman's ritual for the madman. Life-cycle rituals meant different things depending on a participant's social position. Prosperous households associated them with displays of their prestige and largesse. Poorer families could partake of ritual feasts but could not afford to host them. The most profound divisions existed between generations. Ritual had far more significance for many older and middle-aged villagers than for younger people. East Wind Village life-cycle rituals entailed seating and serving arrangements that reenacted Confucian hierarchical distinctions based on age and gender. Not surprisingly, many of the older villagers felt vindicated by the recent interest in "Naxi practices," a category that was fleshed out by discussing once taboo prerevolutionary ritual practice. In impromptu gatherings, such as visits to He Wanbao's courtyard, and during weddings and other social occasions, older villagers commanded the silence of younger villagers as they held forth on shamans, charms, ghosts, exorcisms, and seances. An elderly villager, Old He, reminisced about his grandfather's donkey being cured after the character for "luck" was written on a piece of paper and burned. Another villager told of how his wife became possessed and spoke in the voice of a dead relative. A villager in his eighties recounted witnessing a neighbor with a dislocated arm screaming uncontrollably until he was magically silenced by the appearance of a *dongba*. This ethnicization of *dongba* ritual appeared to take the controversy out of ritual practice. Some of the villagers had worshipped ancestors and house gods during the prerevolutionary and Maoist eras, and for them, elements of a preexisting system of belief were still significant. Other villagers had ambivalent views about ritual practices and made judgments based on particular cases.

The escalation of ritual activity was part of a wider regional and national pattern, and other forms associated with past ritual practice started to appear in the Lijiang basin. In neighboring Heqing, a town occupied by the Bai minority, Buddhist groups began meeting publicly, and there were plans to rebuild local temples. At the annual *jia liu hui*, a popular agricultural fair held in Dali, a Bai minority city some six hours south of Lijiang by bus, geomancers, physiognomists, diviners, and other fortune-tellers offered their services while keeping close watch for local Public Security Bureau officers. There were also new forms of magic. In the late 1980s, a second Mao cult swept across China. While still negatively associated with the Maoist era for some people, Mao's image became a protective talisman for many urban taxi drivers in the early 1990s (Kristof 1992). Mao's second apotheosis reveals these taxi drivers' perception that there is magical power associated with Mao.[15] Drivers would recount stories of devastating accidents in which only people riding in taxis with Mao talismans survived (see Barmé 1996).[16] In Dali and Kunming, independent vendors were selling Mao buttons from the Cultural Revolution and taxi amulets featuring Mao, although in 1991, the second Mao craze had not spread to Lijiang.[17] The shaman's conjuring of Mao, then, was not an isolated event but part of a broader phenomenon in which elements of past ritual practices were revived alongside syncretic forms combining state symbols with magical practice.

This complex history of ritual practice in East Wind Village indicates that there were discontinuous layers of belief systems in a broader arena of varied practice. The identification of these elements of religious meaning, none of which commanded the consensus of villagers, enables us to track the evaluative processes that led to the villagers' acceptance or rejection of the shaman's ritual as a crystallization of social experience. The history of Naxi religious practice reveals that religious meaning had been forged in a fluid arena infused with state power, local interpretations of state power, and village power dynamics. The divisions between local and national discourses were not clearly drawn, in part because the interests and projects of village elites were compatible with state aims to standardize ritual meaning. Thus, the significance of ritual knowledge is tied not only to a persistence of belief but to the contemporary uses of ritual to forge authority within East Wind Village.

Following in the footsteps of He Wanbao, the older men of the village sought to legitimize ritual meaning as a path to authority. Their authority had been substantially tested during the Maoist era and, more recently, by children and grandchildren who eloped and set up new households in defiance of their parents. But generational cleavages were not the only ones that defined East Wind Village life.

VILLAGE DYNAMICS: ILLNESS, CLASS, AND COMMUNITY CRITIQUE

The appearance of solidarity in East Wind Village formed a thin veneer over a community characterized by differences and undercurrents of discontent. The pillars of the community, the financially successful families with impeccable political backgrounds, were often the focus of these tensions. In the early 1990s, the most successful families in the village were those with family members who were retired Party officials or retired or salaried workers. Their additional sources of income and connections enabled many of their families to find nonagricultural work for grown children and, in some cases, to obtain residence permits for Lijiang Town through unofficial channels.[18] Throughout China, residence located a person in a spatial hierarchy that corresponded to a particular standard of living. Villagers with family members who had made the transition to town or urban lives were the economic elite of East Wind Village.

In the early 1990s, there was a sharp difference in the standard of living for families with and without outside earnings. The least prosperous families often lacked fenced courtyards, owned no draft animals, and had only one building, which was both used for living quarters and shared with a few smaller animals such as pigs and chickens. These families were usually unable to provide their outmarrying daughters with a substantial dowry (managing at most one quilt or a single set of clothes) and did not celebrate their sons' marriages beyond providing a simple dinner for the immediate family. Neighbors who were more prosperous owned two or three buildings, neatly walled-in courtyards, and generally many animals. They celebrated the marriages of their sons and daughters with villagewide banquets and elaborate displays of dowries and gifts (multiple sets of clothing, quilts, thermos bottles, bicycles, bedding, and even furniture in some cases).

The growth in village solidarity and village-based identity was partially a response to the economic inequalities that had become particularly pronounced since decollectivization. According to villagers' accounts, the life-cycle rituals revived in the 1990s, to which the entire village was invited, contributed to a sense of solidarity that stressed the equal status of villagers and muted the past and current inequalities among them. Additionally, kin assisted one another on the basis of affective ties and membership in a patriline. Less formal but often emotionally deeper ties were founded on village-based age-mate networks. Age-mates played a defined role in helping with marriage celebrations, but they also assisted one another informally in a variety of contexts based on the strength of particular friendships. Age-mate ties were particularly strong among the somewhat rebellious young men of the village. Many of these men had eloped and established residences separate from their patrilineal kin in a row of houses dubbed "the village of unfilial sons." Many of these "unfilial sons" shared the experience of having lived outside the village and regarded their elders as conservative, or even backward, in their beliefs about social protocol and farming. Yet rebelliousness tended to fade as these young men raised children of their own, mended bridges with their families, and participated in villagewide activities. The ties and sentiments that bound the village as a community were related to practical forms of assistance. In the 1990s, villagers engaged in reciprocal labor exchanges so that they could harvest grain when it was ripe and meet labor demands when family members were ill or had social obligations that took them away from the village.

The growth in economic inequality among villagers dating from the reform era also gave rise to some tensions among kin and within the village. Social ties were often the nodal points where tension erupted. Villagers felt pressured by or could not say no to age-mates or kin who requested loans and often did not repay them. With the abolition of the collective, villagers considered kin, particularly those whose households were financially comfortable, as responsible for assisting their less fortunate relatives. A common theme in the criticism of families unwilling to assist others was the opposition between greed and caring. The discourse that opposes greed with caring for others appears loosely compatible with the ideology of socialist revolution and with behaving as responsible social beings (*zuoren*).

Paradoxically, however, those households that needed to shield themselves against such potential criticism were those with the reddest backgrounds whose members had once vigorously proselytized the ideology of socialist revolution and whose privileged positions during the collective era had contributed to their financial success since decollectivization. Perhaps due to the pressures associated with their relative prosperity, many of these families took a prominent role in villagewide activities and were considered the exemplary citizens of East Wind Village. Their eagerness to contribute to the village promoted an image of social engagement and caring for others and muted discontent over their economic superiority. It was one of these red and exemplary families that was seen as having benefited from the madman's condition and that subsequently responded to village pressure to help with the madman's cure. Hence, the shaman came to East Wind Village to cure not just a madman but a kinsman of one of the village's most prosperous and politically prominent families.

The madman, whose wife had recently died, was about forty years old and lived alone. Before his madness, he was known for being very intelligent and knowledgeable; villagers often consulted with him before deciding when to plant their crops and enjoyed chatting with him because he was considered an expert on world events. The madman's household, one of the village's poorest at the time of liberation, had fared well during the collective era. After decollectivization, however, the household's fortunes had declined, and villagers recounted that the man had gone mad after his wife's recent death. There was a general feeling among the villagers that the madman's case was exceptional and that something should be done.

East Wind Village had another madman, but, in contrast, no shaman was invited and no ritual held to cure him. This second madman had entered a "uxorilocal marriage" (shangmen), meaning he married into his wife's family. He killed his wife during a quarrel, and then had gone mad while in prison. After his release, he returned to the village, where he was known to have occasional "bursts of madness" (feng feng dian dian). A man who marries uxorilocally becomes the classificatory son and heir of his in-laws and, at the same time, loses the right to membership and inheritance in his own lineage. Although villagers viewed this second madman as part of a social body, given his uxorilocal marriage that social body consisted of his wife's kin who had symbolically adopted him and were technically recognized as his patrilineal kin. Hence, this madman had a tenuous, if not nonexistent, claim to support from his natal kin and was already imposing on them by returning and living with his brother. The lack of village pressure on his relatives to intervene ritually was due to the perception that they were already making a sacrifice by taking him back. This was not the case for the first madman, whose relatives did host the ritual: he was indisputably part of one of the three village patrilines and was recognized as having been a valued member of the village community.

However, there is another explanation for why the villagers decided that the first madman's condition warranted particular attention, thereby triggering a rise in village concern. Illnesses during which the body is vulnerable often raise questions about the fundamental basis of social order (Foucault 1980; Comaroff 1981; Turner 1987; Adams 1992), yet not all forms of affliction are perceived as equally momentous. Particular cases of affliction may strike a chord as emblematic of broader dynamics in a fluctuating social order.[19]

The villagers could not ignore the first madman's poverty, misfortune, and affliction, particularly given the conspicuous prosperity of his relatives. His father, mother, little sister, and wife had all died within a ten-year span, which coincidentally corresponded to the beginning of decollectivization in the Lijiang basin. Had his household faced economic hardship during the collective era, it would have received assistance from the collective. But because his misfortunes occurred after decollectivization, he became dependent on relatives whose household had become one of the most prosperous since decollectivization. Their prosperity over the last decade was due to having a family member who was a high-ranking official and others who were salaried workers in Lijiang Town. While they had helped their poorer relation, they had also begun gradually expanding their courtyard into his and started farming his land.

When discussing this situation, villagers focused on the "strangeness" of the multiple deaths in the madman's household. According to informants' accounts, these deaths appeared to be more problematic than the existence of the madman himself. At what may be referred to as a cosmic level, the villagers perceived fertility and productivity as natural phenomena, the reversal of which is conspicuously unnatural. Consequently, the lack of fertility in the madman's wife (they were childless), childlessness of the madman's household, the fact that he was an only son, the untimely death of his young, unmarried, and presumably fertile sister, and the withering productivity of his household unit—taken all together—suggested to the villagers a negativity of supernatural proportions.[20]

The villagers conceive of sì, the life force associated with productive increase or fertility, as the divisible property of a given kinship group. During the pre-1949 era, when a bride joined her husband's household, his family held *siku*, the ritual inviting the bride's *si* to join the groom's family. Similarly, when a household was divided among sons, each would receive a share of *si*, conceived of as that household's prosperity evidenced in children, grain, animals, and so on. Villagers associated excessive wealth with abundant *si*, just as poverty aroused suspicions that someone had taken or "led away" one's share of *si*. Only some villagers articulated the depletion of *si* in their explanations of the madman's condition, but all were familiar with the concept from the recent performance of *siku* at the wedding of He Wanbao's nephew. What most villagers noticed was that the madman's household was becoming impoverished at the same time that his relatives were becoming prosperous, which appeared to support vague constructions of greed and exploitation. At a symbolic level, patrilineal kin could be seen as usurpers of fertility and productive increase who had a particular responsibility to engage in reciprocity in order to restore the madman's unproductive household unit. While circumstances forced the madman to "eat the grain of his relatives," his relatives were seen as "eating the madman's land."

The demonization of misfortune, and its symbolic location in the larger familial unit of the patriline, not only forced the madman's relatives to take ritual action as a matter of self-defense but also effected a symbolic form of redistribution. (For villagers, rituals are always associated with the expenditure of money or its equivalent on the part of the hosting family.) The relatives sacrificed ten duck eggs (equivalent to ¥20, at that time, 30 percent of a monthly rural income), a live chicken, and a modest amount of food offerings. The ritual expenditure of duck eggs, a live chicken, and rice—items that also symbolize fertility and productivity—signified the abundance of fortune the madman's relatives enjoyed. The logic of the ritual is simple: that which has been depleted will be ritually added. By acting as host and paying a ransom to appease the demons, the relatives would symbolically reverse misfortune by redirecting fortune (material offerings and symbols of fertility and productivity) to the madman's household. The performative operations associated with ritual would credit reciprocity and social relations with having created and restored fertility in post-Mao-era East Wind Village.

Such a scenario might seem particularly just in the eyes of those villagers who viewed the source of the madman's affliction not simply as existing in the individual but as located in the larger social body to which he belonged. It is quite common in Naxi villages for relatives of afflicted individuals, prompted by community members, to decide when and how illness should be treated

(White 1993). These decisions are not individual but familial and reveal where villagers locate responsibility for physical well-being.

In sum, the madman's personal misfortune resonated with a wider historical experience of the growth of economic inequality in the village since decollectivization and was itself a striking example of this inequality. Some villagers simply felt that the madman's relatives, given their prosperity, should help their kinsman. By assisting the madman, particularly given their own gains from his illness, his relatives could act as responsible social beings. But many villagers conceptualized these inequalities as unnatural or generated by supernatural sources. Here, supernatural sources operate as an idiom for emergent class inequalities. Whether conceptualized as demons or greed, villagers were faced with these inequalities, which created dilemmas for them as a moral community. Discussion of class had been officially muted by proponents of economic reform since the post-Mao era, which created a climate ripe for an alternative construction of village experiences. At the same time, inviting a ritual practitioner became an attractive option given the apparent rehabilitation of prerevolutionary ritual practice.

RITUAL FAILURE, IDENTITY FAILURE, AND FAILURES IN RITUAL THEORY

What made the shaman's ritual significant despite the fact that it failed to reinvent a symbolic system that was either enduring or, apparently, even shared by its audience? Michael Watts (1992) has pointed out that "identity failures," or failed projects to map the construction of selves onto the creation of imagined communities, have been largely ignored. Gupta and Ferguson (1997, 14) warn that when identity failures are ignored, questions of identity are examined without attention to processes of legitimation and authentication. Such discussions help explain why some identities become salient at certain historical moments, while other marks of difference fail to become the basis of identity (Gupta and Ferguson 1997). What marks of difference, then, led to the assessment of the shaman as an identity failure? Answering this question requires an examination of the identity the shaman tried to create and how the villagers understood this identity.

The shaman's new role as ritual practitioner may have originated from her former position as a low-level Communist Party representative and her subsequent displacement in the post-Mao era. In her capacity as shaman, she may have attempted to reclaim symbols from her days as a Red Guard and Party official by ritually conjuring them as aids in producing a cure. Elizabeth Perry has shown that many Communist Party officials, divested of their former authority in the post-Mao era, have emerged at the forefront of the revival of "unauthorized religious activities" (1985, 183). As a Party official, the shaman undoubtedly played a role in the interpretation of state directives. A new identity as ritual practitioner similarly positioned her as a mediator, interpreting directives from higher authorities and explaining the workings of the imagined social landscape over which these authorities presided. Yet, unlike the powerful local elites who spearheaded the authorization of new deities in the late imperial era, actors like the shaman were marginal.[21] Marginality has long been associated with shamanism as a vocation. Before 1949, it was poor farmers who took on the role of shaman and only after life-threatening traumas, which might be likened to the dislocation experienced by obsolete Party officials in the post-Mao era. The marginality of the shaman who came to East Wind Village to cure the madman must have made her performance particularly crucial to assessments of her identity.

The ritual replacement of the shamanic hierarchy with prominent national figures, themselves symbols of Chinese socialist morality and power, resembles what James Watson refers to as an act of "superseding local gods" with what the shaman conceptualized as "state-approved deities." In Watson's analysis of the process by which local gods were superseded by a handful of state-approved deities in south China during the Qing dynasty (1644-1911), the "standardization of gods" (such as Tien Hou) paralleled the "rise of state authority over China's southern coastal region" (1985, 293–94). He interprets the spiritual triumph of state over local gods as "a metaphor of political domination in the real world" (Watson 1985, 311). The shaman had tried to replace local gods with Mao, Zhou, and Deng, who were much like state-approved deities. Had this been successful, state symbols could have superseded local symbols, with results similar to those achieved by the standardization Watson describes. Such a transformation could have fused powerful symbols of the socialist state with the shaman's cosmology and created a new ritual form expressing the political dominance of the state.

However, unlike the case described by Watson, the shaman's attempt to replace local gods with state deities was unconnected to any state project aimed at political domination. Indeed, the state would have condemned the shaman, despite what appeared to be her pro-state pedagogy. The state condemns shamanism as feudal superstition. Moreover, the shaman's ritual actions went beyond a simple resurrection of Maoist-era symbols. By disengaging the figures of Mao, Zhou, and Deng from the realm of state authority and deploying them in shamanic practice, the shaman transformed their meaning. For both the shaman and the villagers, a Mao, Zhou, and Deng identified with shamanism and relocated in a celestialized hierarchy could not be semantically equivalent to flesh-and-blood state figures or even larger-than-life, Maoist-era icons with auras of personal power. What, then, did it mean when symbols of the state, unbeknownst to state authorities, shaped local practice? Is it the power of the state or the shaman's agency that was evident in this ritual? To different extents, it was both.

By inserting Mao, Zhou, and Deng into the ritual context, the shaman enabled their manipulation according to the logic of symbolic ordering and propitiation implied by ritual formulas known to the Naxi and other regional ethnic groups. In a sense, their cosmological relocation rendered them exploitable as perceived yang sources of, and mediators for, magical power, gods that the shaman could then harness for practical use through acts of ritual propitiation. The shaman's actions created a formalized space for the interpretation and manipulation of state symbols that was outside the state's control. Had it succeeded, the ritual might have become a context for the local co-optation of state symbols that drew on and reinforced preexisting ritual formulas by using them to manipulate new forms of power. It would also have reinvented an identity for the shaman as a powerful healer and transformer of popular ritual practice.[22] In either scenario—state deities eclipsing local gods or the co-optation of state symbols for local uses—the shaman was not simply subject to state hegemony but expressed her own experiences of state power: she was an agent acting upon the contradictory structures and values of the Maoist and post-Mao eras.

Most villagers, however, saw the shaman as a throwback to the Maoist era. For many villagers, symbols of the state—like the shaman's Cultural Revolution paraphernalia—had lost their aura of power in the post-Mao era. Many of the villagers perceived state leaders, even deified, as impotent in addressing the madman's plight. By revisiting the Maoist past, the shaman's anachronistic Maoist identity and ritual performance reminded villagers of the virtues of the post-Mao era. In the East Wind Village of the early 1990s, the attempt to craft a Maoist identity—even within a shamanic framework—could only fail.

Decollectivization had brought about a marked improvement in the standard of living in the village, as well as an enthusiastic return to family-based farming. Although there were contradictions between village experiences and state logic, villagers welcomed the potential for "getting rich" that the state had promoted since decollectivization. When the growing prosperity of individual families created tensions within the village, discussions about misfortune of "unnatural" proportions and "greed versus caring for others" provided a means of venting frustrations over forbidden topics, such as growing economic inequalities and emerging class cleavages. Since the advent of the post-Mao era, the topic of class has been effectively buried because of its association with painful memories of Maoist-era political extremism and community bloodletting. East Wind Village accounts of history define the post-Mao era (characterized by decollectivization, tolerance of ritual and ethnic identity, new prosperity, and sharp economic inequalities) in opposition to the Maoist era (characterized by collective farming, an ethnically muted national identity, poverty, class struggle, the Cultural Revolution, and tumultuous political campaigns). But the moratorium imposed on discussions of class necessitated an idiom for expressing new problematic sentiments. In this context, shamanic remedies and village solidarity gained a momentary popular appeal. But rather than a ritual that redressed inequality and affirmed a village-based identity, the East Wind Village audience interpreted the shaman's ritual as conjuring a Maoist era in which class struggle had divided and dominated the village. In contrast to the now permissible Naxi identity embraced by villagers, the ritual called for national identity, individual responsibility as opposed to community-based decisions, and a cosmological order that resembled a celestialized Maoist state. While the villagers welcomed a shamanic resolution of experienced inequalities, they could not tolerate the volatile mixture of Maoist symbols and class differences. The shaman's ritual reveals something about the realms of possible interpretation and the conflicted fields of power that intervened to preclude their legitimization. East Wind Village interpretations of the shaman as an "identity failure" issued from a disjuncture of experiences. The following factors all worked to challenge the legitimacy of the shaman's identity and the imagined community she tried to invoke: identification with Republican nationalism during the Sino-Japanese War, historical experiences based on positionality during the Maoist era, models of shamanic healing, collective-era experiences, and the rhetorical efficacy of state discourse during the post-Mao era.

The shaman's ritual unintentionally led to a polarization of options, either a return to the tightly controlled and impoverished life evoked by the symbols of the Maoist past or an alternative model that harmonized and elided inequalities. Her performance provided a model against which villagers constructed an identity that was tolerant of emerging class inequalities, inequalities that had prompted the ritual in the first place.

FAILED RITUAL AND FAILED THEORY

What does this failed ritual contribute to the understanding of ritual theory? In a landmark article, Helen Siu has perceptively argued that ritual in the post-Mao era can never be a simple revival of preexisting forms innocent of the experiences of a "monopolizing state power" (1989). She further states that the ritual revitalization under way in reform-era China is taking place with the complicity of the state and has resulted in rituals that are comparatively recycled, diluted, secularized, pragmatically motivated, and lacking their former depth of meaning (Siu 1989, 132–33).

Although the shaman's ritual revealed experiences of a "monopolizing state power," as Siu suggests, her second observation about contemporary ritual revitalization does not apply. The shaman's ritual did not take place with state complicity, nor does it fit Siu's description. Rethinking some theoretical presuppositions in Siu's argument reveals a functional bias that gives priority to ritual outcome over ritual process. In addition, her analysis of contemporary ritual is based on an implicit comparison with standardized rituals that integrated state and popular culture during the late imperial and Republican eras. While Siu acknowledges the existence of other ritual forms, such as pre-1949 ritual practice used to subvert state authority, she excludes them from her theorization because the thrust of standard ritual practice was integration. Limiting analysis of ritual to standardized or normative—and integrative or functional—forms tends to produce representations of society that primarily focus on consensus and homogeneity. These representations simultaneously overlook forms of contestation and conflict that are a regular feature of social arenas. By categorizing standardized and integrative ritual as somehow more authentic, analyses tainted with functional bias are prone to reify hierarchical arrangements of power as "cultural essence." And by privileging ritual outcome over ritual process, the conflicts and lineaments of power that are part of the processes of even successful rituals often escape notice.

A theory of ritual must allow for the inclusion of rituals aimed at transforming social order, whether or not they are successful, as well as those that result in the maintenance of social order. Without theorizing rituals of transformation and failed rituals, analysts eliminate from their depictions of social arenas many forms of agency that contest and resist power. In addition, analyses that categorize rituals according to outcome often ignore the contradictory elements that are common in ritual practice. As Ahern has explained, ritual may be seen as serving both the ends of political power in some ways and the ends of the powerless in other ways (1981, 106). A theory of ritual that adopts a functional, all-or-nothing view cannot account for the shaman's ritual for the madman of East Wind Village, which wed state power to counter-hegemonic interpretations and shamanic agency. Such a theory is further ill positioned to address the complex contingencies and fluid dynamics that led to the failure of the shaman's ritual. The inclusion of failed rituals would be an important step in understanding social processes. It is, however, equally important not to let outcome—in either failed or successful ritual—govern our focus, as doing so would impair our ability to find conformity in failed rituals as well as conflict in successful ones. Including a spectrum of practice in the analysis of ritual will enhance our ability to account for how conflict, contestation, conformity, and unity all shape social processes and ritual outcomes.

**DONGBA CULTURE
AND THE
AUTHENTICIZATION
OF MARGINALITY**

Dongba culture purports to describe a set of practices equated with the culture of the Naxi ethnic group. In the twenty-first century, virtually everyone in Lijiang Town and in the rural villages of Lijiang County is familiar with this term. Naxi children learn about *dongba* culture in their schools, and it is used in branding an array of goods and performances marked as ethnically Naxi. Most young urban residents who continue to live in Lijiang will be employed in some way that is linked to Lijiang's tourism-dependent economy. It is the state's plan to make the tertiary economy (which includes tourism) a pillar of the national economy. *Dongba* culture has become a central part of the vocabulary identifying Lijiang's distinctiveness, and references to it can be found on the numerous websites that market tourism to China. Lijiang has become one of the top ten or so destinations featured on almost all China tourism websites, but this was not always the case.

This chapter discusses *dongba* culture in the early 1990s, before it became broadly equated with Naxi culture and before Lijiang developed into a major tourist destination. The articulation of dongba culture may be understood as a consequence of reform-era biopolitics: the way in which the Chinese state created ethnic categories by encouraging and funding the projects of ethnic groups to discover, record, and narrate distinctive ethnic characteristics. Dongba culture was the particular project of Naxi government officials and intellectuals who sought to beneficially define the distinctiveness of the Naxi ethnic group. This project, which sought to empower the Naxi, has also had the unintended consequence, through its interpretation of the past, of legitimizing and naturalizing a hierarchy of difference.

From 1990 to 1992, I lived at the Dongba Cultural Research Institute, which is located in Lijiang Town, the capital of Lijiang Naxi Autonomous County. The Institute is a work unit that translates pictographic Naxi ritual texts into Chinese. Foreign scholars who seek to study the Naxi are regularly steered toward the study of *dongba* culture, which is portrayed as the cultural heritage of the Naxi. Although my interests were in contemporary Naxi gender construction and ritual practice, I was advised that these topics could be sufficiently explored at the institute and that research in the countryside was unnecessary, because the four resident *dongba* and eleven resident Naxi scholars could provide sufficient information. Gender could be studied through the analysis of female characters in Naxi myth, which is a part of *dongba* culture. Naxi "culture" was not the domain of ordinary people but rather was identified with specific practices that were best articulated by the institute's specialists.

Dongba were not part of an organized religious institution but individual practitioners who performed a variety of rituals including exorcisms, healings, funerals, and annual sacrifices. The *dongba* acquired his skill (women have historically been excluded from this vocation) through a long apprenticeship with a *dongba* master. In some cases, he was the son of a *dongba* or even descended from a long line of *dongba*. Young apprentices often spent years living and laboring on the farm of a *dongba* master while learning to read and write the pictographic script recited during *dongba* rituals. While *dongba* received some compensation for their ritual services, usually in the form of a gift, they were essentially peasants (*nongming*) who supported themselves by farming and merely acted as ritual specialists on the side.

The Cultural Revolution had a devastating effect on the *dongba* religion.[1] *Dongba* were criticized for practicing "feudal superstition," and, in some cases, their children were blocked from receiving any education beyond the primary level. The Red Guards roamed the countryside confiscating or burning *dongba* texts and religious paraphernalia. Many of the texts that survived this period are now housed in the Dongba Cultural Research Institute's library. The training of new *dongba* came to a complete halt during the Cultural Revolution, and, given their experiences, former *dongba* did not encourage their sons to even consider learning *dongba* ways. By the early 1990s, there remained only about thirty to forty *dongba* from those trained before 1949, and virtually all were elderly men in their sixties, seventies, and eighties.[2]

Even the relaxation of the state's anti-religion policy during the post-Mao era of the 1980s and 1990s did not contribute to a revival of *dongba* ritual practices. For the Naxi in Lijiang Town and in the areas southwest of it, bordering the Golden Sand River, there were no actively practicing *dongba* to be found. In these areas, the resurgence of ritual practice had consisted primarily of Chinese-style marriage and funerary rites.[3] The popularity of indigenous Naxi practitioners, such as the *dongba* (priest) and *sanba* (shaman) had already begun to decline in the basin in the 1920s and 1930s, and the Cultural Revolution nearly dealt them a final blow. In the mountain regions, *dongba* and *sanba* continued to practice until the Cultural Revolution.

While there are still isolated incidents of shamanic practice in the rural Lijiang basin, these shamans tend to be from other ethnic groups such as Bai or Han. In the 1990s, it was only in the sparsely populated "mountain districts" (*shan qu*) that dongba were to be found at all, and even in these villages, *dongba* ritual performances were infrequent. In Baidi, the sacred founding place of the *dongba* religion located in the adjacent Tibetan Autonomous County, *dongba* rituals are reportedly still performed, but the frequency and importance of these practices are undocumented.[4]

ETHNIC DIFFERENCE AND IMAGINING THE NATION

How is it that the category "*dongba* culture" came to be promoted by Naxi officials in Lijiang Town at the very moment that *dongba* religion was on the verge of disappearing? The transformation of *dongba* religion into *dongba* culture in the early 1980s may be understood as an "invention of tradition" (Hobsbawm 1983) aimed at bolstering Naxi ethnic identity and prestige, an invention that was inspired by, and took place in concert with, a broader national policy aimed at documenting and celebrating ethnic diversity in post-Mao-era China. In the early 1980s, the Chinese government heavily invested in the "collection and editing" of compilations of the folk culture of ethnic minorities, including their ancient books, folk tales, literature, music and art (Information Office of the State Council of the People's Republic of China 1999, 17–19).

Since the beginning of the post-Mao era, official representations of China as a "nation of many nationalities" (*duo minzu guojia*) have emphasized an image of internal ethnic diversity. This representation marked a sharp turn from the active suppression of ethnic difference pursued by the state during the Maoist era (e.g., Dreyer 1976; Grunfeld 1985, 64–65; Heberer 1989, 23–29). Although people actively sought to forget the Maoist era, its looming presence foregrounded and fueled the imagination of its successor. The lived experiences of the Maoist era summoned memories of internal divisiveness, suspicion, and fear of internal enemies—within the community, among one's neighbors, and even within one's own family (Chao 1996; Mueggler 2001). At the same time, the national body was remembered in terms of uniformity achieved through forced conformity: masses in blue clutching Mao's red book and reciting slogans in a single voice. While the "official" explanations of the chaos of the Maoist era placed blame at the feet of the Gang of Four, people resisted such oversimplification. The process of remembering juxtaposed and causally correlated Maoist nationalism, as seen through disillusioned eyes, with the powerful lived experiences of social discord.

The re-presentation of the nation during the post-Mao era, accompanied by images of plurality and ethnic difference, created a break with the uniformity of the Maoist past. The post-Mao era's reimagining of the nation fostered an expectation of a new order of social experience that would be internally harmonious and consonant with the official promotion of diversity, although this applied only to *representations* of ethnic diversity rather than to any actual cultivation of diversity or grant of autonomy to ethnic groups.

The importance of ethnicity to this new imagining of the nation should not be overstated. The mass disillusionment at the end of the Maoist era required a rupture with the past, which has demanded much more than the symbolic rehabilitation of ethnicity. Anderson has suggested that "nationalism has to be understood by aligning it . . . with the large cultural systems that preceded it, out of which—as well as against which—it came into being" ([1983] 1992, 12). While Maoist nationalism may be understood as having been constructed against the Republican nation and the dynastic realm, attempts to reimagine the nation in the post-Mao era were similarly constructed against the Maoist era by reaching farther back into the imperial past for sources of power and knowledge with which to align and legitimize a new national identity for the present. This re-creation has entailed an appropriation of what the Maoist era sought to destroy: ethnic difference, historical landmarks, imperial antiquities, Confucian obedience, and even religious systems.

Anagnost (1993, 586) has described how theme parks that have opened since the post-Mao era began—such as Splendid China (*Jinxiu Zhonghua*), which features displays of national minority groups and miniature models of antiquities, traditional architecture, and historical and religious sites—demarcated a new space of representation within which the contemporary nation is imagined. These images of the nation concealed its origin, which was defined in opposition to the dynastic realm, as the dynastic realm now ironically came to represent the socialist nation.

Beyond fueling the new discourse of national identity, the promotion of ethnicity involved local and state efforts to appropriate, invent, and re-present ethnic tradition for the purposes of controlling religion and fostering economic development. An examination of the emergence of *dongba* culture—which has come to define the official representation of the Naxi minority—demonstrates how representations of ethnicity are embedded in structures of power and how local efforts to rehabilitate selected elements of the indigenous practice are permeated by sedimentations of imperial and contemporary state discourse.

AGENCY, IDENTITY, AND *DONGBA* CULTURE

What is *dongba* culture? How and why has it come to be equated with Naxi culture? The term "*dongba* culture" was coined in 1981 with the founding of the Dongba Cultural Research Institute. Naxi officials wanted a name for an institute responsible for preserving and translating *dongba* religious texts but that made no reference to the politically dangerous subject of religion.

Since the founding of the People's Republic of China, religion (*zongjiao*) has been alternately discouraged and prohibited. Today the state tolerates the limited practice of religion, which is narrowly defined to include only Buddhism, Daoism, Islam, and Christianity. In the early 1980s, folk religious practitioners and magical healers such as diviners, shamans, sorcerers, geomancers, and so on, were categorized by the state as purveyors of "feudal superstition" (*fengjian mixin*) and were strictly prohibited. Magical healers have been categorically targeted as a force impeding scientific thinking, thwarting the process of modernization, and seeking to defraud unsuspecting citizens. In the early 1990s, such healers faced between two and seven years of imprisonment if caught practicing (Spiegel 1992, 12; Anagnost 1985, 154). Measured strictly by the state's definition of religion, *dongba* ritual practices would fall *outside* the category of religion, according it the status of feudal superstition.

FIG. 2.1 Colored *dongba* pictograph sold to tourists (*above*);
Dongba ritual text (*below*)

The rise of dongba culture is often attributed to the efforts of He Wanbao, the earliest First Party Secretary of Lijiang, who was accused of "ethnic nationalism" (minzu zhuyi) during the Anti-Rightist Campaign in 1957–58 and was rehabilitated in the post-Mao era. A savvy political veteran and the force behind the founding of the Dongba Cultural Research Institute, He Wanbao promoted dongba culture as a means of preserving the dongba religious heritage in a form that the Chinese state could accept. As one of the few Naxi educated in a university before the revolution, He was well aware of the prestige accorded written language in Chinese culture and its strong association with the Chinese concept of culture, or wenhua.[5] While frequently translated as "culture" or "education," the term wenhua closely approximates the notion of civilization: it is closer to the Western idea of high culture than to the contemporary anthropological definition of culture as everyday practice.[6] The Naxi's claim to wenhua was founded on their distinctive status as one of the few minority groups in China with their own system of writing; this system includes a pictographic script (dongbawen) and a phonetic script (gebawen).[7] These forms of writing, however, had been used exclusively by dongba for ritual purposes and were generally unintelligible to the broader Naxi population.[8] The Naxi had no other written language.[9] The ability to conjoin the terms "dongba" and "culture" was predicated on the dongba's association with literacy and the invocation of residual imperial constructs of civilization.

For many Chinese, the category "dongba culture" conjured images of civilization at the same time that it detached the dongba from the realm of religion and superstition. In 1981, the founding of the Dongba Cultural Research Institute set the stage for the reappearance of the Naxi dongba. But like the Jesuit followers of Matteo Ricci, who were shunned as priests, dongba could cross the threshold of state legitimacy only by donning the robes of scholars. Hence, the dongba who was re-embedded in a discourse of Naxi ethnic identity was re-presented as an expert on Naxi "cultural traditions" (fengsu xiguan), while his former history as a perpetrator of "feudal superstition" was muted.

Dongba texts underwent a similar transformation. Formerly used exclusively for ritual purposes, they were re-presented as objects of scholarly analysis and sources of indigenous knowledge. An early pamphlet from the institute describes dongba texts as forming an "encyclopedia . . . that covers a wide range of knowledge including philosophy, history, religion, medicine, astronomy, folklore, literature, art and philology" (Tang 1988). With the dongba recast as a scholar and the ritual texts redefined as an informational compendium, Naxi officials easily re-presented the *dongba* religion as *dongba* culture, wellspring of Naxi tradition and the modern Naxi people.

The invention of *dongba* culture was also supported from another direction. In the 1920s, Joseph Rock, an Austrian American explorer and botanist, settled in Naxi territory. He initially came to collect local plant specimens but soon became more interested in the ritual practices of the Naxi, particularly the *dongba*. Rock spent twenty years meticulously recording rituals and translating *dongba* texts into English. The voluminous works that attest to his labors have both sparked Western interest in the Naxi and significantly contributed to the local Naxi and Chinese social scientific claims of the importance of Naxi culture as a distinct and worthy subject of scholarly investigation (e.g., Rock 1947, 1963, 1972).[10]

In the 1990s, a few copies of Rock's books were proudly exhibited in a locked glass case in the center of the Dongba Cultural Research Institute museum. These English-language editions of Rock's works were unintelligible to the Naxi scholars who labored for decades to reach the institute's goal of translating all remaining *dongba* pictographic texts into Chinese. In the 1990s, though Rock's works remained untouched, they were a treasured source of pride: emblems of the importance of *dongba* culture and the Naxi people, who had commanded the attention of a Western scholar associated with the world-renowned Harvard University.[11]

By 1991, *dongba* culture was still far from being internalized as the basis of identity at the local level. People categorized as Naxi rarely constructed their identity with knowledge of or reference to the *dongba* religion, which many of the town-based Naxi had never experienced and which was only a vague memory among the older rural basin residents. Even in the home village of He Wanbao, the institute's founder, *dongba* ritual was unknown to most of the younger villagers, who often playfully referred to He as "Head Dongba" (*dongba tou*). For many of the younger villagers, the idea that He sought to valorize the practices of the *dongba* was considered odd; *dongba* were thought of as from another time, and promoting them was associated with moving backward rather than toward modernization and the future. In the basin villages, imperial discourses of civilization informed a socio-cosmological order. In Lijiang Town and the rural basin, dating from the Republican era, Han rituals (marked not as Han but as local) were the practices associated with culture. Folk practitioners such as the *dongba*, who were considered "backward" (*luohuo*) according to the older state discourses on religion, generated little interest.

Thus, the celebration of *dongba* culture was not a popular cultural phenomenon; it was not something that articulated a primordial sense of identity or way of life that tenaciously survived the historical transformations since 1949 to suddenly percolate upward and manifest itself in the post-Mao era. Although the representation of *dongba* culture as the living cultural heritage of the Naxi minority suggests continuity between the "authentically ethnic" Naxi practices of the *dongba* and popular practice, among most Naxi there is none. So what was the meaning of this emerging category to the people it allegedly represented? In the early 1990s, as a resident at the institute, I frequently encountered Naxi farmers and town dwellers who would ask, "What does *dongba* mean? And what is this *dongba* culture?"

At first I was puzzled as to why so many Naxi were completely unaware of their own cultural practices and heritage. The resident Naxi scholars would explain this apparent contradiction by saying that the farmers "lack learning" or that fellow town dwellers "have become just like the Han and no longer know about Naxi culture." Yet even the Naxi who live in the mountains and are heralded by Naxi scholars as the "real Naxi" identified themselves in terms of origin myths and a sense of place that were not necessarily associated with *dongba* or *dongba* practices.

If the conception of *dongba* culture did not faithfully correspond to the local Naxi's construction of their identity in the 1990s, then how can it be understood? How did the creation of *dongba* culture influence or transform *dongba* religion and Naxi culture? To what extent may promoters of *dongba* culture be seen as having been doing the bidding of the state, or should they be understood as involved in a project of local representation that articulated a subaltern subjectivity?

THE APPROPRIATION, PURIFICATION, AND RE-PRESENTATION OF THE PAST

Dongba religious practices were conveniently beyond the memory and experience of the majority of contemporary Naxi, which allowed for the creation of *dongba* culture. The repositioning of *dongba* as the scholars and wise men of Naxi society gave them a voice of authority with which to speak for the Naxi past. However, it was actually not the *dongba* who spoke; rather, in the early 1990s, institutions such as the Dongba Cultural Research Institute *articulated dongba* culture. The institute's goal was to preserve the rich Naxi cultural heritage recorded in ritual texts before there were no longer any elderly *dongba* to aid in the process of translation. While the Naxi scholars had some understanding of *dongba* pictographic script, none had completely mastered the language or was capable of translating the texts without the aid of the elderly *dongba* who were essential to the translation process.

The process of textual translation produced two levels of alteration. Not only were Naxi religious texts converted into written Chinese, but there was also a mutation of the ritual form and its purpose. In the past, ritual texts were sacred and could be interpreted only by the *dongba*, who evoked an imagined community and cosmos through their performances, but this evocation was never simply equivalent to the texts alone because ritual relied on song, dance, and other performative operations. The texts were only one element of ritual, and rituals were coherent only when performed in a particular context or enacted for specific social and historical occasions. Although the act of translation purports to rescue and preserve, it actually selects and transforms ritual, thereby rendering it a benign medium for a limited scholarly audience.

The state's institutionalization of *dongba* ritual texts and the *dongba* themselves accomplished several transformations. It aligned the state with a religious system that had once informed local identity and, at the same time, emphasized the decomposition of that religious system. In the 1990s, the *dongba* religion was safely dead for the vast majority of the Naxi population and was even in decline in the remote mountain villages on the periphery of Naxi territory. *Dongba* culture was something to be exhibited in museums, a prestigious emblem of heritage to be stored and interpreted. But the invention of *dongba* culture transformed fragments of that religious system into something else: a scholarly encyclopedia of putatively primordial knowledge, a relic of the past appropriated and rewritten for the purposes of Chinese scholarship, a new form of antiquity to be claimed and wielded by the Chinese nation-state, an exhibit for the promotion of international tourism.

An article in *China Daily*, a newspaper written for international audiences, underscores how *dongba* culture was beginning to be deployed as a source of national prestige and antiquity: "The hieroglyphic scripture of the Dongba . . . is believed to be more primitive than the wedge-shaped language of the Babylonians, the Mayan characters of Central America and the inscriptions on the bones and tortoise shells of the Shang Dynasty (16–11 century B.C.E.).

But whereas the latter three cultures have long since disappeared, the *Dongba* scripture is alive and well" (Gong 1993).

By creating institutions for the study of *dongba* culture, the state laid claim to the once powerful fragments of the Naxi past. In doing so, it expanded the scope of its own antiquity while simultaneously allowing the Naxi people to identify the state's history as their own.

NARROWING NAXI HISTORY

With the valorization of *dongba* culture as the essential core of Naxi heritage, the diversity of religious and cultural practice that existed in Lijiang before 1949 had to be either subsumed under *dongba* culture or eradicated from the Naxi past. Tibetan and Chinese Buddhism, vegetarian temple sects, geomancers, shamans, diviners, and the like were thus banished from official Naxi history. Moreover, the *dongba* themselves went through a process of sanitization in order to reappear as scholars. Those *dongba* practices that smelled of superstition, including entering a trance state during rituals, were played down, while the *dongba*'s historical adherence to written texts was emphasized. The reinvention of the *dongba* was partially achieved through the vilification of his historical predecessor and contemporary, the *sanba*. In fact, the *dongba*'s new identity—which stressed that the profession is "male," "learned," and "literary"—was a specific contrast to a contemporary construction of the *sanba* as "female," "backward," and "illiterate." The act of setting up an opposition between *sanba* and *dongba* obliterated the historical similarities between them and the implication that the *dongba* himself is a transformation of the older form of *sanba* shamanism.

Rock described *dongba* and *sanba* between the 1920s and 1940s performing joint rituals and pointed out that many *dongba* were also *sanba*. Moreover, in the mountain districts, former *dongba* and elderly villagers informed me that there were older practitioners of their fathers' and grandfathers' generations who performed both roles. Practitioners who had doubled as *dongba* and *sanba* were simply considered ritual practitioners with a different repertoire of skills. Informants said that in the past, there were no negative associations with practicing both roles.

Contemporary reconstructions of the *dongba*, however, resisted any association with *sanba* shamanism. In the 1990s, *dongba* made a point of disassociating themselves from *sanba*, although some mentioned that their former *dongba* teachers performed both roles. Although *dongba* had been eliminated as targets of suppression after the founding of the Dongba Cultural Research Institute in 1981, a decade later, many still felt vulnerable to changing political winds and were eager to disassociate themselves from *sanba*, whom the state still categorized as purveyors of superstition. *Dongba* were more aware of these distinctions than the broader population. In the early 1980s, the institute invited all *dongba* in Lijiang Prefecture to a major conference, where participants discussed the institute's purpose and the role of the *dongba* in Naxi history. Although not every *dongba* in the prefecture attended the conference, all the major areas were represented, and those who attended informed others of what had taken place. In Pagoda Hill Village I interviewed a *dongba* who had not attended the meeting but had been informed of its import, which he summed up as: "Now *dongba* are good, but we are different from *sanba*; *sanba* are bad." This conference was crucial to the re-presentation of the category "*dongba*" to the *dongba* themselves.[12]

According to institute accounts, "literacy and orderly ritual" are key characteristics of *dongba* practice that sharply contrast with the "unorderliness and chaos" (*luan qi ba zao*) that define *sanba*. *Dongba* rituals require the performance of specific operations in conjunction with the sequential recitation of written passages from *dongba* texts, which vary according to the ritual performed. An elderly *dongba* explained that "*dongba* do not just do what they please; they learn to be *dongba*: to dance, to sing, to write pictographs, and to hold rituals in a prescribed and orderly manner." In contrast, the rituals of *sanba* differ according to personal styles, rely heavily on spectacle, and have less emphasis on precise performative sequence. *Sanba* are associated with trance states, frenetic activity, and fantastic—now deemed crazy—activities such as washing their hands in boiling oil, licking burning-hot swords, and speaking in a secret language that is now thought of as "nonsensical mutterings" (*hu shuo ba dao*).

It is not that new representations of the *dongba* dating from the 1990s were entirely fabricated; there is certainly a basis for associating *dongba* with maleness since women were excluded from the profession and were even, in some regions, forbidden to attend certain *dongba* rituals. The association of *sanba* shamanism with femaleness, however, seems curious, given that, among the Naxi, male practitioners have dominated *sanba* shamanism since the 1920s.[13] Rock, who spent twenty years in Naxi territory studying their religious practices, believed that there no longer were female *sanba* as he was unable to find a single one.[14] The construction of *sanba* shamanism, then, reached back to the origins of the practice in order to feminize it. The *Naxi Pictographic Dictionary* translates the pictograph for *sanba* as a diviner and shaman who was originally female and does not use books (Fang and He [1981] 1982, 216).[15] The pictograph for *sanba* is identified by *dongba* and scholars of *dongba* culture as unquestionably female, as evidenced by the portrayal of the *sanba*'s hair. In contrast, the *dongba* is defined as a male shaman who recites from books. The characteristics of the *dongba* and *sanba* in the dictionary translation and interpretations dating from the reform era must be critically assessed as an essentialization that places emphasis on gender and literacy while omitting other distinctions and similarities related to specific ritual operations, mental states, the conditions under which one undertakes the vocation, and so on.[16] The distinction made in the 1990s between the *dongba* and *sanba*, then, entailed a re-presentation of historical categories based on distinctions perceived as most important according to *Chinese* criteria.[17] Literacy in the Naxi language had not been a marker of distinction within Naxi communities. Since only Naxi men could train to be *dongba*, literacy in Naxi script was a gendered distinction,[18] but not one that divided the Naxi population according to gender. There were only a small number of *dongba*; rural villages rarely had their own *dongba*. Dongba did not have a particularly high social standing within the Naxi community and tended to be from relatively poor farm families (He Zhiwu, personal communication).

The creation of a distinction between *dongba* and *sanba* was "framed by an opposition and exclusion of gender" (Strathern 1988; Tsing 1993, 33) and underscored the way in which the construction of "ethnic and national marginalities is gendered" (Tsing 1993, 18; Chao 1996; Makley 2002).[19] As Marilyn Strathern has pointed out, there is often a mutual metaphorization between gender categories and the larger prestige system (Strathern in Ortner and Whitehead [1981] 1984, 17). The genderization of ritual practitioners was relevant to the repositioning of the Naxi past vis-à-vis the broader Chinese prestige system. The conceptual bifurcation of Naxi ritual practitioners into masculinized (orderly and literate) and feminized (chaotic and illiterate) categories resonated with popular local representations of Naxi women as traditional, illiterate, and backward, in contrast to Naxi men, who are associated with Chinese practices, literacy, and civilization.[20]

As Schein and others have pointed out, representations of ethnic difference

FIG. 2.2 Pictograph for *dongba* (left) and *sanba* (right)

in post-Mao China characteristically feature minority women (Schein 2000; Harrell 1995, 10; Gladney 1994). It is minority women—wearing "traditional" dress in performances, in museum exhibits, or in glossy guidebook photos and tourist pamphlets—who flesh out the national representations of ethnic diversity. To what extent is the genderization of ethnic difference a complete fabrication rather than a construction with practical referents? There is a contradiction in the use of Naxi women as markers of tradition when men, who actually dominated religious practice prior to the incorporation of minority groups into the Chinese empire,[21] manage to escape this characterization.

The identification of women with tradition and authenticity was a consequence of imperial expansion that was later reinforced by the invention of *dongba* culture. Genderized constructions of ethnic authenticity were not solely oppositional formulations invented for the purposes of promoting national identity in the reform era. They were also residual conceptions embedded in the historical process of incorporating minority or tribal groups into the Chinese empire that began during the Yuan and Ming dynasties. The Chinese established tributary relations with indigenous elites, which included attempts to "civilize" and culturally transform them by instilling a Chinese model of hierarchy and socio-cosmological order. But this transformation was not understood in ethnic terms, in the sense of imposing Chinese practices on ethnic others, but of effecting the transformation of barbarian rulers into civilized subjects. Indigenous elites were simultaneously situated as rulers in local hierarchies and as subjects in imperial hierarchies. Chinese-appointed Naxi rulers[22] learned Chinese, adopted Chinese ritual, and donned mandarin robes and golden girdles, gifts from the emperor. The girdles, which bore Chinese characters such as "loyalty to the nation" (Rock 1947, 101–6), are suggestive of an imperial determination to literally inscribe such sentiments on their subjects.

Literacy (Wright 1968, 38) and ritual (Watson 1988, 3–4; Rawski 1988, 32–33) were key to the process of inculcating Chinese values and became the markers of prestige that contributed to the legitimization of a local hierarchical order sustained by alliances forged with the powerful encroaching empire. In 1723, when the Qing empire implemented direct rule over the Naxi, a similar process to transform the broader Naxi population from barbarians into civilized subjects of the empire was instituted. Schools were opened in Naxi territory with the goal of universal male education; they not surprisingly focused on literacy and ritual (Rowe 1989).[23] It was no coincidence that literacy and ritual, integral to the division between an exterior "barbarian" realm and an interior "civilized" imperial domain, were taught in order to lead, first, indigenous rulers and, later, indigenous populations (males) into the fold of the Qing empire. Naxi women were probably forced to adopt Qing prestige structures as well but were differently situated within them. The process of Qing imperial expansion, then, may be directly correlated with the growing hegemony of Han forms of prestige among Naxi rulers and the Naxi male population at large.[24] In contemporary Lijiang, traces of the gendered incorporation of the Naxi are still visible. In Lijiang Town in the 1990s, virtually all elderly Naxi men spoke Chinese and most were literate as well. Naxi men wore clothing indistinguishable from that worn by local Han men. In contrast, virtually all elderly women were illiterate, spoke only Naxi, and wore distinctively Naxi clothing. Generally, as one moved from Lijiang Town to the rural basin and then to the mountains, there was increased reliance on spoken Naxi and fewer Naxi spoke or read Chinese. In mountain districts, Chinese speakers were predominantly males educated after 1949.[25]

The symbolic association of Naxi maleness with literacy, ritual, and civilized practice is the legacy of specific imperial strategies of domination and local Naxi strategies of self-representation constituted in the context of an eclipsing imperial order. The imperial Chinese civilizing project and means of incorporating "barbarians" (ethnic others) were *gendered processes* that have shaped the sedimented layers of local subjectivity in which Naxi men became more identified with literacy and civilization relative to Naxi women. The creation of *dongba* culture, which entailed a genderization of past ritual practitioners, was similarly a process by which we can see how "gender difference is created through state and ethnic discourse" (Tsing 1993, 34). The gendered bifurcation of Naxi ritual practitioners in terms of the opposition between "backwardness and illiteracy," on the one hand, and "civilization and literacy," on the other, has particular persuasive force because it resonates with preexisting conceptual distinctions created by the process of imperial incorporation, which was gendered and which created forms of incorporation and marginality along lines of gender. The inclusion of *dongba* within constellations of maleness, literacy, and civilization was integral to the articulation of prestigious Naxi ethnicity in the context of the reform era, during which the Chinese state placed new emphasis on categorization by difference.

In contrast to the policies of the Qing empire, which sought to transform "barbarians" into civilized subjects for the purpose of incorporation, and of the Maoist era, during which ethnic diversity was downplayed and suppressed, in the reform era, ethnic groups were encouraged to emphasize distinctive characteristics. Yet Chinese evolutionary discourse, shaped by late imperial discourse, still reserves the space of civilization for the Han, leaving minority ethnic groups to claim only various gradations of less civilized status leading up to the Han, or Chinese, ideal.

The genderization of the spaces of backwardness and civilization has symbolic implications for the internal reconfiguration of the category Naxi and the rehabilitation of *dongba* practices at the expense of (metaphorically) fostering the marginalization of femaleness, illiteracy, and *sanba* ritual practitioners. The discovery of constellations of ritual and literacy among the Naxi invoked residual imperial criteria of civilization and created a space for the invention of Naxi *dongba* culture, which in turn re-presented elements of the Naxi past characterized by "maleness," "ritual," and "literacy" as "civilized." The bifurcation of *dongba* and *sanba* was a reinterpretation of the past that relegated the *sanba* to the realm of backwardness and feudal superstition while allowing the *dongba* to be reinvented as scholar and sage. The dismantling and restructuring of images of the past occurred in concert with the creation of ethnic identity in the 1990s. A Naxi past imagined in terms of "primitive religious practice" corresponds to the depiction of the Naxi people in the present as a "backward minority." Similarly, a depiction of the Naxi past in terms of *dongba* culture, "one of the few early written sources of knowledge,"[26] supports a re-presentation in the present of the Naxi people as a "civilized" and "advanced minority."

The forms of Naxi ritual practice and the variety of ritual practitioners chosen for rehabilitation and valorization by the local authorities were not arbitrary. Many *dongba* rituals promote values parallel to Confucian doctrine. While *dongba* culture was represented as the essential form of Naxi culture, it is actually only one form of Naxi ritual practice; it is, however, a form more suitable for increasing Naxi prestige (in the eyes of Chinese-educated Naxi intellectuals) because of its relative proximity to Chinese practices.[27]

POWER, MEANING, AND THE MARKET

Much of the power to rewrite Naxi history flows directly from the translation of Naxi myth and *dongba* texts into Chinese. While myth may serve as an important source of local identity, the standardization of myth by scholarly institutions has to be scrutinized as an exercise of state power. Published versions of Naxi myths and folktales taken from *dongba* texts were valorized as the "authentic" and "correct" versions of Naxi myths, folktales, and sources of Naxi history. When the oral accounts of stories or myths that I had collected from rural residents conflicted with or diverged from official translations, scholars and resident *dongba* at the Dongba Cultural Research Institute stated that the oral versions were incorrect and that the correct versions were only those that the institute itself had translated directly from *dongba* texts.

While there may be no engaged struggle over the meaning of different versions of these popular narratives, the attempt to delegitimize unofficial versions underscores the existence of alternative popular interpretations, as well as state attempts to dominate representations of Naxi authenticity. *Dongba* culture was invented by extracting select elements from the *dongba* religion that were easily wielded for this purpose both because the institute possessed the lion's share of the remaining texts and because the texts were unintelligible to the broader Naxi population.

The translations and interpretations produced by the institute created standardized versions, edited and domesticated according to the state's criteria. As Miller (1993, 7) has noted, the official translation of folk tales in China involves the systematic *editing out* of material that is sexually prurient, superstitious, or hostile either to other minorities or to the Han. Although Naxi scholars may not have colluded to alter *dongba* texts, they made editorial decisions informed by sensibilities gained from having been trained in universities and institutes and from having internalized Chinese scholarly discourse. The process of transforming *dongba* religion into *dongba* culture inherently entailed an alienation from the religion's former expression and purpose. Many of the institute's scholars were aware of the contradiction between wanting to study *dongba* practices and contributing to the decline of those practices by denuding the countryside of its few remaining *dongba* texts. Yet the institute is embedded in hierarchies that shape its function to the purposes of the state. While the local Naxi exercise some control over the institute, all Chinese institutes are parts of nested hierarchies: the Dongba Cultural Research Institute is overseen by the Yunnan Academy of Social Science, which is in turn directly under the aegis of the state's Ministry of Propaganda.

Since the founding of the Dongba Cultural Research Institute, the collection and preservation of *dongba* texts for the Naxi people had actually narrowed the Naxi public's access to those texts. The institute's library was not open to the public, and the use of *dongba* texts was restricted to select scholars. Although limited editions of *dongba* texts translated into Chinese could be purchased in bookstores and stalls, they were unintelligible to the predominantly illiterate elderly Naxi who were the only ones with any memory of *dongba* practices or their meaning. The institute held *dongba* rituals, but it did so only for the purpose of recording them as ethnographic data. In the 1990s, these rituals took place behind the institute's walls and locked main gate.[28] As one of its scholars explained: "We are a scholarly work unit; we cannot appear to be practicing feudal superstition here." The institute's museum had no posted hours and was rarely open to the public, although it was customarily unlocked for the perusal of visiting government dignitaries or foreign tourists willing to pay. There was a sad irony in the institute's attempt to build a bridge between the past of *dongba* religion and the present of Naxi culture, which gave rise to a hybrid "*dongba* culture" that may have hastened the decline of its predecessor.

In the 1990s, the uses of *dongba* culture began to take a turn from representation and prestige to commodification.[29] *Dongba* culture became both an object for scholarly consumption and a national and international tourist attraction. Inspired by the scholarly interest expressed in the Naxi in the 1980s and 1990s, the institute made plans to build a dormitory in anticipation of the large number of scholars it expected to be drawn to the study of *dongba* culture. In 1991, it began charging scholars ¥50 (about 10 dollars) per viewing to watch videotapes of rituals performed and recorded at the institute. Hoping to cater to a broader audience of local, national, and international tourists, the institute transported and reassembled a "traditional" Naxi house from the mountains and charged admission.[30] Next to the exhibit, a souvenir stand sold cloth shoulder bags printed with *dongba* script. The *dongba*, too, were summoned to the task of tourist promotion. Foreign tourists, attracted by guidebooks that described the "unique *dongba* culture of the Naxi," were charged ¥100 (about 20 dollars) for ten minutes during which one of the *dongba* would dress up and dance for a photo opportunity. Exhibits of so-called *dongba* culture were more and more in demand. Local exhibits gave way to national and international exhibits, such as at the Asia Games (Ya Yunhui) and the Folk Cultural Village (Minzu Cun), an ethnic theme park in Shenzhen replete with village scenes of twenty-one minority groups including the Naxi, and, in 1993 the Dongba Cultural Festival was held at the posh Beijing Lido Holiday Inn complex (Gong 1993).[31]

A *China Daily* article addressing research in the field of *dongba* culture describes how Joseph Rock had "expected to find peculiar plant species in the area, but instead, found a peculiar culture" (Gong 1993). The article goes on to describe the Naxi as one of the world's few remaining pristine cultures with a unique, ancient, but living, pictographic script. The reader's eye is caught by an arrangement of striking photos of *dongba* script, a painted scroll from the Dongba Cultural Research Institute museum, a photo of a dance troupe performing "primitive" *dongba* dance, and a contemporary painting—all examples of so-called *dongba* culture. While the article purports to be announcing scholarly discoveries, it was strategically planted in *China Daily*'s entertainment section in a thinly veiled attempt to market tourist activities and the Naxi people themselves as a tourist attraction. By its references to Joseph Rock and Peter Goullart, the article invoked Western authorities and images of timeless primitivity. The dance described as a "*dongba* dance" was actually an improvisation by professional dancers; this appears to be part of the broader genre of minority dance invented by Chinese dance experts (see Dreyer 1976, 163; Wu 1993). The "modern *dongba* painting," which incorporates distorted *dongba* pictographs, was strategically named after the title of Goullart's early book about the Naxi, *Forgotten Kingdom*. There is little doubt that representations of *dongba* culture as featured in English-language publications such as *China Daily* were tailored to expectations of what would attract foreign tourists. These representations of *dongba* culture suggest that its genesis was in part shaped by the constructions of Western authors and contemporary market forces.

Dongba art sold in twenty-first-century Lijiang is virtually anything that incorporates Naxi pictographs. In the late 1990s, Lijiang residents complained that many merchants (*shangren*) and creators of *dongba* art were Han or of the neighboring Bai minority, although their crafts were sold as "Naxi" ethnic arts. In 2011, the businesses in Lijiang are predominantly owned by outsiders (*waidiren*) from central, eastern, and northern China. Han shopgirls, dressed as Tibetans or Naxi, sit at looms demonstrating weaving while selling largely factory-manufactured shawls and scarves with *dongba* pictographs to visitors who are mostly tourists from metropolitan areas in China and overseas Chinese. Lijiang shops sell T-shirts, stationery, jewelry, and clothing bearing *dongba* pictographs, which they market as examples of *dongba* or Naxi culture.

Scholars at the Dongba Cultural Research Institute complain that the *dongba* script appearing on new commercial products labeled "*dongba* cul-

FIG. 2.3 T-shirts with *dongba* pictographs

FIG. 2.4 Dongba's Yak Meat market

FIG. 2.5 Pseudo-African art

ture" is incorrectly written and makes no sense, but these errors have hardly detracted from the products' marketability. Carved wooden statues in museums and Lijiang shops purport to represent *dongba* culture, but mimic African art and reflect contemporary artists' fantasies of Naxi primitivity rather than historic designs with any relationship to Lijiang's past. Hence, as tourism has grown, the category "*dongba* culture" continues to evolve in different directions, seized by private market forces eager to capitalize on "the ethnic."

MARGINALIZED AUTHENTICITY AND UNREPRESENTED OTHERS

How has *dongba* culture affected the representation of Naxi culture? A key tenet in the Chinese system of ethnic classification is that ethnic groups are presumed to be discrete in the sense of being defined by strict boundaries. Moreover, what represents a minority group must be distinct from that which is Han. The category of "Naxi" is defined in contrast to that of "Han" and the characteristics of other officially classified minorities. The *dongba*, then, was a convenient focal point for defining what is essentially Naxi because it is asserted that no other ethnic group has practitioners like the Naxi *dongba* or a system of pictographic writing like *dongba* script.

In an apparent contradiction to this claim, however, an ethnic group whose members call themselves "Lulu" (classified as a subgroup of the Naxi) has *dongba* priests and an identical *dongba* script. The Lulu have a separate, mutually unintelligible spoken language, which in some areas has been replaced by Naxi. The Lulu identify themselves as distinct from the Naxi, even though they have intermarried with the Naxi for as long as they can remember and are not seeking independent classification.[32] Studies of the Prmi minority suggest that they, too, had ritual practitioners similar to the Naxi *dongba*, as well as a religion they call "Hangui" (Harrell 1995; Wellens 2010). There was in the 1990s apparently a movement afoot among Prmi (also known as Premi) scholars to build a research institute similar to the Dongba Cultural Research Institute for the investigation of Prmi culture (Harrell 1995; Yang Xuezhen cited in Wellens 2010). Similarities such as these suggest that the distinctive religious "tradition" of the Naxi minority may in fact be a form of religious practice common to an entire region, since the Prmi, Lulu, and Naxi peoples inhabit areas bordering one another (Chao 1996). Thus, state categories, which insist that ethnic markers be unique to a singular group, *cultivate*

FIG. 2.6 Naxi culture yard where a *dongba* performs weddings for tourists

differences and inventions where common practices may have existed (Chao 1996).[33] It is unlikely that areas in which religious practices took place will be neatly coterminous with state-determined ethnic boundaries. As ethnic groups seek to articulate the bases of their uniqueness according to state criteria and engage in local projects of empowerment such as creating institutes for displaying, studying, and historicizing their new identities, it is likely that inventing "traditions" will continue to take priority over discovering histories of regionally shared practice (Chao 1996; see Wellens 2010).

AUTHENTICIZED MARGINALITY

Identifying "*dongba* culture" as the core of Naxi heritage had significant implications for the representation of the Naxi people. According to Naxi scholars, the "living representatives" of Naxi culture—the "real Naxi"—could be found only in the mountain districts, far from the influence of the Han. Dating from the 1990s, the Naxi of Lijiang Town and the basin areas were not considered "authentic" Naxi but were referred to as "sinicized" (*hanhua*) because they had largely adopted Han ritual practices.[34] Thus, that which is "Naxi" was essentialized and confined to the peripheries of Lijiang City.

Why were uneducated Naxi women and the geographically and economically marginal mountain Naxi singled out to be both valorized as authentic models of Naxi culture and, at the same time, relegated to occupying a space of backwardness?[35] To some extent, post-Mao-era ethnic essentialization was rooted in specific historical processes of imperial expansion and the incorporation of the Naxi into the Han empire. The gendered strategies of transforming the Naxi into Chinese subjects had consequences for the differential location of men and women relative to Chinese power and contributed to the marginalization of Naxi women. Similarly, the mountain Naxi—who lived in areas geographically remote from the centers of Chinese power within Naxi territory—were comparatively less subject to imperial intrusions than their basin- and town-dwelling neighbors. The basin's suitability for wet-rice cultivation made these areas far more desirable to control, and their proximity to towns made this logistically more plausible. The pacification of town and basin Naxi had gone hand in hand with their schooling in Chinese and conversion to Chinese ritual practices. By the Republican era, the Naxi who were literate in Chinese were disproportionately male and residing in Lijiang

Town or the basin (Rock 1963a, 29).[36] After 1949, equality in education was promoted, but women and mountain people continued to be associated with illiteracy because this perception continued to reflect actual divisions within the older and middle-aged Naxi population. Literacy in the Naxi language was never a marker used to hierarchically differentiate between individual Naxi.[37] However, with the reform-era categorization of groups by ethnic categories, town and basin Naxi accentuated literacy in Chinese as a marker of civilized identity, which in turn created hierarchical distinctions among the Naxi based on Chinese literacy. The illiteracy of Naxi women and mountain people contributed to the popular perception of them as trapped in the past, backward, and primitive.

The discourse of imperial expansion had contributed to the negative depiction of mountain Naxi. Rock states that the Chinese "left the aborigines alone after they had been chased from the rich plains to rule themselves under their own chiefs . . . [who were] nominally under some Chinese magistrate often many days' journey distant" (cited in Sutton 1974, 56).[38] In some cases, those who resisted imperial expansion were driven to the least desirable ecological zones, which subsequently contributed to their impoverishment relative to their counterparts in the basin and town areas.[39] From the era of imperial expansion through the early 1950s, the mountains were identified as "wild" zones inhabited by "barbarians," "bandits," and "brigands." During the Ming and Qing dynasties, the characterization of rebelling native populations as "bandits" and beyond the pale of "civilization" justified the looting and burning of their villages (Rock 1947, 66–162). This demonization and suppression facilitated the project of imperial pacification and expansion. Siu (1990, 47) points out that official documents lumped together "untamed natives," "bandits," and "resistors of imperial taxes." Native magistrates who broke with the Chinese retreated to mountain bases to foment rebellions. The conceptual association of mountain areas with danger, banditry, and lack of civilization continued throughout the Republican era[40] and into the 1950s.[41]

In mountain areas in the 1990s, there were visible differences between mountain and lowland Naxi, as well as between older Naxi women, who wore distinctive ethnic clothing, and older Naxi men, who dressed like the Han. These differences reinforce their categorization as immune from the power of the state and as a site of timeless primitivity.[42] Nevertheless, the creation of Naxi women and mountain people as objects of marginalization cannot be attributed to substantial differences between these groups and the broader

Naxi population. The diminished degree of state control over Naxi women and mountain Naxi (originating from a legacy of imperial civilizing projects) fostered some actual differences that contributed significantly to popular and state conceptualizations of these groups as "uncivilized," "backward," and, more recently, "authentic." Popular and official representations of ethnicity have been fueled by these sedimented conceptualizations, which have taken on new force in the post-Mao-era search for ethnic difference.

The search for ethnic difference, however, was not solely informed by historical differences; it was also shaped by contemporary discourse. Corresponding to the rise of the market economy, popular and state discourse differentiated between China's rural and urban populations. Su Xiaokang's *River Elegy* (Heshang), a television series broadcast nationally in 1988, depicted China's peasants as steeped in superstition and backwardness. The show provided urbanites and intellectuals with an explanation for China's relative poverty in a 1980s global arena. Fifth-generation filmmakers similarly depicted rural Chinese culture as intransigent and averse to modernization.[43] While these films were set in prerevolutionary China, they were interpreted as allegories relevant to understanding contemporary China. Depictions in official documents of China's rural population as "low quality" have been interpreted by Anagnost as an explanation for rural poverty in the face of growing urban prosperity (2004, 193). In the 1980s through the early 1990s, the differences between the rural and urban populations were a subject of national scholarly speculation and became increasingly pronounced at the ground level. It is not surprising that Lijiang scholars, echoing biopolitical distinctions between urban and rural Chinese, would imagine the differences between rural and urban Naxi using similar forms of essentialism.

When Naxi nationalists such as He Wanbao were given the opportunity to articulate what was distinctively Naxi, they sought to use this opportunity to empower the Naxi. Yet, as intellectuals educated in Chinese universities, they themselves had long ago internalized Han constructions of prestige, which were informed by imperial prejudices toward minority ethnic groups. There is little doubt, particularly among minority groups who have long been incorporated into the Chinese state, that being identified with Han culture commands more prestige than being identified as an ethnic minority, despite the contemporary Chinese state's valorization of ethnic difference.[44] In contrast to imperial times, however, the contemporary discourse of ethnic pluralism has erected boundaries between ethnic categories that can no longer be crossed.[45] Such boundaries not only fail to recognize the substantial flow of cultural practices between ethnic groups but also erase the history of inter-marriage among them.

With the end of the Maoist era's homogenization of ethnic groups into a singular national identity, Naxi leaders were faced with the problem of creating a distinctly non-Han identity that was nevertheless "civilized." Their solution was to create a space for a new form of "civilization" that would have the overall effect of situating the Naxi closer to the Han according to the contemporary Stalinist-influenced evolutionist trajectory. Similar to the process by which the Han have designated themselves as modern and scientific in contrast to the perceived traditional, superstitious, and backward minorities, the creation of a "civilized space" within the category "Naxi" was an oppositional process that led to the discursive marginalization of what was imagined as Naxi femaleness, illiteracy, and superstition. But while the civilized space of *dongba* culture provided reflective glory for Naxi intellectuals—and all Naxi—the intellectuals were not themselves representatives of *dongba* culture. Instead, mountain Naxi were made to symbolize living *dongba* culture. The discourse of *dongba* culture directs Naxi intellectuals to romanticize mountain Naxi because difference may be positively equated with authenticity. Yet the intellectuals themselves avoided being categorized according to the precursor and negative side of authenticity, that is, backwardness. The designation of mountain people as authentically Naxi drew on popular and historical discourses in which women and mountain people were identified with extremes of difference, allowing men and town-dwelling and basin Naxi to be comparatively associated with learning, culture, and "civilization" within the new, fixed national order of ethnic kinds.[46] According to reform-era state criteria, difference could be valorized as authenticity. Yet the tenacious grip of imperial discourse rearticulated in new forms of biopolitical categorization continued to situate Han practice as the most prestigious and to label difference in terms of distance from this ideal, creating a double vision of difference as both authenticity and backwardness. The search for difference actually reinforced marginalization of some Naxi by reinscribing imperial constructions in reform-era ethnic categories. Such reinscriptions in turn negated the situated histories and shared ethnic and national experiences of women and mountain Naxi.

This is not to say that Naxi agents knowingly created representations of Naxi women or mountain people that symbolically denigrated them according to the residual logic of imperial and contemporary criteria.⁴⁷ Rather, the spatialization and genderization of difference are a by-product of the efforts of Chinese-educated Naxi men to empower all of those in the category Naxi through the invention of a civilized space that contributes to that category's prestige by invoking Chinese conceptions of civilization. *These unintended consequences illustrate the way in which local agency cannot exist outside the space of state hegemony and, indeed, was shaped by it.* The invention of mountain Naxi and Naxi women as objects of authenticity and marginality was fueled by a state evolutionary discourse that constructs difference in terms of unblurred ethnic boundaries and a trajectory of hierarchy, by the reform-era biopolitical project of categorizing populations according to ethnicity, and by local agents seeking ethnic empowerment within the social order of reform-era China.

In the reform era, the quest for a new national identity encouraged essentializations of ethnic difference. There is little doubt that ethnic groups have found the state's enthusiasm for difference infinitely preferable to the suppression they experienced during much of the Maoist era. Yet the representation of a distinctly Naxi identity, as separate from a shared Chinese identity, placed Naxi nationalists at odds with members of the broader Naxi public, who had come to see themselves as indistinguishable from other Chinese citizens. With the revival of popular Han ritual observances among town and basin Naxi, popular identity has aligned with broader popular cultural practices that are understood as local but were of Han origin. The creators of *dongba* culture sought to elevate ethnic difference by re-presenting elements of the Naxi past—particularly *dongba*—and by drawing on Han notions of civilization for the purpose of bringing prestige to the articulated category "Naxi." Depicted as a relic surviving only among mountain Naxi, *dongba* culture lent itself to the reflective valorization of all Naxi but avoided directly implicating town and basin dwellers as representatives of Naxi authenticity or backwardness. It was in the mountains, on the periphery of the state, where *dongba* culture was more than just a remote memory, that an identity based on ritual practices performed by *dongba* might again be capable of informing popular subjectivity. Yet with few *dongba* or *dongba* texts remaining in the mountains, Naxi officials and scholars improvised *dongba* culture and Naxi identity in the 1990s in ways compatible with state discourse.

In 2011, *dongba* culture is equated with Naxi culture nationally and locally. In contrast to the early 1990s, today many Lijiang residents identify *dongba* culture as their heritage. This new identification is likely a product of the Lijiang educational system, combined with local government propagandizing and the pervasive tourist industry. *Dongba* culture is used primarily to sell souvenirs and market attractions for tourists. Tourist goods, some of which are artifacts decorated with *dongba* script, are ethnicized as Naxi or branded as *dongba* culture regardless of any connection to *dongba* practices. Tourists can purchase tickets to watch *dongba* performances or pay to have a Naxi marriage performed by a *dongba*, complete with a wedding feast. All the Old Town businesses are required to use *dongba* script in their signs even though most Naxi are incapable of reading it. As a scholar at the Dongba Cultural Research Institute noted, the Kentucky Fried Chicken sign is phonetically translated as *ken de ji*, simulating the sound of the word "Kentucky," but is infelicitously or ironically translated as "cut dog meat." Most of the *dongba* in Lijiang Town have not served in communities as religious practitioners but are young men who began training in the profession only after tourism created opportunities for urban employment in the mid-1990s and have limited knowledge of the broader array of *dongba* practices. As the institute's retired director put it, "All the *dongba* are dead; no one knows about *dongba* culture anymore." Most of the *dongba* who actually practiced rituals before 1949 are in their eighties or older.

There have been efforts to bring about a revival of *dongba* culture in mountain villages. Yang Fuquan, a scholar of Naxi culture and history at the Yunnan Academy of Social Sciences, obtained funds from the Ford Foundation and the Nature Conservancy in 1999 to create a program to train young *dongba* and has attempted to bring about a revival of *dongba* culture in the Lijiang countryside (Yang 2003, 483). A few of the young men who participated now assist with translation at the Dongba Cultural Research Institute. These young *dongba* occasionally return to their home villages and hold rituals there, but they are now primarily urban residents who cannot effect a revival of *dongba* ritual from afar.[48]

The Dongba Cultural Research Institute, which coined the term "*dongba* culture," is perhaps the only place in Lijiang where there is reliable knowl-

FIG. 2.7 Pizza Hut sign with *dongba* pictographs

edge of the meaning of *dongba* script and *dongba* ritual practices. Though the institute's scholars have translated all the *dongba* texts in China, they are now translating texts from the Harvard-Yenching Library as well as texts from other countries. Given that it is not a commercial enterprise, its future in Lijiang's new tourism-driven economy is uncertain. Throughout the rest of Lijiang, *dongba* culture is primarily a brand with little connection to a regional history of ritual practice.

ETHNICIZING MYTH, BRIDE ABDUCTION, AND ELOPEMENT

"Coqbbersa," a story that tells of the marriage between Cei-heeqbbubbeqmil and Coqsseililee, is described as the origin myth of the Naxi people which explains the importance of the Heaven Worship Ceremony (Meebiuq) to Naxi familial, spatial, and social reproduction (McKhann 1989, 157). The myth is one of the most important, if not *the* most important, *dongba* texts (Cheng 2001; He 1992; He 1993; Tang and Jin 1983; Wang 2003; F. Yang 1993; F. Yang 2003, 481). The following oral version from Pagoda Hill Village, in one of Lijiang Prefecture's western mountain districts, is still recited today:

> Ceiheeqbbubbeqmil, a celestial maiden, descended to earth in order to avoid marrying her mother's brother's son. Coqsseililee, a [mortal] young man, was in search of a wife. In gratitude for Coqsseililee's assistance in cross-ing a river, a rat directed him to a place where he could find a mate.[1] The rat advised Coqsseililee to ignore the other women and to select Ceiheeqbbubbeqmil. Since Ceiheeqbbubbeqmil was a celestial woman, she had earrings with wings that would allow her to fly back to heaven. In the beginning, the rat warned, she will not like you. So you must pull off her wings so she cannot escape and then drag her off. The rat also warned that Ceiheeqbbubbeqmil would use pine sap to reattach her wings and try to escape, but when the sun came out the sap would melt and she would fall back to earth. Ceiheeq-bbubbeqmil flew up three times but fell back to earth each

time. After the third time, she realized there was no escape and that she had no choice but to live with her mortal captor.

Because Ceiheeqbbubbeqmil needed to fly up to heaven to tell her parents of her union, Coqsseililee used glue to reattach her wings. At first, embarrassed by the situation, she hid Coqsseililee, but Zzeelaqapv, her father, smelled iron and brass and realized that a mortal being was among them. Zzeelaqapv told the young man he could marry his daughter only if he completed a number of impossible feats. Assuming he would fail to complete them, Zzeelaqapv made plans to kill him after each feat. But with the aid of Ceiheeqbbubbeqmil, her mother, and armies of rabbits and ants, Coqsseililee was able to complete all the tasks. So his father-in-law gave him various types of grain and animals to take back to earth. But since Zzeelaqapv did not give the couple the cat [hualleiq] or the turnip [manjing], Ceiheeqbbubbeqmil stole them. In retribution, the cat and turnip were cursed by Zzeelaqapv: from that time onward, the cat makes an irritating and repulsive sound [purring], and the turnip weighs a lot but is full of water and gives you gas.

Ceiheeqbbubbeqmil and Coqsseililee had three sons who were born mute. Ceiheeqbbubbeqmil overheard her father and mother talking. The mother told Zzeelaqapv not to be so cruel because the couple was now a family. He replied that they only needed to worship him once a year by holding the Heaven Worship Ceremony. [Ceiheeqbbubbeqmil relates this conversation to Coqsseililee, enabling him to learn the secret of how to undo Zzeelaqapv's curse.] Coqsseililee then held the Heaven Worship Ceremony, after which the three children each began to speak a different language—Tibetan, Naxi, and Chinese—and they became these respective peoples.

The privileging of the Coqbbersa story as the Naxi origin myth may be understood as part of the project of creating "dongba culture," that is, the reform era essentialization of ancient Naxi history and culture.[2] Dongba culture is equated with an originary, authentic, primordial, or ancient form of Naxi culture that represents all Naxi. Naxi scholars identify dongba culture as persisting in the contemporary practices of some rural mountain villages, particularly in the beliefs, narratives, and rituals that appear in the texts of dongba priests who practiced in the mountains.[3] In the 1990s, Lijiang Town and basin residents were unfamiliar with the Coqbbersa myth.

Rather than treating the Coqbbersa myth as representative of the entirety of Naxi culture and history, an alternative interpretive strategy would be to consider it as saying something particular about the history and practices of the regions where the text circulates and continues to be part of an oral tradition. Drawing on the ethnography of marriage practices in three regions—Lijiang Town, the rural basin, and the mountains—I will reconsider Coqbbersa as a text that situates bride abduction within a history of regional practice. The ethnicizing of the Coqbbersa myth as part of *dongba* culture calls attention to a parallel process whereby marriage practices such as "bride abduction" (*guaihun; mil jiuq* in Naxi) and elopement (*paohun*) came to be imagined as "ethnic practices."

Rather than being ethnically distinct forms of marriage, bride abduction and elopement represent a continuum of economically driven marriage strategies. After-the-fact efforts to legitimize bride abduction and elopement indicate that these strategies were deployed in arenas where they were perceived as inferior to ideal marriage practice. Criticisms of abduction and elopement as "uncivilized," "unlearned," or "backward" had coherence only in a larger arena in which another form of marriage was imagined to be "civilized," "learned," or "modern." The criticism of elopement, informed by state discourse, led proponents of this practice to claim defensively that it was an "ethnic practice" of the Naxi. The representation of historical practices of bride abduction and reform era elopement as ethnic practice was persuasive because it was consistent with the new significance of the Coqbbersa story concurrent with the invention of *dongba* culture. This was an outgrowth of the state's promotion of ethnic categories during the reform era. It was also consistent with the state's explanation that ideological and cultural factors are responsible for economic inequality. By identifying nonconforming marriage practices as instances of the persistence of intractable and backward cultural proclivities, the state need not address the way in which class and ethnic marginality are closely correlated and increasingly pronounced in reform-era China.

IMPERIAL EXPANSION AND THE LEGACY OF MARITAL PRESTIGE IN LIJIANG

An understanding of marriage practices in the Lijiang region requires some cognizance of late imperial expansion into what is now southwest China.

During the Ming and Qing dynasties, distinctions between groups were based not on ethnic essence but on political allegiance and the adoption of cultural practice. Those defined as barbarians (unpacified ethnic others or politically recalcitrant Han) could transcend their barbarian status through political submission and adoption of Han, or Chinese, rituals (Dikötter 1992, 2). As Siu has pointed out with reference to Guangdong, ethnic labels were deployed for the purpose of marginalizing non-Han groups or asserting superiority (1990, 49). Groups that did not incorporate cultural practices promoted by the Qing empire were denigrated as "uncivilized." Crossley (1990) and Rowe (1992) observe that the imposition of Han family structure and Confucian ideology was a powerful tool for the cultural domination and "civilizing" of non-Han tribes.[4]

It is difficult to discuss the cultural practices that ethnic groups may have had before the late imperial era, both because historical records relating to these areas are scant and because contemporary categories such as "Naxi" did not exist during this period.[5] The Lijiang area was, during the Ming and Qing dynasties and up until 1723, governed under the tusi system, in which native chiefs ruled in the name of the imperium. The native chief of the Lijiang region, which was known as the Mu Kingdom, was the Mu Tusi, who went to great lengths to keep records of their filial devotion and conversion to Confucian practices in order to justify the renewal of their patents to rule (Rock 1947, 118).[6] But in 1723 the tusi system was replaced by direct Chinese rule. Under the Yongzheng emperor, Chinese magistrates replaced native chiefs, and newly established Chinese schools attempted to "civilize" (i.e., rectify) what was perceived as the backward sexual morality of minority people by mandating Han-style marriage and child betrothal (Rowe 1989, 16; He Rugong 1988, 102–9). Gender segregation, a concern for sexual propriety, and a sense of bodily shame were legacies of Zhu Xi's school of Neo-Confucianism, which was taught in schools opened under the Yongzheng emperor (Rowe 1989, 15).

Guan Xuexuan, the first Chinese magistrate of Lijiang, opened three Chinese schools[7] and imposed child betrothal and arranged marriage (baoban) on the Naxi (Rock 1947, 219; Rock 1963a, 31; A. Jackson 1971, 60; Tang and Jin 1988, 34). Qing dynasty records indicate that parents who failed to betroth their children were punished. Han models of female purity were promoted by such means as the recorded narratives of "virtuous women exemplars" (lie nü) in Qing dynasty Lijiang prefectural records. The equation of Confucian gender values and Han marriage ritual (which included betrothal, the use of go-betweens, dowry, bridewealth,[8] and celebrations) with a system of prestige in the larger Lijiang area has to be understood as the legacy of imperial expansion during the Qing dynasty. The adoption of marriage practices became a cultural strategy for social mobility for some, and, at the same time, a means for excluding others (see Siu 1993, 22).

While the Naxi generally complied with dominant Chinese marriage forms, there was also evidence of resistance. Despite mandatory betrothals, the Lijiang region[9] became infamous for the suicides of women resisting arranged marriages (xunqing in standard Chinese; ieqvq in Naxi). The persistence of clandestine courtship and romantic love led Naxi women to commit suicide instead of marrying men they had not chosen, killing themselves either alone, with female age-mates, or with their lovers (Chao 1990; Goullart 1955, 155; A. Jackson 1971; Rock 1939, 3; Zhao 1985a).[10] Love suicides both rejected arranged marriage and mimicked it. Young couples who went off to die in the mountains wore their best clothes and brought food and often tents, so that they could live together as married couples, albeit briefly, before killing themselves. By the Republican era, Han marriage practices had become central to the expression of a "civilized" and "learned" identity, even though incidents of Naxi suicide in resistance to arranged marriage continued.

During the Republican era, marriage in Lijiang Town required that households engage in elaborate marriage rituals in order to enhance their prestige. In contrast, my informants' accounts of rural basin marriages during the same time period demonstrate that although rural residents also aspired to Han marriages, they practiced modest exchanges and less elaborate procedures that included betrothals, go-betweens, and simple celebrations. An elderly woman from East Wind Village recalled receiving a betrothal gift of two silver bracelets, but after she arrived at her new home, an embarrassed relative, from whom her husband had borrowed the bracelets, came to claim them. Simple celebrations (with a concern to incorporate elements associated with "marriage") and borrowed betrothal gifts suggest that poor families went to considerable lengths either to imitate aspects of the prestigious marriage ritual or to feign prosperity so that their sons could marry.

At the same time, impoverished men abducted brides or eloped and then sought to legitimize their practices after the fact with the rhetoric of betrothal gifts, bride service, and bridewealth, which blurred the distinction between their practices and prestigious arranged marriage. The shortage of women and the high cost associated with marriage during the late imperial and Republican eras were related to the strategy of bride abduction among a minority of town residents, but the practice was more prevalent in impoverished basin villages (like East Wind Village) and in the even poorer mountain regions. In mountain villages, bride abduction was legitimized in expressive forms such as the Coqbbersa story and the Heaven Worship Ceremony. The story explains the creation of the world as beginning with an act of bride abduction. This first marriage led to the birth of the mountain-dwelling groups: the Tibetans, Naxi, and Han.[11] The Heaven Worship Ceremony, practiced thereafter by mountain Naxi, was the means by which descendants of the bride-abducting couple ritually honor their affines, in order to quell affinal anger over the originary act of bride abduction and ensure the health of their own descendants.

POVERTY AND BRIDE ABDUCTION IN
PRE-REVOLUTIONARY LIJIANG

Sometimes when it happened there was such a scuffle that they weren't sure who they really grabbed until they got her home. Grabbing took skill: you had to grab the upper body and the pants.—an elderly market woman, Dayanzhen

An older man from East Wind Village told an abduction story:

I think it was in the mid-1930s when Liwen abducted a sixteen-year-old girl. She was on her way to fetch water when, assisted by some of his age-mates, he carried her off to his house. His family had been watching her routine and decided dusk would be the best time to grab her. The girl did not want to be Liwen's wife. She put up a good fight; she screamed and kicked and bit my friend's hand [*my informant raises his hand to his mouth, bares his teeth to demonstrate the action, and laughs uncontrollably*]. Then we brought her to Liwen's home and locked her up. Two of her brothers came to Liwen's house to fight; they were very furious. They threw stones at the walls of the locked courtyard and the roof of the house. After they broke the courtyard door down, neighbors stepped in to restrain them. Liwen's mother stood with her arms spread, covering the door to the living room; the girl was tied up inside. The girl's mother was the last to arrive. She was livid; she yelled and spit at them before leaving. Because the girl's family was so mad, those of us who had helped grab her went home to hide.

The story of Liwen's marriage is a typical account of East Wind Village bride abduction. The abduction had been planned by Liwen's mother, who wanted to secure a daughter-in-law before his sister married because she needed help making the linen shoes that she sold in addition to farming.

Bride abduction—"grabbing a woman" (Naxi, mil zzerq) or "marriage by grabbing" (standard Chinese, qianghun)—was a locally tolerated marriage strategy practiced in pre-1949 Naxi territory. It involved major differences from arranged marriage (marked by go-betweens who negotiated marriage agreements, betrothal gifts, dowry, bridewealth, and celebration), but also mimicked ceremonies and marriage protocol (cf. Bates 1974). Bride abduction reflected the comparative poverty of many Naxi, who could not afford the expenses associated with arranged marriage.

It is not clear when the practice of bride abduction first began. The Coqbbersa story refers to how abduction prevented parentally arranged cousin marriage, implying that abduction was an alternative marriage strategy. In informant accounts, bride abduction and arranged marriage were both found within the same communities. The practice of apologizing and seeking to appease in-laws after an abduction supports the perception that the practice was somehow transgressive.

Before 1949, bride abduction was common throughout Naxi-inhabited areas. Older Lijiang Town residents estimated that it accounted for a small number of marriages. Its incidence appears to have been much higher in rural areas, according to East Wind Village elders.[12] The precise frequency of abductions in rural areas was difficult to determine. In East Wind Village, due to the stigma associated with bride abduction, it was often a person's neighbor rather than the person himself or herself who identified a marriage as having been effected through bride abduction.

In East Wind Village, a girl would be watched for days in order to determine when she would be alone. The abductor usually rallied a group of young men who would assist with the abduction and ensure its success.[13] The girl was seized and then dragged or carried to the man's family's courtyard. There, a basin of water was dumped over her head while someone proclaimed "great auspiciousness, great strength" (da ji da li), referring to the triumphant action accomplished by the groom and his household. In bride abduction, the groom was celebrated for the feat of subduing the girl, which his family and age-mates characterized as a display of his masculine vigor and virility. The act of pouring water over the girl symbolized the irreversibility of the act and referred to the popular saying "A daughter married out is like water poured out; you can't retrieve it."[14] Informants told me that if the woman managed to escape or was rescued before she entered the man's courtyard, the abduction would not be valid. In Lijiang Town, women from the groom's family would spend the night with the abducted woman, comforting her and persuading her to accept the inevitable union.[15] The abductee was usually locked up for a number of days until she or her family acquiesced to the match. Women who continued to resist were eventually raped by their groom-abductors. At that point, the humiliation and shame, combined with the irreversibility of the abduction, gave her no alternative but to accept the circumstances. In rare cases, brides killed themselves or tried to run away (the latter occurrence was rare, however, because of the inevitability of recapture).

Abductions were extremely traumatic for most women. Many older women were obviously still resentful when they spoke of their experiences. One older woman proudly told me that she did not eat or leave the room for seven days after being dragged to East Wind Village; she appeared to savor the temporary distress she had been able to inflict on her anxious husband's family. Many women were reluctant to talk about abductions. Two women whom I interviewed several times described their marriages in detail yet did not mention that they had been abducted. When asked about it directly, one tearfully recounted being grabbed and nearly dying of pneumonia after cold water was dumped on her and she was left tied up and shivering. The other woman merely smiled and said, "That's just the way marriage was."

After the abduction, the man's family would attempt to create the semblance of marriage by sending go-betweens to the woman's household. They would offer profuse apologies for the improper actions of the young man and implore the abductee's family to consent to the union by accepting betrothal gifts or bridewealth, usually substantially lower in value than the betrothal gifts and bridewealth given with an arranged marriage. Unlike bridewealth in an arranged marriage, abduction bridewealth was not expected to return to the groom's household in the form of indirect dowry. In most cases, what was given did not resemble the bridewealth of arranged marriages but usually consisted of the standard betrothal gifts of wine, rice, and brown sugar.[16] There was considerable variation in the value of gifts given by men's families depending on their financial situation. The woman's family rarely agreed after the first attempt at negotiation, and the man's family might make several trips before abandoning the effort.

Whether or not gifts were accepted, societal opinion was on the side of the abductors, and the abducted woman would eventually be regarded as the daughter-in-law of the man's family. Insofar as bride abduction was considered disrespectful and an affront to the abductee's household, her family was expected to be enraged and was not responsible for providing a dowry.[17] If a woman's parents consented to the union, which they often did because they were essentially being presented with a fait accompli, she might be permitted to return to her natal home for a visit.

In Lijiang Town and in basin villages, the man's family customarily celebrated the union, and thereafter the couple was considered "married." Such celebrations ranged from a simple family dinner if the groom came from a poor family, such as those in basin villages, to a larger wedding celebration if the groom's family could afford it.

Although glorified peer accounts often depicted the son's conduct as heroic, bride abductions involved a number of young men overpowering an unaccompanied girl. In at least one case, the prospective groom actually cowered at the back of the gang of abductors and had little to do with the seizure. And despite a general attribution of principal agency to the son, informants' accounts often had women (mothers or aunts) masterminding the abductions. In comparison, men (fathers and mother's brothers) figured prominently in the after-the-fact negotiations. Narratives seem to portray the different phases of abduction as symbolically gendered: the transgressive phase was associated with junior (nonadult) males and women, coupled with injunctions prohibiting the participation of senior men on the grounds that such participation would be unseemly. The legitimizing phase was orchestrated by senior men who were naturalized as inherently knowledgeable about social propriety. In these phases, youthful male and female transgression was symbolically remedied by the subsequent intervention of senior males who repaired transgression though negotiations with the abducted girl's parents in a sequential reaffirmation of senior male authority over women and junior males, underscoring a hierarchy based on age and gender.

Despite the sequence of ritual, in which older males played the most important role in the restoration of moral and potential affinal relations, bride abductions most conspicuously articulated a construction of gender that valorized overblown youthful masculinity. Given the frequent involvement of kin and age-mates, it is curious that grooms were singled out for recognition. The glorification of young men who abducted girls might be explained in terms of a need to overcome their identification with economic impotence. In cases of abduction, perceptions of impotence were dispelled by the performance of masculine potency in overpowering and abducting the girl and feminizing her family by forcing them to submit to the union.

Bride abduction took place in a variety of situations, but the overarching explanation was financial hardship. In cases of arranged marriage, if the man's family could no longer afford the agreed-upon bridewealth or the woman's family could no longer afford to provide a dowry, bride abduction often followed. Many of the abductions in Lijiang Town occurred after the woman's family canceled the engagement and returned the bridewealth because the groom's family was no longer of comparable social and economic standing.[18] In both town and rural areas, a girl's family commonly returned bridewealth and canceled an agreement if the boy she had been engaged to as a child or infant turned out to be physically or mentally disabled as an adult. If abduction followed the cancellation of a marriage agreement, it was itself often followed by a period of serious resentment or hostility, although families tended eventually to establish relationships with their affines, particularly if they lived nearby or were kin to begin with.

When the woman's family approved of the marriage but could not afford the dowry, abduction took place with the tacit consent of the woman's family—who put up a fight just to make the abduction seem authentic and save face; families did not want their neighbors to know they were incapable of providing their daughters with dowries. An older woman from Lijiang Town described some of the circumstances under which bride abduction took place:

> It usually happens that the girl's family is so poor they have no money to give her gifts—no money for a dowry (peijia). In the old times [the Republican era], weddings took three days; you had to have money or you'd lose face. Many people had to sell land to take care of wedding expenses. You had to have a pink wedding dress of silk that was long in back so that two people had to help carry the dress; you also needed embroidered shoes. Brides had to have two chests, an iron brazier and wood coals, a table and stools, quilts and a complete set of bedding. Most of those abducted were already engaged; usually the man's side had already sent some betrothal

gifts. There were two types of abduction: when families were too poor and had to grab; another when the [girl's] family is rich and think they can find a better match for their daughter.

In some cases, a woman's family did not break an agreement but merely sought to prolong the engagement, which usually meant that the family could not afford a dowry or the loss of the daughter's labor. Men's households in Lijiang Town gave bridewealth that was returned to them with the brides in the form of an indirect dowry.[19] Officially, bridewealth was supposed to be used for purposes related to the marriage of a daughter, but the families of poorer women often retained a portion of it to finance the marriages of their sons or pay for household expenses. In such situations, the subsequent inability to produce a dowry suggested financial hardship on the part of the woman's family.

In some bride abductions, there was no marriage agreement between the woman's family and the man who abducted her. In Lijiang Town, since most women were engaged in childhood or infancy, the women most commonly abducted in this way were those from poorer rural families,[20] or town widows abducted by widowers.[21] If a widow was young or if her husband's household had not yet "divided the assets of the corporate household" (fenjia),[22] there was considerable incentive for a brother to outmarry his brother's widow. In doing so, he would ensure a larger share of the corporate estate for himself after the division of the household.[23] If a widow was unwilling to remarry, colluding with an abductor would settle the matter.[24]

It appears that kidnap-type abductions (guaihun) were more common in the rural mountains than in either Lijiang Town or the rural basin. An elderly male informant in Pagoda Hill Village gave an account of one such abduction:

In 1949, a few months before the liberation, Xu's younger sister was abducted while working in the fields. Twenty men came to get her; she fought them, but it was no use. When she arrived at their house, they didn't lock her up, and she escaped and secretly ran back home. The man and his friends came a second time and grabbed her again when she was in the fields. This time, they tied her up and locked her in the house. The next day, the man's family brought new clothes for the girl's parents, wine, tea, and a pig that they had slaughtered and cured. [Bride-giving] families tended to be very exacting about the entire pig being included. If the groom's family neglected to include the heart, they might say "Does my daughter lack a heart?" The parents agreed to the marriage, and she was married the day after they grabbed her. Xu's younger sister was very unhappy about this, but there was nothing she could do because her parents agreed to the marriage. The man who grabbed her was from a mountain region poorer than their village.

In this type of abduction, compensation legitimized the practice as marriage, and such marriages were often described as "selling a girl."

In Pagoda Hill Village, informants estimated that arranged marriages accounted for about 60 percent of marriages.[25] The remainder of unions could be described as having taken place on a continuum from violent capture, as described above, to elopement, as in East Wind Village in the 1990s. An elderly man who had married in the mid-1930s gave the following account of his marriage:

My parents did not arrange a marriage for me because they were too poor. Ana [Grandmother] and I found each other. I led her home, and then my family sent two go-betweens (mi la bbuq in Naxi) to my in-laws. The male and female go-betweens brought one [empty] bowl—now it's two bowls—and one jin [17 ounces] of wine—now it's two jin. Nothing else was given, and neither side celebrated the marriage.

Another elderly man described the importance of the go-betweens, who helped with the after-the-fact apologies that legitimated bride abduction:

The female go-between [mi la bbuq mei in Naxi] and male go-between [mi la bbuq bba in Naxi][26] went to the girl's parents' house with the young couple. They [the young couple] waited quietly outside, and the go-betweens would enter first. They apologized politely to the parents [for the young man's theft of their daughter] and then the go-betweens would sing. It was a beautiful song [the Coqbbersa story] about how, in the beginning, a wife is brought home. There was heaven and earth, and this is how we bring brides home. It was after they finished singing that the couple would enter the room.

The go-betweens' song bears witness to the relationship between bride abduction and elopement and the Coqbbersa story. Like Coqsseililee and Ceiheeqbbubbeqmil, the bride and groom must apologize for their transgressive union. After the plea for parental forgiveness, the go-betweens sing the story of Coqbbersa. The song ends with Coqsseililee and Ceiheeqbbubbeqmil's marriage, which results in the birth of the Tibetan, Naxi, and Han peoples. At the end of the song, cued in advance, the young couple enter the room. The girl's parents find themselves facing their daughter and the rash young man she seeks to marry. The apology scenario echoes the way in which Coqsseililee and Ceilheeqbbubbeqmil stood before Zzeelaqapv (the celestial father of Ceilheeqbbubbeqmil) in the Coqbbersa story. The acceptance of their daughter's abduction or elopement is likened to the act of forgiveness that enabled the creation of the world (i.e., the birth of the Tibetan, Naxi, and Han peoples). The circulation of the Coqbbersa story in mountain regions and the practice of the Heaven Worship Ceremony strongly suggest that bride abduction was not an anomaly but had come to be identified in the mountains with familial and social reproduction. The Heaven Worship Ceremony ensured Naxi social reproduction through the worship of Zzeelaqapv (a celestial being who symbolizes heaven). Before the ceremony is performed, the Tibetans, the Naxi, and the Han—the progeny of Ceilheeqbbubbeqmil and Coqsseililee—come into being, but they are mute and speak only after Coqsseililee holds the Heaven Worship Ceremony. This ceremony continued to be practiced in Pagoda Hill Village until it was classified as a feudal superstition in the early 1950s. In 1985, however, it was reidentified as part of the newly legitimate *dongba* culture, enabling villagers to resume its practice.

The high incidence of bride abduction in mountain communities appears to have been a pattern. In Xinzu, a community of mountain villages several miles away from Pagoda Hill Village, residents remembered bride abduction as a common form of marriage. An elderly *dongba* recounted that bride abduction where he lived was so common during the Republican era that "half of the village's girls and young women did not dare walk outside their homes unaccompanied." In Xinzu, as in the Pagoda Hill region, people recited the Coqbbersa story and held the Heaven Worship Ceremony annually until it was banned after the revolution. While it is not clear what portion of the population married by bride abduction, it was prominent in the memories of elderly villagers in the Xinzu area. In both mountain communities, abduction was associated with poverty and considered inferior to arranged marriage.

COMPARATIVE VIEWS OF BRIDE ABDUCTION

There are many parallels between Naxi bride abduction and its practice as a marriage strategy elsewhere. Like bride abduction in other parts of the world, Naxi bride abduction may be positively correlated with households facing financial hardship and those with disabled or otherwise stigmatized males.[27] In this respect, Naxi bride abduction may be interpreted as a patterned strategy for overcoming social and economic inequalities.

The practice of abduction was sometimes also associated with romantic love, that is, decisions made by couples instead of parents.[28] In Lijiang Town and in the rural basin and the mountains, bride abduction was rarely associated with romantic love on the part of women. Abductions in East Wind Village were portrayed as driven by the desires of young men, even though parents might have actually masterminded them. In all of these areas, however, people committed love suicide, and suicide pacts were associated with clandestine courtship, romance, and resistance to arranged marriage. Love suicides reflected the decisions of young people who made their own choices in marriage. Significantly, young people often mimicked marriage by purchasing wedding bracelets and special clothing and then fleeing to the mountains to live as married couples before killing themselves. Hence, while not explicitly linked to bride abduction, ideas about marriage based on romance and independent decisions were present in contexts where bride abduction took place. And in Pagoda Hill Village, elopement-like practices (which existed on a continuum with bride abduction) were characterized by romantic love and decisions made independently of parents.

Reports of the conflict between parentally arranged marriage and romantic love in Lijiang resemble the observations made by other anthropologists, who attribute bride abduction to local conventions that were significantly different from the rules of arranged marriage (e.g., Bates 1974, 272). It is not clear, however, what the local conventions were in Naxi-inhabited areas before the imposition of direct Chinese rule in 1723.

While it might be imagined that bride abduction was standard Naxi practice before Chinese contact, it is more likely that bride abduction resulted from, rather than preceded, adoption of the Chinese system of prestige.

Brukman observes that bride abduction among the Koya of southern India takes place in a context in which the conventions of an encompassing, powerful ethnic group have defined the ideal of local practice (1974, 308). In the case of Naxi bride abduction, Qing imperial expansion, followed by the imposition of Han marriage practices, created a situation in which Han practices came to define the local ideal in Lijiang. However, two questions are still unresolved. First, what context gave rise to practices of bride abduction, and, second, what can account for the regional differences in Lijiang Town, the rural basin, and the mountains?

PRESTIGE AND REGIONAL VARIATION

Beginning with direct rule of the Lijiang area by Chinese magistrates in 1723, the Naxi were forced to adopt Han marriage and burial practices. The late imperial "civilizing" project sought to incorporate ethnic groups into the Qing empire by transforming them through the inculcation of Confucian ritual and education. In Lijiang, marriage and child betrothal were key to converting members of "uncivilized" groups into "civilized" and morally reliable subjects. It is not clear when bride abduction began in Naxi-inhabited areas, but according to Mann, eighteenth-century China was characterized by a widespread shortage of women. This shortage created a "relentless demographic pressure" resulting in the "kidnapping and abduction of young women" (Mann 1997, 125). If the Coqbbersa story can be understood, in the Lévi-Straussian sense, as the "remains and debris of historical events arranged into a structure," it may provide some clue as to when bride abduction first occurred in Lijiang. According to the elders of Pagoda Hill Village, their ancestors (nineteen families) migrated from rural Tai an (now Nanshan) and Baisha some ten generations ago. The elders who provided this account in 1991 described themselves as the eighth generation and their grandchildren as the tenth. Villagers identify Coqsseililee and Ceiheeqbbubbeqmil as the second generation of their ancestors. Calculating backward based on thirty years per generation, it would appear that the Coqbbersa story might be about a bride abduction that occurred in the early eighteenth century. If this were the case, then bride abduction began roughly in the early 1700s—a time that Mann characterizes as marked by a shortage of women throughout China.

According to Pagoda Hill Village elders, their ancestors were the Mu Tusi's soldiers who had been given the right to choose where they wanted to settle after their regiment was disbanded.[29] The higher incidence of bride abduction might also have occurred because these Mu soldiers did not have wives and resorted to seizing local women to marry when they established the village.

These villagers can hardly be described as primordial or geographically isolated, since their ancestors (the Mu *tusi*'s regiment) originally came from the Lijiang basin and migrated to the mountains. Regardless of whether shortages of women and bride abduction persisted until the early nineteenth century, Joseph Rock reported a shortage of women in Lijiang in the 1940s; this was corroborated by oral histories of bride abduction recounted by elderly informants in the mountains and the basin (1963a). It is also true that the ritual memorialization of bride abduction in Pagoda Hill Village was geographically specific, even if the practice of bride abduction was not.

In Lijiang Town during this period, arranged marriage had become the form of marriage associated with prestige. As elsewhere in China, marriage without betrothal and gift giving was marked as inferior (Mann 1991, 221; McLaren 2001, 955; Wolf and Huang 1980, 72).

Regional variation in the practice of bride abduction may be accounted for in the following ways. Lijiang Town was characterized by state penetration and intensive market activity, which fostered economic fluidity, stratification, and—through schooling—Confucian constructions of gender. In particular, the town had a high concentration of schools. East Wind Village had a private Confucian school during the late Qing dynasty, and during the Republican era, a public primary school was established. In contrast, there were no schools in the Pagoda Hill Village region during either period.

In Lijiang Town, Confucian schooling gave rise to more demanding standards for betrothal gifts, bridewealth, and symbolizations of marital legitimacy. While households preferred brides of comparable social and financial standing, given the shortage of women referred to by Rock, men who were too poor to find town brides (as verified by informants) could resort to finding brides in the basin or the mountains. In the rural basin, despite the preference for intra-basin marriage, impoverished basin men could find brides from the mountains who were even poorer.[30] The regional marriage market had an overall negative effect on males from poor mountain households who were at the bottom of the marriage hierarchy.[31] The following pattern—a low incidence of bride abduction in Lijiang Town, a higher incidence in the rural Lijiang basin, and the highest incidence of practices ranging from bride abduction to elopement in the mountain villages—supports the theory that these practices occurred more frequently in areas with the most economically marginal men.

This economic explanation is borne out in the accounts of older town residents who described bride abduction as less common in the town and often taking place when engagements were broken or delayed by the abducted woman's family. In contrast to bride abduction, arranged marriage was more elaborate (costlier than bride abduction) and uncommon in impoverished households, which could not attract brides.

In the rural Lijiang basin villages, there was a distinct awareness of the prestige associated with marriage ritual. Simpler basin marriages, as well as abductions, in many cases sought to incorporate such elements of Han marriage practice as gifts and, in some cases, bridewealth and celebrations. At the same time, abduction emphasized an exaggerated masculinity that was symbolically equated with abductors and their families. Impotence (in an economic sense) was addressed through gendered spectacle, in which the abductor and his family feminized the girl and her family through dominance, which in turn masculinized the son and exhibited his household's collective strength.

In the rural mountains, practices similar to bride abduction did not draw heavily on Han marriage because these regions were too geographically distant from the local center of Han influence in Lijiang Town. In the mountains and basin, however, an abduction reflected favorably on the abductor's household—which was perceived as "strong" or "capable" (qiang). Perhaps because they had migrated from the basin in the late eighteenth or the early nineteenth century, the first Naxi men to settle in Pagoda Hill thought of abduction as an illegitimate act. The Coqbbersa story and the Heaven Worship Ceremony give voice to both of these aspects by emphasizing the impossible feats performed by Coqsseililee and by undoing the transgression of abduction by performing the Heaven Worship Ceremony, which enables social reproduction.

Although elopement was not explicitly described as "bride abduction" in East Wind Village in 1990–92, the practices closely resemble each other. An examination of elopement and the contexts in which it took place provides clues to interpreting older practices of bride abduction.

RUNAWAY BRIDES

During the reform era, marriage in the rural Lijiang basin increasingly took the form of elopement, referred to as *paohun*. The elopement craze lasted about a decade, beginning with isolated accounts in 1985, reaching a fever pitch in 1990, and then ending in 1995. Elopement took place primarily in poorer basin villages and constituted approximately 80 percent of marriages in East Wind Village during this period.[32]

Paohun, literally "running-away marriage" or "running at dusk," can be translated only loosely as "elopement" and conjures up the image of a marriage brought about by a girl (guniang) running away to marry. Only girls can elope in the sense conveyed by the term paohun; a boy (xiao huozi) "leads a girl home" (ling guniang hui jia) and is not perceived as capable of eloping.[33] Elopement is a feminized practice that attributes agency primarily to girls or women. When referring to marriage by elopement, villagers never described the boy's or man's role in elopement as "leading a girl home." The accentuation of female agency may be rooted in patrilocal kinship, in which sons cannot be perceived as running away because they are eloping to their own houses. It appears that the young men who promoted this practice coined the term and that it reflects their bias by representing the girl or woman as freely choosing to elope. Interviews with informants, however, confirm that elopement encompassed a spectrum of practices, ranging from bride abduction to consensual unions based on courtship and romance.

The following accounts of this diverse practice fall into the categories of "trickery," in which elopement involved coercion and no consent; "persuasion," in which elopement was to some degree consensual; and "forbidden kin," in which elopements involved patrilineal kin whose marriages tended to be consensual but were prohibited according to cultural conventions and the marriage law.

Trickery

A young woman described what happened the night of her elopement:

One evening, Bao, a young man I was acquainted with but whom I had never courted, invited me to his house. Several of his relatives were visiting, and he told me the food would be plentiful and the evening lively. I initially declined, but after much discussion, it was getting dark and he insisted we go. His family members would walk me home later. I went with him reluctantly because I had no other choice.

When we arrived, they treated me well; they gave me chicken leg and lots of other good food. There were many people celebrating what I later learned was "my arrival" as the new daughter-in-law of the house! Bao's family sent a messenger to tell my parents that I had arrived at his house and had agreed to be their daughter-in-law. Bao's family members refused to escort me home, as he had assured me they would. I did not know [if I wanted to marry him]; I was scared. What could I do, my own home was so far away. Bao's family is very powerful and I thought . . . I don't know what I thought. What could I do? I couldn't walk home by myself, it was dark, late, and I was scared.

That night I shared a room with several of his female relatives. After the go-between went to my parents' house several times [and brought betrothal gifts], my family consented, and I realized my fate was with this household.

Persuasion

A young man, nicknamed "Hong Kong" for his martial arts skills and chaotic nature (both associated with Hong Kong films), persuaded a girl to elope:

> My mother told me I needed to think about marriage, that I couldn't perform martial arts my entire life. I first met Yuhua at the movies. She was with five other girls. I walked up to her, and we talked and joked with each other. It was love at first sight. I didn't want to let her go. I told her and her friends that I'd be performing in a Chinese martial arts [wushu] exhibition the next evening, then asked her where she lived.

Yuhua said that Hong Kong went to her house the next day and hung around the courtyard door.

> I was afraid my parents would be angry if I invited him in, so we talked outside the courtyard. That night my girlfriends and I set off to see a movie, but then they told me they were taking me to see Hong Kong's martial arts performance. They insisted we wander around after the performance until we saw him; then my friends left the two of us alone. He walked me home. As we walked, I fell in love with him. When we reached my house, I told my sister I was leaving [would elope].

Hong Kong had seen a friend at the performance and asked this friend to let his family know he would be bringing a girl home that night. His family prepared a room and good food and arranged for relatives to act as go-betweens the next day. They brought the four traditional betrothal gifts: rice, two cones of red sugar, wine, and tea. The go-betweens apologized for Hong Kong's behavior and begged Yuhua's parents to allow the groom's family's to save face. They did not agree but permitted the go-betweens to leave the gifts since they had come so far. On each of the following visits, the party again apologized and brought more of the same gifts. Hong Kong described this practice as "begging for kin" (qiu qin). On the fourth visit, Yuhua's family agreed to set a wedding date. "Four times wins gold," Hong Kong exclaimed, as a way of explaining their success.

Forbidden Kin

A young man describes how he and his wife, Xiu, became married:

We both grew up in East Wind Village. Thirty generations ago, our families were brothers. Since we have this kinship relationship, we first asked our parents if we could marry. They opposed it, so we had no choice but to elope. I discussed this with Xiu and male age-mates [xiao dixiong], and they pledged their support. Not necessarily money, but maybe labor and friendship.

I led her to my house at night. Why at night? You can't elope during the daytime! We both went to work in the fields as usual; then at midnight, she came to my house. I had spoken with my mother beforehand and she was opposed to it, though she likes Xiu. The two of us were always together from a young age. In the morning after the elopement, my mother was pleased. She told us we could relax, that she would help convince my father.

After a few days, my father returned, and I told him. He didn't say anything—he knew it would happen. The day after the elopement, we sent go-betweens to Xiu's house. The party consisted of a maternal aunt [biaosu] and uncle [biaoniang] and a cousin, my father's younger sister's son. They brought a plate of rice, two cones of red sugar, liquor, tea, and cigarettes. Her father opposed the marriage even more than my parents. Her mother disagreed on the surface but underneath supported us. The go-betweens didn't leave the gifts at her house. After six trips, they gave up. My in-laws still hadn't agreed. My grandmother and Xiu's younger brother both agreed. Only my father-in-law refused to accept us.

We waited three months after the elopement, hoping my father-in-law would change his mind, asking him continuously. During this time, we couldn't go out in public or to other people's houses. We were allowed to work in the fields and friends could come see us. [These are the rules associated with elopement.] Finally, we went ahead and held a wedding banquet. The next day, the day when the bride usually goes home [hui niangjia], Xiu's mother, her father's brother, her younger siblings, and many other relatives came to our house for a special meal instead. We didn't go to my father-in-law's house because he didn't agree. My wife's family sent us nothing.

In an elopement, you have to look at the circumstances. Two people both like each other, but because of their families' and society's opposition, we could only elope. Without elopement, I couldn't get a wife. We had to elope because I would marry only her. Since you can marry only once, it's a lifetime business. We courted for a year. In marriage, you have to love each other or it's no use trying to make a family. It doesn't matter if you face hardship; to make a family, one shouldn't fear hardship. Parents raised us, but they're old and can't watch us all their lives. We don't fear the law. This was the only road for us.

THE SPECTRUM OF ELOPEMENT

Elopement in the Lijiang basin did not conform to a single pattern but developed as a broad continuum of practices characterized by old forms of coercion and new forms of agency. As illustrated in the three narratives above, the circumstances and the level of consent involved varied considerably. In Bao's wife's case, the elopement was virtually identical to bride abduction. His family sent go-betweens to apologize and persuade the woman's family to accept betrothal gifts and ratify the union. The woman's family was presented with a fait accompli and could do little to resist, other than prolonging negotiations or refusing to accept the union as legitimate. In either case, their daughter was gone and would eventually be considered married regardless of their views. Bao's account, an example of trickery, shows how elopement, like bride abduction, could entail coercion and the absence of consent. Consistent with abduction, many women described girls who had eloped as "having been tricked" (bei pianle).

One woman with an unmarried son opined that elopements were largely coercive:

I teach my son *not* to trick a girl into coming home. He must do it the right way—be the right age, then marry. The girl too. . . . If they both like each other, he must go to the girl's house to ask her parents to agree and her brothers, too. Cheating a girl at night isn't right. In elopement, sometimes the girl is willing, but sometimes she is not willing, and the boy will force [rape] her. It's wrong, a boy forcing a girl to go to his house. Some are dragged there.

A twenty-two-year-old woman offered a similar opinion:

There were these situations. A man forces a girl to have sex. He fears the girl won't marry him, so he'll force her, so she won't go with others. In cases of rape, if the girl is angry, the man will threaten to ruin her reputation [if she doesn't marry him]. I heard of this happening even during the collective era. With elopement, sex is common. If they have sex, their reputations are negatively affected.

In colloquial usage, the term *bei pianle* also implies that a young woman was seduced, perhaps raped. The expression girls use to describe an elopement, "he's locked up a girl" (*ta guanle yige guniang*), also equates elopement with coercion. It was difficult to establish how many elopements had actually been abductions because women thus married were members of their husbands' households, and they faced potential repercussions if the details of their elopements became public. Among people in East Wind Village, there were strong suspicions of coercion in cases of elopement because the girls were frequently under the legal age to marry, between sixteen and nineteen, and the men were between three and six years older. Critics portrayed these men as preying on young girls who were likely to be inexperienced and vulnerable. The older bachelors generally were from poorer households; their families could not afford the cost of marriage or could not attract a potential wife due to their poverty.

The elopement of Yuhua and Hong Kong was typical of accounts described as consensual. The rationale for elopements involving persuasion indicates generational shifts as well as pragmatic financial motivations. Beginning in the post-Mao era, images in films, magazines, and advertisements invitingly portrayed new ways of life and modern identities.[34]

The villagers' subjectivities, informed by films and other popular media, echoed a shift throughout reform-era China toward reimagining courtship and marriage in terms of "romantic fulfillment" and "wedded love" (Rofel 1999).[35] All the usual criteria employed by young women's parents seemed old-fashioned: a man whose land had good soil quality and was close to the town, who was a dependable worker of few words, the only son of a family with assets. A young woman remarked, "How I can spend a lifetime with a man who doesn't talk or smile?" Parents interpreted elopement to a poorer household as downward mobility, based on a family's land or material assets. But some eloping young women used a different measure of upward mobility or "hypergamy" (Constable 2005, 10). Romantic young men with style, verbal sophistication, and masculine cachet more closely embodied modernity in the imaginary of the reform era, making them more attractive than the mundane choices of the young women's parents.

The accounts of individual men did not always square with the romanticized views of courtship that many young men initially portrayed. What constituted "courtship" ranged from a single meeting to more than a year of meetings. In Hong Kong's case, the couple had met twice and eloped at the end of their third meeting. Other young women, sixteen years of age, described eloping at the end of a single meeting.[36] For Hong Kong, it was not exclusively romantic feelings but also his mother's prodding that set him on a course to find a wife. Common explanations for elopement given by men include the following: the family needed the labor of a daughter-in-law; elopement would hasten marriage to a girl or woman with several unmarried older siblings who would otherwise have to wait years to marry; the man had an undesirable (e.g., lazy, violent, or alcoholic) family member who placed an unusual burden on the household; the man was comparatively less attractive (from a poor village, lacked good land, had no inheritance or financial resources, had bad housing, or was disabled).

And while most men described elopement as convenient for their particular situation, they did not want their own children to elope. One man disclosed his preference that his son marry after engagement and the negotiation of bridewealth. Another woman pointed out that a daughter whose in-laws had "begged for her" had a higher status, while a bride who had eloped could be perceived by her in-laws as "coming empty-handed."

Elopement with patrilineal kin was the one form in which financial circumstances were not necessarily foremost. In Xiu's case, her patrilineal cousin, who was in danger of becoming an aging bachelor, persuaded her to elope. She was underage but knew that elopement was the only means by which she could marry her cousin, given her father's orthodox views on kinship propriety. Intralineage elopements may reflect a strategy on the part of women to remain in their natal villages, affording them a better support system and closer connection to their parents, including the ability to assist them. As Norma Diamond has pointed out, women who stay in their natal villages are often more likely to rise to roles of public leadership in their communities (cited in Judd 1989, 541).[37] However, other cases of post-revolutionary intravillage and intralineage elopements suggest that such unions were employed by impoverished men's families (see Chan, Madsen, and Unger 2009, 190-92).

In another case, Wen, a schoolteacher, eloped after a courtship with Jiao, her patrilineal nephew (despite their different generational status, the nephew was actually older than her). She had become gradually aware of his interest when he began addressing her as "Village Sister" instead of "Little Aunt," which he had used for most of their lives. With Wen and Jiao, their families elevated what would otherwise have been an unprestigious match by employing the rhetoric of marriage protocol. Wen's family provided a large dowry and bridewealth, and both the bride and groom's families celebrated the union with huge banquets and much fanfare. Wen and Jiao had lived together for months before the wedding, yet the families insisted that the bride be sent home so that they could go through the rituals of fetching the bride and even hazing the newlyweds in the bridal chamber, or *nao xinfang*.[38] By including all elements of Han marriage protocol (albeit not in order), their families sought to make elopment as prestigious as marriage.

Wen and Jiao's wedding was unusual as well in its syncretic approach to marriage, including both Han marriage ritual and *dongba* ritual. The marriage celebrations included two days of activities and two banquets at the bride's and the groom's parents' houses. At the groom's banquet, *dongba* performed *siku* (discussed in chapter 1), which none of the people in East Wind Village had seen. This ritual, which was held in the mountains before the revolution, was presided over by He Wanbao, founder of the Dongba Cultural Research Institute and a relative of the bride and the groom, and represented as an authentic "Naxi wedding." The entire staff of the institute was invited to the feasts and filmed the *dongba* rituals for its archive. All of East Wind Village was invited to the wedding, which was intended to be an opportunity for the villagers to learn about *dongba* culture and their "ethnic heritage."

Most elopements did not resemble Wen and Jiao's, which took place in order to circumvent conventions about patrilineal kinship. The import of celebrations, bridewealth, dowry, and ritual, however, was clearly linked to prestige. Unlike most of the East Wind Village elopers, Wen and Jiao were from two of the most prosperous households in the village. And to the extent the households of other elopers could afford any of these practices, they were usually on a smaller scale and involved far less expense; they were also used to regain respectability and legitimize unions after elopement.

MAPPING ECONOMIC INEQUALITY IN REFORM ERA CHINA

In the 1980s, elopements occurred sporadically throughout the basin surrounding Lijiang Town.[39] According to the leader of East Wind Village, elopements sharply increased in the late 1980s and became the most common means of marrying from the mid-1980s to the mid-1990s. The rise and fall of elopement has to be understood in the context of the major changes that took place during the reform era. The decollectivization of agriculture and the establishment of the Household Responsibility System contributed to the creation of new prosperity as well as growing economic inequality among rural residents in the Lijiang basin. Economic inequality became pronounced both between villages and within them, and was particularly an issue in marriage negotiations and visible in marriage celebrations. During the Maoist era, there were fewer differences in the prosperity of individual basin households because land was farmed collectively. The state advocated simple marriage celebrations, which were considered politically de rigueur. This changed significantly after decollectivization. Increases in the standard of living were coupled with the reappearance of popular cultural practices, including life-cycle celebrations such as marriage. Marriage was again associated with the production of prestige, and households translated their prosperity into prestige through marriage ritual and celebrations. Historically, marriages in East Wind Village were largely intra-basin. While there continued to be a preference for intra-basin unions, starting in the reform era, the new expenses associated with marriage made it difficult for rural men on the bottom of the economic hierarchy to marry.[40] East Wind Village was among the poorest in the basin, and therefore its men were at a disadvantage in terms of finding brides.

Reform-era changes at the national level also had reverberations for poorer rural families in the Lijiang basin. Between 1985 and 1995, when the Lijiang elopements took place, income inequality in China was exceptionally high (D. Davis 2005),[41] and Yunnan was among China's poorest provinces. Hence, Yunnan was targeted as an area where one could easily attract young women because movement out of the province signified upward mobility. During this time, Lijiang women were lured into long-distance elopements with promises of jobs or marriage into prosperous households (see Chao 2005). The rise of economic inequality, and the attendant high cost associated with marriage in other parts of rural China, additionally fostered the growth of elaborate organizations that engaged in the long-distance kidnapping and sale of women, primarily from ethnic minority areas in China's southwest (Chao 2005). The Lijiang Public Security Bureau was aware of a number of cases in which Lijiang women, primarily from the countryside, had been tricked (i.e., seduced, raped, and sold) into going to Zhejiang and Jiangsu, coerced into remaining there, and even pressured into luring other Lijiang women to similar fates. The unidirectional flow of young women out of the Lijiang basin to other provinces, either due to long-distance marriage or kidnapping, further diminished the number of available rural basin women and worsened the marital prospects of East Wind Village men at the bottom of the marriage market. The economic marginality of many village men precluded them from arranging marriages and potentially doomed them to lives as aging bachelors, incapable of attaining masculine adulthood.

Popular representations of elopement suggest that many villagers understood that the practice was linked to economic marginality. However, echoing gendered representations of bride abduction, proponents of the practice valorized it as a hypermasculine feat rather than an act of economic impotence. Male age-mates celebrated men who "led girls home" as daring, virile, masculine, and physically forceful. These traits were exemplified by their ability to attract, overpower, lock up, or domesticate their captives—transforming the girls into wives. In contrast to the depiction of these young men as "cheats," put forward by the women's families, the men's parents viewed their sons as "clever" and were proud of the young men's skill with the "honeyed words of

FIG. 3.1 Parents of a 1990s runaway bride

courtship." As in abduction, one's perspective on a particular elopement was likely to be positional, reflecting whether one's household lost or gained. For a poor man's family, elopement was equivalent to receiving a free bride, but for a woman's family, it meant being forced to accept a marriage they had not chosen or face the prolonged public disgrace of their daughter's continued sexuality outside of marriage if they attempted to oppose the union.

Local understandings of elopement, however, were shaped not only by a son's or daughter's involvement but also by state discourse and the way it informed village perception through the structures of village governance.

ELOPEMENT UNDER PARENTAL ATTACK

The reform era marked a shift in governmental discourse; political campaigns now blamed local tensions arising from material inequality on culturally driven or ideological shortcomings. Government campaigns like the Five Good Families Campaign (*wuhao jiating*) emphasized "the education of social morals," "respect for the old," "observing the law," and "family virtues." The Civilized Village Campaign articulated topics ranging from rebottled Confucian morality to unplanned births (Anagnost 1997, 363).[42]

During East Wind Village governance meetings, residents were urged to understand state campaigns in terms of local issues. Drawing on state rhetoric, girls who had eloped came to be condemned for "uncivilized behavior" (*buwenming de biaoxian*), "not registering marriages" (*buban jiehun zheng*), and "not listening to their parents or the state" (*buguan fumuqin, buguan guojia*). An elderly informant recounted one of the many discussions at meetings of the Village Elders Association (*laonianxiehui*):

Zheng, a cadre, brought up the problems caused by young people. He said, "Now youths are disobedient; their behavior is beyond words [*bu xiang hua*]. Boys going off drinking and girls going to elope [*paohun*]—these are problems of education. We must educate our kids!" Another person added: "We tell girls, don't elope. We tell them, When you get to a certain age, then look properly for a fiancé. This is the right way." Finally, a cadre concluded: "There is a lot of elopement, especially among young girls who are seventeen and eighteen. We must tell them, 'Don't elope,' especially if they are young."

These concerns about underage marriage and disobedience among young people corresponded to the state-mandated marriage age and state discourse promoting models of patriarchal family relationships.[43] For people in East Wind Village, daughters who eloped were conspicuous targets of village moral education projects because they failed to consult, or even defied, their parents regarding marriage and, in cases of underage marriage, violated the 1980 marriage law.[44] Eloping girls were condemned as "chaotic" or "unfilial" or having a "low cultural level." Boys and men suspected of engaging in coercion were criticized as engaging in acts that were "uncivilized" and "illegal." Anti-elopement discussions ultimately laid the responsibility for regulating marriage on parents, who were supposed to educate their children about adhering to state-defined marriage guidelines.[45] Underage elopement and subsequent unplanned births directly violated both the 1980 marriage law, which set the minimum marriage age at twenty for women and twenty-two for men, and national population policy, according to which only married couples may legitimately reproduce.

ELOPEMENT AS ETHNIC

Elopement is the cultural custom of the Naxi minority and our ethnic characteristic.
—former Lijiang Communist Party secretary

He Wanbao, once the highest-ranking Communist Party official in Lijiang Prefecture and founder of the Dongba Cultural Research Institute, was raised in East Wind Village. He explained that elopement was an ethnic trait. The categorization of a practice as "ethnic" accomplished two objectives. First, it placed the custom in a special category that China has embraced and showcased, nationally and internationally, since the reform era. Specifically, it suggested elopement could be considered part of *dongba* culture. Second, it exempted elopement from the realm of the political, from being considered "chaotic," "unlawful," and "uncivilized," and from being in violation of population policy (due to births out of wedlock) and the marriage law (due to its association with underage girls and unregistered marriages).

The evidence against elopement having been a distinctively Naxi practice is manifold. It was not practiced among the Naxi of Lijiang Town, and although elopement-like practices took place in mountain areas such as Pagoda Hill

Village, they were regarded very differently because villagers there did not resist or stigmatize elopement.

In the town, where Chinese influence was stronger than in the rural villages, people practiced parentally arranged and individually contracted (but parentally approved) marriage, and elopement was nonexistent. Sons and daughters in Lijiang Town customarily sought their parents' permission before making plans to marry. An informant explained that since parents are the ones who arrange marriages, it would not be possible to marry unless they agreed to the match. While it was becoming more common for young people in Lijiang Town to find their own spouses, parents still wielded considerable authority over such decisions in the 1980s and 1990s and, in many cases, could veto what they saw as inappropriate alliances.

The authority of town parents over marriage matters could be attributed to the financial dependence of the younger generation. From the end of the Maoist era to the mid-1990s, there were fewer work unit jobs and the unemployment rate was high. At the same time, banqueting and life-cycle ceremonies were becoming more elaborate and costly in town than in the surrounding rural basin. Stores specializing in "red and white" (marriage and funerary) decorations and services were common. In an effort to reduce the costs of banqueting associated with marriage and funerary obligations, street associations had begun collectively purchasing land, chairs, and tables, so that residents could use them in rotation. In the 1990s, marriage celebrations had become so lavish in Lijiang Town that the Communist Party asked its members to set an example by limiting the number of tables at their children's marriage banquets.

Marriage celebrations in the reform era had become essential to the production of social prestige and the maintenance of social networks. When asked about elopement, town residents indicated that such a practice would be "laughed at" in Lijiang Town and that families would be considered uncivilized (buwenming) or unlearned (mei xuewen) if their children married in this way.

Elopement was also unheard of in rural Pagoda Hill Village, located in the mountains, far from both Lijiang Town and the Lijiang basin. As in the basin, young people were free to court whomever they pleased and chose their spouses without parental interference. On weekend nights, young people gathered by a small store where they built a bonfire and played music. As the evening progressed, couples paired off and "walked together with the man's arm around the woman's neck" (*luobozi*). Couples went off to the mountains to court, which could include talking or more. When young people stayed out all night, their parents generally regarded these activities as their son's or daughter's business. According to convention, a woman could refuse by insulting or even scratching an aggressive suitor.[46]

Couples in Pagoda Hill frequently bypassed marriage and began their relationships with cohabitation. A young man might perform bride service by working periodically or for a number of months at his future in-laws' farm before a marriage celebration would be discussed with any of the parents. Sometimes couples lived at one of their families' households for several months to a year before deciding to proceed with a marriage celebration. Parents still orchestrated the preparation of betrothal gifts, dowry, and marriage celebrations, but there was less negotiation between affines. Pagoda Hill courtship and marriage practices differed from elopement in that they were not marked as new or aberrant. They were not associated with the theft of a daughter, a girl's disrespect for her parents, or any moral taint connected with premarital sex. Nor was the young man characterized heroically as bold, daring, and masculine or negatively as a cunning trickster. If Pagoda Hill unions could be described as elopements, they were without the taint of immorality associated with the basin practice of *paohun*. The courtship and marriage practices in the village were, from the perspective of basin and town standards, scandalous. The Public Security Bureau officers (themselves from other parts of Lijiang) who were stationed near Pagoda Hill clearly expressed this viewpoint. The officers described the courtship practices on the mountain as "uncivilized" and "chaotic," and they had made several unsuccessful attempts to stop these practices. However, they were stationed several hours' walk downhill from the courtship sites and lacked the continual presence required to police courtship practices.

The variation in marriage practices among Lijiang Town, the rural basin, and the mountain villages corresponded to the extent to which Han marriage practices were equated with prestige and the extent to which men seeking wives could afford the prestigious practices. In East Wind Village, many households aspired to Han marriages but, unable to afford the required practices, incorporated elements of Han marriage into elopement and claimed that elopement and marriage were indistinguishable.[47] In mountain villages like Pagoda Hill, an area poorer than most basin villages, a groom provided the bride's household with labor and edible resources, and marriage celebrations did not appear to be a venue for the production of household prestige.[48] Economic differences between households did not strictly impinge on the marital prospects of impoverished men, at least in the sense of a household blocking a daughter's marriage, because young people made their own decisions about marriage. It was not the case, however, that poor men faced no difficulties marrying. Some Pagoda Hill Village men remained bachelors (they had sexual relationships but never married), and some of them married women from adjacent, and even poorer, Lisu or Tibetan households.

Elopement and bride abduction are not distinctly Naxi practices. They take place across ethnic boundaries and among a number of ethnic groups. One or the other of these practices has occurred, and continues to occur, among the Bai, Lisu, Manchu, Yi, Pumi, Lahu, Zhuang, Jingpo, Achang, Tujia, Va, Miao, Tibetan, Ewenki, Kazakh, Uyghur, and Mongols, and possibly among other ethnic minorities in China. Despite the perception that bride abduction was an archaic practice associated with China's minority ethnic groups, Ann McLaren's study of Republican-era bride abduction in rural Pudong-Nanhui suggests it was common among Han inhabitants of these areas (2001, 953) and of other regions of China (citing Gates 1996, 131; Honig and Hershatter 1988, 278, 288, 359n; Elvin 1984). McLaren argues that because bride abduction is associated with the "past of the Han Chinese and the present of the 'non-Han minority nationalities,'" there has been a lack of interest in China in pursuing it as an area of scholarly inquiry. She concludes that bride abduction was a local institution that responded to the irrationalities of the dowry-bridewealth (caili) system by the poorest classes and was an accepted custom among the Han Chinese (2001, 957, 953, 982).

McLaren's research shares similarities with ethnographic studies of bride abduction in cultural contexts outside of China, which strongly correlate abduction with families unable to pay the expenses associated with prestigious marriage practice. The strategies of bride abduction and elopement in East Wind Village were utilized largely by the families of impoverished men who wished to see their sons married without the expense associated with marriage, and its expectations of betrothal gifts, bridewealth, dowry, and celebrations. In the sense that Naxi men engaged in these practices, it might be argued that these were "ethnic" practices. This raises the question of the import of classifying practices as "ethnic." Paul Gilroy has cautioned that such classifications contribute to "ethnic absolutism" (1987). Thus categorized, ethnic customs are reduced to the cultural proclivities of a particular ethnic group and stripped of the contexts in which they are deployed. Based on the evolutionary and primordialist definitions of ethnicity that reign in China, the classification of bride abduction and elopement as "ethnic" reinforces the idea that minority ethnic groups are situated in the past. Chinese scholars may be reluctant to study Chinese bride abduction precisely because of the implied epistemological contradiction presented by the Han occupying positions of both "primitive" and "modern" within the hegemonic evolutionary framework. Ethnicity (associated with custom and culture) is not so much a means of marking difference in contemporary China as it is a means of marking hierarchy. Though the Han and minority ethnic groups are coevals, in Chinese evolutionary discourse only "ethnic groups" (*shaoshu minzu*) have customs associated with China's past. The contemporary anthropological understanding of ethnicity disputes essentialist definitions of ethnic groups "as given" or characterized as having primordial origins. Ethnicity is understood as originating in "relations of inequality" (John Comaroff 1996, 166). The designation of ethnic practices, then, is a means by which "the dominant are able to define the subordinant" and, it might be added, justify that subordination (Wilmsen 1996, 5). Jan Pierterse has argued that ethnicity might be better understood as a contemporary invention, a "product of nation rather than its forerunner" (1996, 11). The ethnicization of practices such as elopement is not an inevitability of national orders but a product of crafting a reform-era national identity based on multiethnic heritage. More specifically, it is a project encysted in the creation of *dongba* culture as the essence of Naxi heritage.

The representation of bride abduction and elopement, as Naxi traits, reflects only how such practices are portrayed at a local or a national level. It does not depict the basic circumstances or motivations that gave rise to these practices. Bride abduction and elopement are better understood as class strategies than as cultural forms—such an understanding accounts for why the practitioners of abduction and elopement have been, and are, disproportionately ethnic minorities.

One of the salient characteristics of many ethnic groups in China is that they occupy much of China's most agriculturally marginal land (Heberer 1989, 16) and are among China's poorest citizens. Poverty among China's minority ethnic groups has disproportionately grown since the reform era compared to the larger Han population. In 2010, close to 50 percent of China's poorest citizens were members of ethnic minorities. If we understand marriage as taking place within and between economically heterogeneous regions, such as Lijiang Town and basin, in which some households were impoverished, it is not surprising that members of those households would have encountered difficulties finding spouses or contracting marriages. During the reform era, marriage desirability was increasingly correlated with economic criteria. Meanwhile, the expenditures associated with marriage (which marked prestige) increased, making it virtually impossible for impoverished households to find brides for their sons. Just as poverty and shortages of women gave rise to bride abduction in the late imperial and Republican eras in Lijiang and elsewhere, the reform era growth of economic prosperity and inequality in the Lijiang basin and the surrounding mountain districts led to marriage practices perceived as "uncivilized" or otherwise aberrant by the standards of more prosperous neighbors in Lijiang Town or in the rural basin. If we understand "aberrant marriage practices" in economic rather than cultural terms (i.e., as class strategies), then it is not surprising that these practices occurred in areas as different as the Lijiang basin and Republican-era Pudong-Nanhui.

Finally, one cannot ignore the potential political dimensions that shape the analysis of popular practice—that is, to suggest that elopement arises from economic inequality, as opposed to ethnic motivations, implicitly critiques state policy since the reform era. Aberrant marriage practices may be understood as a new index for tracking poverty. The elopement craze of 1985–95 certainly suggests that reform-era shifts in policy had negative reverberations for many East Wind Village residents.

By the mid-1990s, the elopement craze was over. The mid-1990s marked the beginning of Lijiang Town's transformation into a major center for national and international tourism. With the opening of the Lijiang airport in 1995, tourists began flooding into the town, which became a major destination for tourism in China. The growth of Lijiang's new tourism-based economy required laborers for construction and to provide services, and the area became a magnet for young rural villagers eager to work in the city. Lijiang's expansion into the surrounding countryside, or urbanization (cheng-shihua), mirrored the national redistribution of China's population from rural to urban areas. Young people from East Wind and other villages in the basin found jobs in town as maids, cooks, performers, bar hostesses, guides, shop attendants, guards, construction workers, taxi drivers, or sex workers. Their enhanced earning power increased their authority, including the right to make decisions about marriage. But more significantly, basin villages like

East Wind ceased to be multigenerational communities. Courtship and agreements to marry took place off-site, away from parents and the rural basin. People from East Wind Village who worked in Lijiang Town or other cities usually courted workers of rural origin from a much broader range of places than the basin. East Wind Village parents appeared to have much less authority over children of marriageable age. Women who had eloped fifteen years earlier complained that young people were chaotic; in some cases, couples cohabited openly with no intention of marrying. The practice of women eloping or being kidnapped and taken to Zhejiang or Jiangsu, as occurred in the 1980s and early 1990s, ended with the development of tourism in Lijiang. Given Lijiang Town's rapidly growing economy, migration to faraway places could not compete with local options for economic mobility. By 2005, East Wind Village was emptied of young people. Only the elderly, middle-aged women, and children remained. In 2011, the few who remained in the village complained that young people "dumped their kids" with their parents, having neither the time nor the proper conditions to care for them while they worked in the city. The remaining young people in the village were making marriage decisions independently of their parents, but many still expected their parents to cover the cost of marriage celebrations.

In the 1990s, eloping basin villagers were one among many, largely ethnic, groups in China who engaged in "aberrant" marriage practices. This did not escape the notice of the central government. Article 50 of the 2001 marriage law created the possibility that ethnic groups[49] living in autonomous regions would be "given the right to formulate certain adaptations [to the marriage law] in light of the specific conditions of the minority nationalities in regard to marriage and family." In this revision of the marriage law, the state again identified the economic inequalities that led to the strategies of bride abduction and elopement as having been caused by the cultures of the ethnic groups themselves.[50]

RETHINKING MYTH AS "ETHNIC"

The Coqbbersa story may be reinterpreted through the lens of practices such as bride abduction and elopement. It provides an account of overcoming bride abduction or, more specifically, quelling affinal anger resulting from the theft of a daughter. The remarkable parallels between Ceiheeqbbubbeqmil's abduction in the story and bride abduction in mountain villages such as Pagoda Hill support this conclusion. Bride abduction resonates with many elements of the story: daughters are perceived as tending to be willful and resisting marriage; bride abduction takes place in lieu of arranged marriage (specifically cousin marriage, identified in the myth and Pagoda Hill history); it is the groom's, and not his parents', agency that brings about his marriage; the groom's family is socially inferior to his bride's family (symbolized as the difference between heaven and earth in Coqsseililee's case); Ceiheeqbbubbeqmil initially resists abduction but ultimately acquiesces and becomes a loyal wife; once a woman's wings (virginity) are taken, she will be disinclined to escape and too embarrassed to reveal her situation to her parents (a woman's reputation is damaged as a result of capture); affinal approval depends on a potential son-in-law's successful bride service (labor for his in-law's household); for women's families, bride abduction is equated with trickery and theft (symbolized by the purloined cat, turnip, and Ceiheeqbbubbeqmil herself).

If abduction were the ideal form of marriage practice, Coqsseililee would not have been required to perform extraordinary feats in service of his father-in-law or to worship him annually. Yet the persistence of the story and the Heaven Worship Ceremony underscores that both were of particular significance to the Naxi communities in Pagoda Hill and Xinzhu.

Oral transmission of the Coqbbersa story and practice of the Heaven Worship Ceremony in these rural mountain areas suggest that bride abduction played a significant role in social reproduction. Service to the bride's family, stressed in the story, was an important element associated with abduction and marriage practice, but this was related to the region's history. In contrast, bride service did not play a significant role in rural East Wind Village or Lijiang Town. In the town and basin, go-betweens did not recite the Coqbbersa story as part of their apologies.

In the three communities of Lijiang Town, East Wind Village, and Pagoda Hill Village, geographic differences simultaneously marked economic hierarchy and different degrees of Chinese influence, but it should not be assumed that ethnic authenticity as opposed to history accounted for these differences. Not all Naxi communities located in the mountains perform the Heaven Worship Ceremony or emphasize the Coqbbersa story. In Baoshan, a Naxi mountain village built on a stone precipice some eighty miles north of Lijiang and which dates back to the Yuan dynasty, villagers worship the Gaa bu (*zhan shen*), the god of war, and do not practice the Heaven Worship Ceremony. In Muli county's Eya township, a mountainous area in Sichuan, Naxi villages similarly do not practice the ceremony (Li Ying, personal communication, 2011). The practices in these Naxi villages suggest that the Heaven Worship Ceremony and the Coqbbersa myth reflect the particular histories of Naxi communities and are problematically taken to be indicators of primordial Naxi practice or representative of the history of all Naxi communities.

In East Wind Village and Lijiang Town (which had Confucian schools and was the center of Han political authority in Naxi-inhabited areas), the remedy for bride abduction not surprisingly involved Han marriage ritual (go-betweens, dowry, bridewealth, and celebrations) combined with apologies for the transgressive act. In contrast to the mountain areas, in Lijiang Town and predominantly throughout the rural Lijiang basin the story of Coqbbersa was unknown and the Heaven Worship Ceremony was not performed. While this may in part be explained by the adoption of Han ritual forms, it was also true that the Coqbbersa story and Heaven Worship Ceremony were directly tied to the incidence of bride abduction, which was not central to social reproduction in Lijiang Town or as central in basin areas. Regional variation in the practice of bride abduction underscores the historical and economic dimensions of this practice. The highest standard of living in Lijiang has always been associated with the town, followed by the rural basin areas, while the rural mountain regions have been considered the poorest. The ancestors of Pagoda Hill villagers who were disbanded Mu *tusi* troops may have practiced bride abduction because they lacked access to local women. The soldiers' transgressions and relations with their in-laws appear to have been ritually memorialized and justified in both compensatory groom service and ritual deference to in-laws, on whom the men depended to some extent for their livelihoods.[51]

These cases underscore the importance of thinking about marriage as a dynamic institution shaped by both political and historical conditions. In all its variants, bride abduction and the later practice of elopement took place in arenas where other practices—arranged cousin marriage or parentally arranged marriage with betrothal (often, child betrothal), bridewealth, dowry, and celebrations—were the ideal. In Pagoda Hill Village, Xinzhu, East Wind Village, and Lijiang Town, those arenas were shaped by a history of the imposition of Han marriage practice, which, over the course of two or more centuries, became the most prestigious form of marriage.[52]

The privileging of historically situated practices as originary (which state-promoted projects of essentialization such as the defining of *dongba* culture have done) ironically contributes to an erasure and homogenization of Naxi history. The Ceiheeqbbubbeqmil story, the late imperial and Republican-era practices of bride abduction, and reform era elopement came to be identified as ethnic. This ethnicization obscures the ways in which these practices were regionally variant and informed by the Han prestige system. Rather, abduction and elopement strategies were part of an arena in which Han marriage marked the difference between "civilized" and "barbarian" and between Han and Naxi, and then later marked class differences between Naxi that corresponded to regional and intraregional marginality. The contexts of abduction and elopement narrate a history of a "civilizing project" that began with political subordination and resurfaced at moments characterized by pronounced economic inequalities. The ethnicization of marginality continues to conceal what is behind the ethnic marker: in some cases, nonconformity to hegemonic Han marriage ideals; in others, the poverty that initially led indigent Lijiang residents to engage in abduction and elopement as strategies of marriage and social reproduction.

In the mid-1990s, the one-child family policy and the related national shortage of women gave rise to the kidnapping and sale of women as brides for rural households in central and eastern China. As was true of bride abduction and elopement in Lijiang, the phenomenon is directly linked to the difficulties faced by impoverished rural households in finding brides for their sons. Articles appearing in Chinese newspapers condemn the kidnappers as criminal but are often sympathetic to the economic circumstances motivating households that purchased brides. Given the ethnicization of bride abduction and other "aberrant marriage practices" among China's ethnic groups, it is particularly interesting that these Han practices are *not* ethnicized or understood as the cultural proclivities of Han households predisposed to abduct brides.[53] No one would propose that the kidnapping of women should be classified as a Han ethnic practice.[54] As the Naxi case demonstrates, the ethnicization of bride abduction and elopement can result in the misrepresentation of class marginality as ethnic difference, which reinforces contemporary biopolitical categorizations. Such categorizations assume minority ethnic groups to be biologically distinct populations that are economically marginal *because* of their culture. They also create a situation in which the state, under the auspicies of embracing the diversity of ethnic minorities, need not address the disproportionate correlation between perceived ethnic marriage practices and poverty.

4

BIOPOLITICS FOX STENCH, GENDER BOUNDARIES, AND THE MORAL ECONOMY OF POSTSOCIALISM

One day a beautiful taxi driver disappeared. Rumors soon circulated about what had happened to her. It was assumed she had been murdered and dismembered, because no body was ever found. The crime remains unsolved.

A young man from a prominent Lijiang family fell in love with a beautiful taxi driver. They courted and planned to marry. His mother, however, thought the young woman had body odor, literally, "fox stench" (*huchou; fuchou* in Lijiang pronunciation). She refused to allow the marriage without an investigation. The man therefore enlisted a young woman, a friend of the family, to get to know his girlfriend well enough to stay overnight at her house. When they shared a bed, a practice common among close friends, the family friend would be able to discover whether the taxi driver suffered from any "abnormalities." The friend spent the night with the driver, verified the odor, and reported back to the man's family. The man broke off the relationship, and gossip about the taxi driver began spreading around Lijiang Town.

I heard these two accounts in 1995 and 1997, when friends and acquaintances were eager to tell me about changes in the local landscape since the early 1990s. Stories about female taxi drivers were conspicuous in gossip and in the news. In 1992, there were no taxis in Lijiang, and most people traveled by bicycle or on foot. By 1997, more than seven hundred taxis were operating in this town of only about three square miles. The large number of taxis, one of the most conspicuous changes, was touted as evidence of "modernization" in Lijiang. In particular, the large number of women drivers, rare in other parts of China, drew the attention of national and international tourists. At the same time, numerous stories about female taxi drivers' violent deaths revealed widespread local ambivalence about the women driving taxis. Less common, but more intriguing, were stories that focused on their bodies, which were identified with danger, immorality, ambiguous sex organs, and pollution. Such stories allegorized how capitalist privatization was straining the social fabric of Lijiang.

As tourism and the number of private businesses increased, state-sector workers and established Lijiang residents lost considerable economic and social standing, and Lijiang's social hierarchy was thrown into flux. Discussions over suitable marriage partners reflected these upheavals. Some residents disparaged old distinctions, now blurred, while others sought to reassert them. Parents debated the sort of daughters-in-law they wanted with an eye to maintaining family reputations in Lijiang; young people seeking marriage partners were giving serious consideration to moral character, material wealth, and physical appearance. Young women, especially those perceived as attempting to use marriage as a way of crossing social boundaries, were closely scrutinized for signs of bodily difference.

Imaginings of bodily abnormality reassert hierarchical distinctions through stigmatizing stories of essential difference—that is, by accusing female taxi drivers of bodily pollution, some town residents attempted to reinforce difference (between rural and urban origins, private- and state-sector employment, immorality and morality, backwardness and modernity, and divergent constructions of the feminine). Global flows and capitalist privatization in Lijiang had brought upheaval, dislocation, and danger to downwardly mobile town residents, experiences they conveyed in the taxi driver narratives. In particular, for the state-sector workers and intellectuals who told such stories, female taxi drivers embodied the negative aspects of Lijiang's economic transformation. The drivers became a convenient surrogate for the otherwise complex and impersonal forces of capitalist privatization, which brought the sensibilities of outsiders to bear on local forms of hierarchy and marginality.

Scrutiny of female drivers' bodily abnormalities followed state campaigns targeting body and population quality (suzhi). In these campaigns, improving reproductive female bodies and public hygiene was presented as a catalyst for national modernity. But bodily improvement required economic means that downwardly mobile state-sector workers and intellectuals did not have. Stories about smelly taxi drivers, which warned listeners against falling prey to deceptive appearances, asserted that bodies are not alterable but are characterized by essential difference—here, fox stench, understood as an incurable medical condition (bromhidrosis) (see Cowie and Evison 1988, 181). Although the connection with medicine is relatively recent, throughout history such accusations sought to enforce boundaries at times of social transformation. Taxi driver stories were intriguing because they voiced a counternarrative to notions of bodily improvement within a national discourse on population and modernity. These stories expressed the bitter experiences of town dwellers who perceived modernity to be beyond their reach. In seeking to contest the upward mobility of new urban residents of rural origin, they drew on popular ambivalence about Lijiang's changing social landscape as they offered older scenarios of essential difference. Ultimately, however, the enduring effect of taxi driver stories for the broader sector of Lijiang Town dwellers was to promote a model of femaleness that privileged a woman's role as wife and mother over her identity as worker.

While capitalism in China is often associated with the decline of the state sector and the appearance of private-sector businesses in the 1980s, the private sector in Lijiang expanded most rapidly in the late 1990s, when tourism grew markedly. Ironically, the biggest boost to tourism came in the form of disaster: a 1996 earthquake that rocked northwestern Yunnan Province, severely damaging Lijiang. Many residents said that national media and international press coverage of the earthquake's aftermath "put Lijiang on the world map." Domestically, the picturesque Song dynasty architecture and willow-lined streams of Lijiang's Old Town attracted those nostalgic for "old China." The town also drew the interest of officials from UNESCO because it was a site of antiquity that, unlike temples and palaces, illustrated how the non-elite lived. Aid poured in to assist rebuilding efforts.

Accounts of the events that transformed Lijiang praised the efforts of authorities and some local residents to make the town attractive, but also criticized the resulting artifice. Most residents thought it necessary to alter the town's appearance in order to appeal to outsiders, thereby demonstrating their understanding of power and Lijiang's place in the nation's periphery. But others—elderly vendors (mostly women), many state-sector workers, and disgruntled onlookers—resented the distortion and the disruption of the community's day-to-day existence.

Key events in this transformation were the 1996 visit of Premier Li Peng, followed by representatives of UNESCO, which a year later conferred the status of "World Heritage Site" on Lijiang's Old Town. Working to ensure the success of these efforts, the town cleaned and dammed streams, raising water levels so that dry areas appeared lush (although the construction of luxury hotels led to frequent water shortages that lowered and even dried up many of the town's scenic streams). It was also said that each dish to be eaten by Li Peng had to be sampled beforehand by food tasters lest he get food poisoning, and that the origin of every ingredient—each soybean, each grain of rice—had to be identified, down to the farmer who had produced it. To some, it seemed that the premier was being treated like an emperor, but others viewed these precautions as a response to the different standards of cleanliness betwen the nation's capital and a "backward, remote" (*pianpi*) place such as Lijiang.

Tourism developers had already expressed concern about Lijiang's standards of cleanliness and hygiene. Delegates to a regional conference in Kunming concluded that the Old Town's outhouses were the biggest obstacle to Lijiang's growth as a tourist site. Thus, Western-style public toilets were built at the town's entrance, providing an alternative without modernizing the Old Town itself. But many Lijiang residents, who like the tourists had to pay to use the facilities (albeit at lower rates), were angered by the new expense.[1] Moreover, so that the Old Town would appear untouched by time, visible electrical wiring was removed from the model houses to be visited by UNESCO officials and a modern movie theater newly built near the old town's entrance was demolished because it detracted from the desired architectural "authenticity." Adding to local inconvenience, the new town—the section of Lijiang without historic architecture—was cleared of the food vendors who usually provided snacks and lunch but whose makeshift operations might strike outsiders as unsanitary. Many residents believed no sacrifice was too great to win recognition from UNESCO; others viewed the changes imposed on the town as a nuisance and resented being made a spectacle for powerful outsiders.

National and international recognition resulted in a cataclysmic reconfiguring of local economics and demographics. Tourists, primarily Chinese nationals, arrived daily by the planeload. In 1997, close to two million visited Lijiang, a town of sixty thousand.[2] Luxury hotels, restaurants, massage parlors, and stores selling souvenirs and antiques opened, catering to tourists from within China as well as to government officials and businessmen who came to attend conferences in scenic Lijiang. International tourists were primarily from Singapore, Malaysia, and Japan, with fewer from Western countries. Many of these visitors were men making business trips, attending conferences, or traveling for pleasure. Chinese from major urban centers—the largest group of tourists—and international tourists were drawn to Lijiang as an ancient town offering a glimpse into China's past.

Lijiang also holds the attraction of being a site of the much-exoticized "matriarchal society" (muxi shehui) associated with the Mosuo, who are categorized by the state—but not by Naxi themselves—as a subgroup of the Naxi. The Mosuo reside not in Lijiang but in Yongning, north of Naxi territory. The matrilineal Mosuo have been described by Chinese ethnologists as "living fossils" occupying an evolutionary stage prior to patriarchy (Yan Ruxian 1982). They are erroneously believed to be ruled by women in a society with no conception of paternity, where women take lovers at whim (see Blumenfield 2010; Walsh 2005). Chinese audiences began to associate the Mosuo with unrestrained sexuality when, in 1988, the noted author Bai Hua published The Remote Country of Women (Yuan fang you ge nü er guo), a novel about a Chinese man's love affair with a Mosuo woman. Chinese tourists to Lijiang frequently expected to find an exotic matriarchal society whose women sought sexual pleasure but shunned marriage. The promise of an existing matriarchy in tourist advertising also enticed Western feminists to Lijiang in the hope of finding a society free of male domination. The Naxi were aware of the romantic imaginings of tourists drawn to Lijiang and argued vigorously that they—patrilineal, with a long history of arranged marriage—were not the Mosuo, whom they considered backward. Nevertheless, recent tourist literature has often referred to the Naxi as matriarchal, deliberately pandering to these marketable fantasies.

Another point of interest used to market Lijiang is its infamous history of love suicide. Numbers of young Naxi women, from the late eighteenth century through the Republican era, killed themselves in order to avoid parentally arranged marriages (see Chao 1990, 1995; Mu 1995; Yang Fuquan 1993). The stories of these suicides, which frequently took place in the alpine meadows of nearby Jade Dragon Mountain, add a tragic appeal to the beautiful sites that have drawn backpacking Westerners since the 1980s. Previously accessible only to the young and robust, visitors may now reach Cloud Summit Grassland (Yun Shanpin)—the most notorious of these suicide sites—by purchasing space on an expensive gondola lift. Local attitudes toward these tourists were mixed. The prestige and capital they brought to Lijiang were welcome, but their sympathetic regard for behavior locally understood as tragic, immoral, and a source of embarrassment was seen as reflecting badly on Naxi morality.[3]

Other outsiders came to Lijang: an influx of Han entrepreneurs from Zhejiang, Shanghai, Sichuan, and Guangzhou, as well as Bai merchants from neighboring areas. They became the proprietors of small businesses that began to crowd the streets and market stalls of contemporary Lijiang. Following the establishment of these businesses by outsiders, Lijiang residents sarcastically referred to Sifang Jie, the former central market square in the Old Town, as Baizu Jie (Street of the Bai Ethnic Group) because Bai merchants selling "newly made antiques" (*fangjiu*) and souvenirs had displaced Naxi engaged in the less profitable business of selling vegetables and copper ware. Longtime residents similarly resented the Han investors and entrepreneurs, whom they saw as profiting more from tourism than the local community did. The newer sections of town swarmed with Sichuanese laborers, part of the floating population of itinerant workers who did much of the low-paid construction work in urban areas throughout China. Dressed in patched farm clothes or dusty, ill-fitting blazers and weathered shoes, they stood out from the more prosperous town dwellers. But the most conspicuous new presence in Lijiang's streets were the prostitutes,[4] wearing miniskirts, hot pants, and see-through lace outfits that ranged from garish to scandalous by Lijiang standards. Town residents claimed that the prostitutes were outsiders—Tibetan, Yi, and Sichuanese from the countryside—though one occasionally heard about a "formidable" (*lihai*) Naxi madam.

With the exception of local peasants and rural migrants who opened restaurants or drove taxis, most Naxi did not operate their own businesses. Many Naxi with homes in the Old Town rented them out to businesspeople, but they stopped short of going into business themselves.[5] For some, particularly those with low-paying state-sector jobs, this lucrative rental was a necessity, not a choice: inflation and high rents had forced many to move to new suburbs on Lijiang's fringe, and those who remained were not permitted to modernize their homes because of the requirements of architectural preservation. They complained that the Old Town was no longer a vibrant community, that it was now occupied by "outsiders" who were neither Lijiang nor Naxi people.

Despite widespread negative opinion about newcomers, there was substantial enthusiasm for newly available consumer goods and services. New businesses selling such novelties as life insurance, wrapping paper, and musical birthday cards were viewed by some as "rare, curious" (xiqi) and by others as unimaginably clever and luxurious. These commodities, along with cell phones, compact disc players, and other forms of new technology, were proudly viewed as signs that Lijiang had caught up with large cities. Many people owned consumer goods once believed unattainable, such as color television sets and washing machines. A small number of extremely prosperous residents even owned cars, considered the ultimate luxury in a town where, in the early 1990s, there were only a handful of state-owned vehicles. Many young residents were pleased with the new sources of entertainment available. By 1997 there were karaoke bars, teahouses, restaurants, coffee shops, and fancy nightclubs in abundance. Less welcome were the prostitutes with cell phones, who had become a regular feature of Lijiang nightlife.

Older residents lamented the deterioration in the quality of life. They complained of overcrowding, air pollution, immorality, extravagant consumption by the newly rich, and the constant din of the ever-present taxis on Lijiang's main streets. The harshest criticism was leveled at the outsiders who were seen as having invaded Lijiang. Western tourists were viewed as oddities by some and as loathsome, excessively hairy, and smelly by others. Western women, who were unusually large by local standards, often inspired debates as to whether they were male or female (Chao 2003; Makley 2007). But the more familiar outsiders, such as the Chinese officials who traveled at public expense, were the most vehemently resented. Locals quipped, "Big bosses and high officials who visit Lijiang as tourists share three characteristics: they don't use their own money, they don't use their own grain, and they don't use their own wives."[6] One hotel manager told me that some officials even asked prostitutes for receipts, which were then submitted for reimbursement as a regular business expense. The issue here was not so much the privileged consumption of food and sex but the illegitimate siphoning off of public resources to pay for it. While this form of tourism—the most prevalent in Lijiang at that time—was profitable to those involved in the tourist industry, local people criticized it as immoral activity conducted at the expense of public welfare. Other social ills were also attributed to outsiders. The increase in violent crimes and theft that accompanied the growth of Lijiang's economy was blamed on the floating population of itinerant laborers, the most impoverished and presumably most dangerous of Lijiang's new residents. Most vilified were the prostitutes, who tainted Lijiang's reputation and caused such embarrassment and disdain that some residents averted their eyes when passing them on the street, as if to avoid being polluted by the very sight of them.

Tourism and capitalist privatization transformed Lijiang's public space into something most town residents experienced as unfamiliar and fraught with sexuality and danger. Streets in the center of town, once geared toward families with children, were taken over by entertainment venues catering to tourists, officials with expense accounts, and pleasure-seeking young adults. After dark, Lijiang became a place for sexual trysts and adult entertainment. Because pleasure seekers, tourists, foreigners, and prostitutes shared public spaces with town residents, the boundaries of local identity were challenged. The commodification and consumption of sex by outsiders radically altered local constructions of gender and power. As sex was increasingly seen as a privileged form of consumption by outsiders, it took on a similar meaning within local constructions of male prestige. Luxury hotel managers and prosperous entrepreneurs, notorious in Lijiang for keeping mistresses, came to be seen as modern men of power. But while the male embodiment of sex, money, and power was the admired capitalist or entrepreneur, his female counterpart was the reviled prostitute whose association with sex, money, and power signified pollution and depravity.

The sexualization of space and power affected local standards of female behavior. Particularly among Lijiang residents who were critical of these developments, widespread prostitution, equated with female immorality, heightened the need to differentiate among local women by categorizing them as sexually pure or polluted (for a similar dynamic among Tibetans, see Makley 2002). Not surprisingly, the new surveillance of women focused on their circulation in the now dangerously sexualized public spaces, as well as on their contact with morally suspect outsiders. The surveilled included not only fiancées and unmarried daughters but also wives. The popular saying about the visiting big bosses and high officials was also a warning to the local male audience, because the corrupt outsiders "who don't use their own wives" were believed to be using the wives of Lijiang men. The town's young men, too, were at risk, particularly when they challenged boundaries of difference by becoming attracted to, and perhaps marrying, suspect migrant women. Lijiang women who repeated taxi driver stories might be understood as acting defensively by differentiating themselves from an emergent sexualized model of ethnic femininity in a context where social and spatial transformation had led to a heightened scrutiny of female morality.

The reordering of prestige and power in Lijiang's economy, now increasingly oriented toward tourism and capitalist privatization, had reverberations within the local marriage market. In the 1980s, the hierarchy of prestige was fixed: rural residents were perceived as inferior to urban residents, people with private-sector jobs were less desirably employed than people with state-sector jobs, and outsiders or recent migrants were socially inferior to old Lijiang families. A popular saying in Lijiang illustrated the inferiority of rural women as marriage candidates: "A country flower can't compare to the city's grass (xiangcun de hua bi bu shang chengli de cao). Town residents had long held beliefs about their cultural superiority, higher standards of cleanliness, and relative modernity in contrast to their rural counterparts. One underpinning of this was dietary: throughout the Maoist era, peasants subsisted on long beans (changdou), while town residents were issued rations for rice, which was considered a superior staple. Town dwellers "looked down on peasants" (kanbuqi nongmin) because they considered long beans to be smelly (chou), and intermarriage between these groups was rare.

But in the late 1990s, economic growth, particularly in the private sector, blurred distinctions between rural and urban residents, making intermarriage more imaginable. As Lijiang spread out into the countryside, the government took land from local peasants, compensating them with money and permits granting them urban residential status. Some of these formerly rural, newly urban residents, or nongzhuanfei, used the money to find ways of making a living in town. Many purchased cars and turned to the lucrative profession of driving taxis, which contributed to the seven hundred or so taxis operating in Lijiang by 1997—with many new residents planning to add to the number.

During the Maoist era, an urban resident earned roughly four times more than a peasant. And although the standard of living for peasants improved substantially in the mid-1980s, when they were allowed to sell their crops in the marketplace rather than exclusively to the state, it still lagged far behind that of town residents. Rural and urban residents rarely intermarried, and they continued to observe a degree of social separation. But from the mid-1990s onward, with the success of tourism and the entrance of some former peasants into lucrative professions, hierarchical distinctions faded.[7] Of the various outsiders in Lijiang, former rural residents had the most in common with Lijiang Town residents. Unlike foreign and international tourists and temporary laborers, rural people who had been granted urban-resident status became permanent residents. In comparison to migrants from afar and most entrepreneurs who were outsiders (*waidiren*), they were Lijiang people (Lijian-gren) with regional and ethnic affiliations that represented significant bases of shared identity in China.

Perceptions of female taxi drivers were also situated within changing con-structions of gender-appropriate labor in late socialist China. Before the early 1990s, goods within Lijiang Town were transported mainly by young and middle-aged rural women pulling three-wheeled carts (*sanlunche*; lit., "carts with three wheels"). Men drove motorized vehicles between the town and the countryside, or between towns, but local hauling was considered women's work. Many women drivers were former rural residents who considered the taxis to be a modern version of the three-wheeled cart. However, ownership of a taxi was additionally marked as a private business (*getihu*), which was identi-fied with masculine activity. Women drivers were seen as "like men," "bold," "risk taking," "daring," and "willing to run around trying to make money." In rural Lijiang, a Naxi woman who fit this profile was praised as *tzoguze*—a Naxi term describing a woman with a man's heart, who does what she says and is tough, willing to gamble, and courageous, particularly with respect to her work. *Tzoguze* had the "spirit" of the "iron girl" (*tieguniang*) of the Maoist era, just as *mirouguo* (Naxi; lit., "female warhorse") had her body. *Mirouguo* (which is sort of an oxymoron, or at least a somewhat ambiguously gendered image, since warhorses were always male) was a complimentary expression for ro-bust Naxi girls whom rural parents praised as ideal marriage candidates. But in Lijiang in the late 1990s, the *tzoguze* and *miruoguo* were eclipsed by an-other model of womanhood that stressed difference from male counterparts. Women were assessed not for their labor potential, but as embodiments of femininity and morality—the characteristics most valued in potential wives and mothers (see Evans 2002). In the broader Chinese context, entrepre-neurial activity and being bold or daring were associated with masculinity. Even as Lijiang's female taxi drivers were drawing the attention of foreign and Chinese tourists and journalists as a curiosity, taxi driving began to be viewed as a masculine activity. A young man explained, "People don't like the idea of their wife or daughter-in-law running around, aggressively searching for money." I was told that fights over a woman's taxi driving were a leading cause of divorce in Lijiang at that time. And while a number of middle-aged women drove taxis in 1997, it was the younger women who drew the criticism.

The image of young female taxi drivers as morally suspect was not grounded in their actual behavior but appears instead to have arisen because of the location of their labor. In a town where decent women did not go out alone at night, and certainly reported their destinations before leaving home, women who drove taxis challenged the standards of female respectability. As public spaces lost their former associations with community and family—transformed into places occupied by foreigners and outsiders seeking night-life, adult entertainment, and prostitutes—a woman venturing into such spaces risked her moral respectability.

Moral overtones attend the location of labor, not just in a literal, geographic sense, but as a matter of the public versus the private sector. During the Maoist era, family political background played a significant role in determining who could obtain a state-sector job "serving the people." Such jobs were associated with model behavior and national identity, and those who held them were desirable marriage partners. The earliest private-sector employees in Lijiang were migrants or town residents with questionable political backgrounds who were ineligible for the more desirable state-sector jobs. Because the private sector was associated with instability and shady dealing, it often employed only people who were least able to find other jobs. But the new wealth associated with the expanding private sector substantially improved its image. According to many Lijiang interviewees, entrepreneurs throughout China were now portrayed as "bold, capable, and willing to work hard," while state-sector workers were feminized as "passive and lazy tea-sippers." Particularly hard hit in Lijiang were the once elite state-sector employees with college degrees who found themselves earning less than half of the income of taxi drivers and fried potato vendors. And it was mostly those educated state-sector employees who recounted the taxi driver stories examined here.

The feminization of public-sector employment had harmed women less than men.[8] Indeed, since Lijiang's economic transformation, women in state-sector jobs had continued to have appeal as marriage candidates. Naxi town dwellers repeatedly told me that "women who were state-sector employees, particularly doctors and teachers, make the best wives." State-sector jobs were "stable" (*wending*), with fixed salaries and set hours. A man working in the private sector explained that a wife with a state-sector job could "better manage household affairs and child care" because she would not have to work at night and could shop for food during the day. Many believed that state-sector jobs were more legitimate and generally held by good citizens of sound moral character, while private-sector jobs attracted people interested only in making money.[9] Lijiang residents advised their daughters to "take up the doctor's knife, not the haircutter's." Beauty parlors and haircutting salons, private-sector establishments known to pay high salaries to women, were morally suspect because some offered massages and were linked to prostitution. In the Maoist era, a woman's identity as a worker was primary, but by the late 1990s, as popular sayings revealed, a woman's future roles as wife and mother were the cornerstone of a feminine identity. Popular sayings also assigned moral valences to female employment and employed females based on whether their jobs were in the state or the private sector.[10] But although educational inequalities or lack of connections barred some categories of women (such as rural migrants) from state-sector employment, a woman's decision to enter the private sector was taken to reveal her "moral proclivities."

TAXI DRIVERS, SPATIAL TRANSGRESSIONS, POISON, AND MARRIAGE BOUNDARIES

There were two prevailing themes in taxi driver stories: either female taxi drivers were in danger as women out of place, or they posed a hidden danger to others. The first type of story includes chilling accounts of the murders of female drivers that focus on the violence done to their bodies. In one such account, a beautiful female taxi driver disappears. Public Security Bureau officers later find her body parts scattered throughout a remote area, and local residents assume she was dismembered by a man who was either a drug addict or had a criminal record. In another variant, a female taxi driver's disappearance is taken to be a case of murder and dismemberment simply because she is never heard from again. In a third story, a beautiful taxi driver picks up two men who ask her to follow their directions. What she thinks will be a short ride becomes longer and longer, until she finds herself driving down a deserted road. Finally, they ask her to stop the car in an isolated spot, where they maim her beyond recognition and murder her. The two men disappear and are never caught. People suspect that the driver may have broken off an affair with one of the men, making jealousy and revenge the motives for the killing. Curiously, many versions of such stories include the driver's thoughts as well as the murderer's intentions and methods, despite the absence of a body or any suspects. The women are deprived of all agency in these tales, although they were familiar with Lijiang and were the ones doing the driving.

Structurally, the last story bears some resemblance to local accounts of female abductions that occurred in Lijiang in the late 1980s and early 1990s. Women promised good-paying jobs or marriage into a prosperous family by a male outsider naively travel farther and farther from home; they are raped, humiliated, and then sold into marriage, or at best they find poverty and isolation rather than prosperity in the homes of the men who have tricked them into marriage. Although they may not die, their lives are likened to death.[11]

In both taxi driver and abduction narratives, women are imperiled through encounters with unfamiliar men, circulation in places unknown and dangerous, and their own naïveté. The similarities suggest that beyond merely reporting tragic events, these stories helped establish standards of appropriate conduct for local women. The community enforced these standards by supervising the movements of women outside familiar and well-frequented spaces, restricting their contact with male outsiders, and assigning blame to women who failed to conform.

In the second type of story, women endanger others. In one such story, a beautiful female taxi driver is suspected of being a *yinyangren*, a term used to refer to a person with ambiguous sexual organs. In Lijiang, it is applied to someone who is perceived as not male and not female. Thus, a woman lacking breasts or female sexual organs and a person possessing both male and female sexual organs are considered *yinyangren* or, simply, *yinyang*. According to local accounts, this taxi driver was believed to be *yinyangren* because she was beautiful, unmarried, and nearly thirty years old. In Lijiang Town, everyone is expected to marry, unless he or she has "body problems"—for example, physical disabilities, epilepsy, or mental retardation. Beauty would presumably enhance marriageability; thus, the unmarried female taxi driver must have had a hidden problem, perhaps involving her sexual organs. There is a reason for that suspicion. Just as men in state-sector jobs were feminized, perhaps women taking on what most Chinese believe to be men's jobs were masculinized. By this logic, women taxi drivers owed their success in a masculine domain to the possession of masculine characteristics.

The robust Western female was also associated with sexual ambiguity and thus also metaphorically embodied the *yinyangren*. While the female taxi driver looks like a woman but may actually possess male morphology, the foreigner looks like a man but may actually be a woman. In the popular imaginary, both images were monstrous: both figures were inherently deceptive, potentially concealing an essential nature that belied its visual presentation. These women's bodies were sites for the signification of difference, but the source of that difference lay outside the body itself, as gendered activities marked the bodies that performed them. Western women seemed masculine because their mobility and independent movement between countries and within China were unhindered, like those of Western men. Town residents say of Western women that "they run around everywhere" (tamen dao chu dou pao), behavior abnormal for women in China. Female taxi drivers displayed a similar hypermobility, associated with the manic qualities of the masculinized capitalist entrepreneur, which made them appear masculine. The connection between female identity and body image was additionally bolstered by a new consumer culture arising in the post-Mao era in large urban centers and in the mid-1990s in Lijiang, as an array of beauty products and services marketed a modern female identity. As femininity was increasingly defined in terms of gendered bodily attributes, the woman who exhibited anomalous behavior was likely to be suspected of having an anomalous body.

In this context, the curious story of the female taxi driver with fox stench begins to make sense. After hearing accounts of taxi drivers alleged to have fox stench, I asked why soap and water could not solve the problem. A college-educated friend of mine explained that fox stench was not merely dirt or the ordinary state of being unclean (bu ganjing). According to a young woman in my former work unit, fox stench smells like the rotting corpse of a dead animal, not sweat. Others explained it as an inherited odor that could not be simply washed off. Most people with fox stench were unaware of it, but those who realized their condition tried to hide it from others. Another acquaintance knew someone who tried to rid himself of fox stench by having the sweat glands in his armpits surgically removed. But even this procedure was reportedly useless because the glands grew back and the odor returned. Near exasperation, an older man responded to my insistent questions by saying: "Marriage with such persons is impossible. Who wants a smelly person? Why, they would pollute your entire ancestral graveyard and be the ruin of the family line."

Although folk healers and Western-style medical practitioners offered to treat fox stench, popular belief in Lijiang held it to be incurable.[12] Yet (to return to the story at the beginning of this chapter, in which the family friend spends the night with the taxi driver), if fox stench is really so powerful that it is like an animal's rotting corpse, why would its detection require such elaborate scheming? Indeed, fox stench is best understood not simply as a bodily affliction but rather as a repository of imaginings of unbreachable difference. Such imaginings took different forms at different times. In the second type of taxi driver story, fox stench functions to mark difference, much like witchcraft in prerevolutionary China.

In southwest China, *gu*, a form of witchcraft that uses poison, has been long associated with non-Han ethnic groups—specifically, non-Han women whose victims were usually men (Feng and Shyrock 1935, 10). The term *gu* is usually translated as "to poison" or "to bewitch," but the phrases "to sexually seduce men" (*gu huo renxin*) and "to cause insanity through sexual exhaustion" (*gu huo zhi bing*) (Mathews 1931, 516) suggest its connotations. Norma Diamond has argued that Han accusations of *gu* do not reflect the practices of non-Han ethnic groups but issue from Han fears of intermarriage between Han and local women who have ethnic ("barbarian") ancestry (1988, 8). She links Qing dynasty witchcraft accusations against Miao women to some 350 Miao rebellions in which Han men with Miao wives were among the anti-Chinese rebels (ibid., 12). Miao women threatened to assimilate Han soldiers into tribal practices, reversing the imperial civilizing project that sought to convert tribal groups to Chinese practices.

In Lijiang, *gu* is pronounced *du*, which is virtually identical to *gu* in terms of practices and symptomology. Those accused of witchcraft, like those suspected of fox stench, were usually beautiful or clever women. In East Wind Village, accusations of witchcraft were far more commonly lodged against women than men, reflecting both patrilocal residence and the ideology that associates daughters-in-law with danger in a patrilineal descent system. Not surprisingly, the danger presented by the daughter-in-law, the carrier of poison, emerges at adulthood and the beginning of sexual activity. It is only then that her poison becomes potent and dangerous. The witch harbors the poison in the form of an animal—a toad, snake, centipede, butterfly, pigeon, or cat—that transmits the poison to others. Someone who carries witchcraft poison does not intend to harm others but spreads the poison when she (only rarely he) can no longer contain it. This condition is indicated by the witch exposing and scratching her underarms, which are considered "polluted." The pollution associated with someone who harbors poison is uncleanliness of supernatural proportions; it cannot be washed away or cut away, nor does it die with its host. Witchcraft poison is inherited by the witch's favorite child or children; it is referred to as dowry because daughters usually inherit it from their mothers, just as, Naxi town dwellers say, a daughter inherits her mother's skill.

In East Wind Village, historical accusations of witchcraft corresponded to instances of interregional hypergamy. Residents considered those in the mountain regions, which had not adopted Chinese marriage practices, to be "less civilized,"[13] and most marriages in basin villages were intra-basin rather than between mountain and basin villages. The mountain districts were not just comparatively poor, but they were also identified with different cultural practices (less affected by Han influence and perceived as more authentically Naxi) and spoke different dialects of the Naxi language. Thus, the interregional marriages crossed class, cultural, linguistic, and perceived moral boundaries. An accusation of witchcraft against an in-marrying woman could harm the village's reputation throughout the entire basin. The dangers presented by such a marriage were experienced as gendered, usually taking the female bodily form of a witch who was imagined to be spreading poison to descendants and those close by, who, in a village composed of three lineages (the maximum in most Naxi villages), are likely to be kin.

The witchcraft accusations in southwest China during the Ming and Qing dynasties parallel those made in Qing dynasty and Republican-era Lijiang in many ways. In both settings, female sexual behavior could bewitch; these women were feared because they were trying to cross cultural, economic, and regional boundaries through marriage. These forms of difference were imagined as "backward," "uncivilized," and dangerously polluting. Yet there is also a significant dissimilarity: Diamond described witchcraft accusations as a Han fantasy, implying they were not shared by the ethnic groups accused; but Naxi living in Lijiang Town, surrounding rural basin villages, and mountain villages—during the late Qing and the Republican eras and, to some extent in the late 1990s—believed in witchcraft and specifically identified its practice with the Naxi and other minority ethnic groups. It might have been the case that witchcraft accusations originated as Han fantasies of ethnic others, but as imperial expansion identified Han cultural practices with civilized practice, the Naxi internalized those fantasies. At least among basin-dwelling Naxi, accusations of witchcraft were used to set boundaries—not between ethnic groups but between groups of Naxi.

The boundaries between Naxi created by accusations of fox stench and witchcraft are strikingly similar, as is the imagery associated with the accused. As previously mentioned, taxi drivers were primarily Naxi from rural Lijiang who were seen as less modern than residents of Lijiang Town. Like the mountain villagers who married basin men, they were freighted with an imagery of backwardness articulated as pollution. People with fox stench sicken those who are close enough to inhale their smell. Similarly, proximity to a witch can cause illness because poisons enter the victim's body through a cut or wound or in food consumed in the witch's presence. Carriers of fox stench and poison are typically attractive, but marriage to such persons harms one's family and lineage. Like fox stench, witchcraft is imagined to be congenital, incurable, inexorably tied to the body, usually more perceptible to onlookers than to the carrier, emanating from under the arms, intentionally hidden if the carrier is aware of it, self-regenerating, and polluting even after the carrier's death. In both cases, the woman represents a form of danger that, especially through marriage, penetrates the individual and social body.

Although female taxi drivers were more prosperous than the town dwellers among whom these stories circulated, they were often perceived as social inferiors because of their rural origins. Accusations of both witchcraft and fox stench stigmatized by invoking the language of purity and pollution. Pollution ideologies are gendered, and they mark difference and hierarchy when marriage boundaries are crossed.

FOX SPIRITS, FEMMES FATALES, FOX STENCH, AND SEXUALIZED ALTERITY

Contemporary dictionaries translate the term *huchou* as "body odor" but do not explain why the smell should be likened to that of a fox rather than some other equally noisome animal. The answer lies not in the fox's stench but in its ability, according to cultural beliefs, to take human form. The belief in "fox spirits" (*hulijing*) makes it easy to characterize people as foxlike and aids in anthropomorphizing the fox. The vast historical literature on fox spirits enables us to explore the various meanings and metaphors of being foxlike, which illuminate why some people were categorized as having fox stench. Simply put, fox stench was an indicator of vulpine characteristics in humans.

When a fox appears, it has been interpreted as a threat to families and homes, a sign that the kingdom was imperiled, and a portent of evil and disaster (Doré 1918, 695–701; De Groot 1907, 576–600). Rarely, the fox spirit took the form of a benign male spirit; more commonly, it was evil, highly sexualized, and female.[14] In legends and popular accounts, the fox was portrayed as a man-bewitching were-vixen who brought delirium and disease. The fox spirit typically insinuated herself into the lives of the unsuspecting, particularly a man, in the guise of an innocent young maiden or a beautiful woman. But she was eventually revealed as a seductress who—following sexual intercourse—poisoned her victim or drove him mad. In these stories, which warn of the dangers of female sexuality that is not channeled into reproducing the family, those who encounter a fox spirit suffer injury or death. Because evil fox spirits were infertile (Monschein 1988, 415), they were conspicuous inversions of legitimate womanhood (identified with the roles of wife and mother). The fox spirit resembles, in Ylva Monschein's words, an "erotic nyphomaniacal mistress" whose desires ultimately bring about the destruction of her male lover (1988, 416). In other tales, the afflicted male lover, under the evil influence of the fox spirit, becomes a maniac who ransacks ancestral graves, beats or injures family members, or—particularly horrific in a Confucian society that privileges filial piety—kills his own parents. Fox spirits also recruited and advised prostitutes. In one tale, a hoary old fox squats in an ancient tomb, updating a list of lewd women and circling in red the names of those who had submitted to illicit intercourse; the man who finds the fox is horrified to come upon his daughter's name on the list (De Groot 1907, 587). Such parables clearly betray popular anxieties about the morality of women, underscoring the need for family members to be vigilant.

The translation of *huchou* as "fox stench" is highly suggestive. The character *hu* signifies the fox in late imperial and contemporary discourse. *Chou*, translated in contemporary dictionaries as "odor," also means "disgusting," "disgraceful," "foul," and "rotten." In terms of the semiotics of smell in Lijiang, *chou*, a Chinese loan word, refers to odor and to supernatural pollution. Smells and odors set the stage for auspicious as well as inauspicious forces. In *dongba* and Buddhist ritual, and in virtually all forms of temple or ancestor worship in Lijiang, incense purifies the ritual space in which people summon and propitiate gods or ancestors. Lijiang residents say that unpleasant odors, such as garlic, repel the gods and are therefore banned from ritual contexts; polluting substances (notably feces and their attendant odors) are kept far away. Some smells encourage a proper moral disposition; thus, lay Buddhist groups in Lijiang used sandalwood incense to put participants in a frame of mind to worship. One might expect the converse also to hold: bad odors—symbols of pollution—signify or promote an immoral disposition. The term "fox stench" may evoke not only the odor of the fox, but also forms of pollution tied to the nefarious aims of the fox spirit, who traffics in sex and death.[15]

In many accounts, foxes dwell in or near old graves. Indeed, Ming and

Qing dynasty codes specifically prohibited people from damaging graves while attempting to smoke out fox spirits (De Groot 1907, 600). Dispatching a fox spirit was no easy task. One method—which culminates in frying the creature in oil—produces a stench that travels for several miles (ibid., 580). Such a stench suggests supernatural pollution, an index of the fox spirit's evil. In the popular imaginings of the late imperial era, the odor of the fox was not a mundane smell but was freighted with pollution of a phantasmic sort. In sum, the fox was both an omen of evil and a malignant agent—significantly, a feminine agent who incorporated deceptive appearance, illicit sexuality, and the potential ruin of one's body, family, or kingdom.[16]

If the fox spirit is a sign, then by tracking its appearance we can find those dangerous moments when gendered boundaries were challenged. Bixia Yuanjun, the goddess of Taishan, did not win acceptance from the state and was perceived as dangerous by Qing dynasty elites, largely because—as the "chief of fox spirits"—she was linked with sexual power and havoc (Pomeranz 1997, 196). Kenneth Pomeranz has argued that Bixia Yuanjun's iconographic portrayal as young and beautiful, joined with the depiction of her power as "vital but dangerous," highlighted the sexual and reproductive capacities of the young wives and daughters-in-law who threatened family stability in a Confucian order (1997, 185, 198, 204). He suggests that Bixia Yuanjun's association with "luxury, beauty, display, and sexuality" made her an unacceptable model for female emulation, just as her marginal followers—the midwives, matchmakers, and healers who were unusually independent women—made her a problematic deity for state canonization (ibid., 185, 196). State and elite perceptions of the chief of fox spirits tell us much about acceptable standards for female behavior and about which groups were thought to fall short of those standards.

Tales of fox spirits are identified as a subgenre of the femme fatale stories common in Chinese literature (McLaren 1994; Link 1989).[17] Fox spirit stories may be similarly understood as critiques of powerful or anomalous women and expressions of popular anxieties at times of political upheaval, foreign incursion, and the blurring of gender boundaries (see Elvin 1989; Handlin 1975; Monschein 1988), as the female protagonists "show ingenuity and strength of mind, and often dominate their husbands and lovers" (McLaren 1994, 1). The stories are set in a fictional world that nevertheless bears a strong resemblance to the one inhabited by readers (ibid.). Fox spirit tales were used from the fourth century through the late imperial era to attack women who wielded political power, but powerful women in the socialist era were cast as femmes fatales—most notoriously Mao's wife, Jiang Qing. Not only was she portrayed as a femme fatale in court, where she was "tried in part as a housewife . . . who exceeded a woman's proper functions and led her husband astray" (Terrill 1984, 391), but readers of hand-copied fiction during the Cultural Revolution claim that the femmes fatales who appeared in those stories were none other than Jiang Qing (Link 1989, 28). The portrayal of male political figures was more rarely used to express their illegitimacy. During the last phases of the Cultural Revolution, fortune-tellers (face readers) claimed that Lin Biao's photographs "revealed the face of a crafty fox" (Chan et al. 2009, 157).

Yet fox spirits have not disappeared. The term "fox spirit" is still applied to women in contemporary China, usually in whispers, when illicit sex or corruption is suspected. In Lijiang, an informant's friend read a collection of pulp fiction stories titled *Fox Spirit*, featuring women who brought about the demise of their male suitors. Its cover depicts a beautiful woman with a stylish modern haircut smoking a cigarette; behind her, the body of a man lies crushed under a car. Educational billboards proclaiming that "foxes cannot turn into fox fairies" further suggest the persistence of popular beliefs about fox spirits in contemporary China (Monschein 1988, 3; McLaren 1994, 16). Like stories about femmes fatales, these narratives were not simply fictional fantasies but could be understood as parables about the social worlds in which they circulate. Femme fatale narratives educate us about acceptable standards of female behavior by depicting their violators, just as the failure of the Bixia Yuanjun cult to attain state canonization revealed which categories of people were barred from legitimacy.

Female taxi drivers may not be referred to as "fox spirits," but the claim that they have the medical condition of fox stench invokes those associations. This diagnostic category may be understood as freighted with culturally specific meanings. Like the "dog" radical, the character *hu* (fox) at the beginning of a word almost guarantees a highly negative connotation in standard Chinese. Some fox-related terms are *humei* (to bewitch or seduce), *huyi* (suspicious, distrustful), *hulang* (evil-hearted), *huyan* (irrational speech), *hu qun gou dang* (gang of scoundrels), and *hu peng gou you* (evil associates) (see Luo 1987, 33; Zhang Qiyun et al. 1967, 175). The use of *hu*, particularly when referring to a woman, pairs her with imagery of sexual immorality, illegitimate power, and transgressed boundaries. The circulation of these images parallels those of fox spirits, stretching from ancient times to the present.

There were suggestive similarities between the fox spirit and the image of the Lijiang female taxi driver of the late 1990s. As independent women characterized by hypermobility, they circulated in the sexualized nocturnal terrain of the town, in public spaces that many Lijiang residents viewed as having become unfamiliar and dangerous, now occupied by outsiders. Particularly at night, the body of the innocent, attractive female taxi driver was imperiled—subject to corruption or attack by passengers, outsiders, or foreigners with suspect morality. The sexual possession of local female bodies became a concern for the community and reflected its impotence in the face of outside forces. And if she were not in danger, perhaps the female taxi driver was already corrupted. Willing to deliver clients to massage parlors and sexual assignations, she was tainted by the immoral activities she facilitated and profited from. Like the fox spirits who monitor and promote prostitution, taxi drivers were part of the chain of operators that included the tour guides and hotel managers who, when asked to "introduce" guests to the nightlife of the town, enabled the flow of people into immoral nocturnal activities. The taxi driver, as a local agent promoting immorality, may be perceived as an enemy within, abetting the decline of the community.

For the vigilant parent, the prospect of a taxi-driving daughter-in-law conjured up images of sexual immorality and the threat of power attendant upon money, along with the standard fears of a daughter-in-law's manipulation of beauty and sex. It brought to mind the popular narrative of the familiar femme fatale, a story that could only end in trickery, female dominance, and male ruin. Reminiscent of tales of witchcraft and femmes fatales, these stories cautioned young urban men against marrying taxi drivers and thereby eroding the system of distinctions on which the older hierarchical order rested. But more broadly, stories of anomalous bodies and supernatural pollution signaled danger and disorder that threatened the community and its way of life. And the stench of a fox invoked in these stories portended more than foxiness.

FOX STENCH AND THE MODERN BODY

The term "fox stench" first appeared in biological and medical textbooks in the early twentieth century, during the Republican era, when the Chinese sought to modernize by incorporating Western science. The medical discourse of the Republican and socialist eras aimed at scientizing Chinese medicine by purging it of the demonology that characterized Ming and Qing dynasty medical discourse (Unschuld 1985). But the demons were replaced by new enemies. In the 1920s and 1930s, medical texts, popular manuals, and handbooks addressed hygiene (*weisheng*) and portrayed the body as under attack by bacteria and other agents of ill health (Dikötter 1995, 122–24). And just as the embattled body would be saved by better personal hygiene, so a body politic too weak to cope with foreign intruders (as demonstrated by its humiliating defeat in the Opium War and the fall of the Qing dynasty) could be strengthened by improvements in public hygiene. The state's promotion of hygiene became a matter of national salvation. Lurking behind metaphors of the body under siege and of the need for national regeneration was a sense of national inferiority or lack in comparison to Western science and military power. Science offered a means of improving the quality of the Chinese body and modernizing the nation.

Definitions of "fox stench" in Republican-era medical, scientific, and political discourse, however, contradicted the dominant discourse calling for such improvements because they presented the Chinese body as essentially superior. Chinese biology texts described fox stench as an "evil odor" emanating from "barbarians" (foreign races) who had numerous sweat glands; the relative absence of underarm sweat glands in the Chinese population was a marker of Chinese racial and evolutionary superiority (Dikötter 1995, 161). The odor of Westerners was also linked to alleged activities such as the ingestion of menstrual blood—perceived by the Chinese as a horrific pollutant (Dikötter 1992, 47). Chinese medicine cast racial difference in terms of animality and sexual danger: Westerners were "closer to the beast" and thus had more "powerful sexual urges" (Dikötter 1995, 159). In racialized constructions of fox stench, boundaries between pure and polluted bodies reinforced distinctions between people ruled by the mind and people ruled by sexual urges, between those "more civilized" and those "less evolved," between Chinese selves and foreign others. Thus, at the same time that discourse about hygiene advocated the possibility of change and mobility, fox stench suggested that bodies were frozen in a hierarchy of difference.[18]

Discourse about fox stench was not confined to the medical and scientific realm; in the 1930s, the noted historian Chen Yinke wrote an essay on the fox stench of Western peoples. In *Fox Stench and Barbarian Stench* (Huchou yu huchou), he argues that body odor in the Chinese population may be traced to intermarriage between Chinese and Western barbarians (Turkic people) during the Tang dynasty ([1937] 1980, 140–42). Fox stench, which Chen also attributes to European peoples, is described as hereditary and incurable. Here, as in contemporary medical and scientific accounts addressing race, fox stench is a marker of essential difference between foreigners and Chinese: the existence of fox stench among the Chinese is blamed on the failure to set boundaries.

There are striking similarities between the China in which fox stench appeared in the 1920s and China during the reform era (roughly from the 1980s onward). Both were periods of political and economic transformation that featured national projects for improving the quality of the body as a means of modernizing the nation. Like national hygiene projects of the Republican era, state discourse after Mao has been directed at improving population quality (renkou suzhi)—that is, at eugenics. Even the equation of hygiene with modernity has resurfaced. In the 1980s, the government bestowed awards on hygienic villages, hygienic work units, and hygienic households, holding them up for emulation as the socialist state's model of modernity. The push to improve the population in the post-Mao era did not address a yearning for national salvation as in the 1920s, but it has been a means of preparing an undisciplined, poor-quality labor force for foreign investment and entrance into a global capitalist economy (Anagnost 1997, 123).

The fervor for improving the body as a means of attaining a desired modern identity is present in popular culture as well. Advertisements for fox-stench cures (aimed at bodily improvement) are common throughout the contemporary urban Chinese landscape. Throughout the 1990s, the focus on the model body drew on and fostered imaginings of its opposite. In Lijiang, government public health billboards warning of contagious diseases featured explicit photos—revealing regions of the body (part of a thigh, a breast, the side of a face) afflicted with sores, lesions, and infected, decaying flesh—and crowds flocked to view the spectacle of disease. In contrast to advertisements picturing models of beauty and health used to sell products (body spectacles that inspire desire and emulation), these billboards were spectacles of loathing that conveyed desire's opposite, that which must be distanced from the self, and provided images in opposition to which identity can be constructed.

A banner advertising a carnival troupe performing in Lijiang, "Traveling exhibit of the world's strange bodies, featuring real people" (Shijian qi ti zhen-

ren you zhan), also roused imaginings of bodily abnormality. It offered two female images: in one, a single head and upper torso were attached to two sets of hips and legs, the figure suggestively attired in a low-cut sleeveless dress with hemline above the thigh; in the other, a woman is wearing a blue bikini bottom and a thin, flesh-tone bra that reveals one breast lacking a nipple and the other with two. By sexualizing female bodies, the depictions cultivated voyeuristic loathing. Also pictured were children: one child with a tail and a cylindrical nose; another with simian facial features and excessive body hair; two sets of Siamese twins; and a boy with multiple stumps in place of hips and legs. An inset showed a pair of distraught parents who had given birth to abnormal children.

The banner bore two quatrains:

Kaleidoscope of the very rare and strange.
Exhibition of the world's deformed bodies.
Profound mysteries revealed by scientific research.
Alarming cases of birth and reproduction.

Excessive alcohol and cigarette use cause great harm.
Harm begins with the uninformed use of medicines.
You're advised to see the exhibit to broaden your knowledge.
Good birth, good nurturing for future generations.

The first quatrain markets the spectacle of bodily and reproductive abnormality, while contriving to present it as a scientific exhibit aimed at promoting public health. The banner, spanning more than twenty feet, hung between two large buildings in downtown Lijiang and could not be ignored by local residents. While a few onlookers regarded the bodies as inauthentic, most cautioned that the horrific abnormalities were real. Residents viewed the children, one with a tail and the other with simian features, as evolutionary throwbacks, monstrosities that mixed human and prehuman animal forms. The second quatrain explains bodily deformity as the result of failure to care for the reproductive body, specifically, the maternal body, and thus echoes the state's discourse on prenatal care and eugenics. Like the taxi driver stories, the banner played on gendered imaginings of bodily abnormality (the banner featured no men while drawing attention to nubile yet aberrant female bodies), stirred anxieties about inferior reproduction (exemplified by bodies

FIG. 4.1 Carnival troupe banner

manifesting congenital aberrations or uncivilized inheritance), and portrayed difference as essential and irremediable.

There is a contradiction between the logic of a discourse predicated on bodily improvement and the logic of discourses about essential bodily difference. The stress on hygiene relies on a Western mind-body dichotomy that assumes the mind's dominance, while fox stench draws on substance-oriented beliefs about the body—in particular, the concept that bodies are what they eat. Hence, the consumption of menstrual blood and smelly beans creates polluted people, much as abnormal bodies produce monstrous descendants. And if the campaign for hygiene reflected the logic of a capitalism that has insinuated itself into Western medicine—holding that the body may be invested with desired qualities and improved, thus making mobility possible—then fox stench, which focuses on inalterability and boundaries that fix difference, may be understood as a critique of that logic.[19] The tension between mobility and inalterable essence expressed in these discourses of the body arose from a historical process: a new economy that created opportunities for mobility at the same time that it threatened a preexisting social order.

The construction of identity against imaginings of backwardness (perceived as immutable) takes place throughout China, but the identification of backwardness with evolutionary primitivity was particularly salient in minority areas such as Lijiang. The Lijiang Naxi, described by Chinese anthropologists as barely more advanced than "living fossils" (i.e., the Mosuo, popularly believed to be a sexually promiscuous matriarchy), have a large stake in representing themselves as "civilized" and "modern." This modern identity has been both enabled and undermined by Lijiang Town's transformation into a site of antiquity for national and international tourist consumption. As the social landscape was reconfigured, Lijiang women confronted the problem of differentiating themselves (as both modern and moral) from bodies characterized as immoral and backward. At the same time, residents' relationships to the new economy shaped perceptions of and access to signs of the modern. In state discourse, modernity was reflected in hygiene, and emphasis on bodily enhancement in urban China converged readily with consumer culture. In Lijiang, commodities and services used to imprint modernity on the body substantially expanded as a result of the capitalist privatization that began in the mid-1990s. The vast majority of these services and commodities were gender specific and targeted women, who were sold cosmetics, permanent waves, facials, girdles, brassieres, perfumes, and eyelid operations.

While privileged consumption enabled such modifications, it was the body itself—rather than what it consumed, as is the case with male consumers—that marked women as modern feminine subjects.[20]

For intellectuals and other state-sector workers whose incomes fell in comparison to those of laborers and migrants, not only were these signs of modernity unaffordable but their possession now inverted older sensibilities of the modern. During the 1980s, the superiority of state employment compared to private employment lay in its association with morality and socialist modernity. Town dwellers then claimed modern identities by setting themselves against their backward and unhygienic rural counterparts, who were perceived as deficient in cleanliness and hygiene (weisheng tiaojian). In the new Lijiang, however, the most visible symbols of modernity were, by and large, rural migrants: the prostitutes walking Lijiang's streets with beepers or cell phones, and the taxi drivers— women driving cars, the most prestigious commodity of all. The connection between material means and bodily improvement was obvious to women employed in the state sector who recited, in detail and with irritation, the prices charged by hair salons and complained that they could never afford such extravagant services. For state-sector workers, intellectuals, and other Lijiang residents who had not benefited from the recent economic growth and increased consumption, the new signs of femininity were not natural but were synthetically crafted—and came at a high price. The nature of the woman who deployed such purchased artifice was imagined as intentionally deceptive because the artifice hid an essence that required disguise.

Like the attractiveness of fox spirits and femmes fatales in familiar stories, the "beauty" of taxi drivers suspected of fox stench disguised abnormal and polluted bodies that were unacceptable for marriage, imperiled reproduction, and were even unsuitable for burial in the ancestral graveyard.

GENDERED ALLEGORIES OF CAPITALIST TRANSFORMATION IN AN ETHNIC ENCLAVE

Examining the specifics of capitalist development in Lijiang will help us understand the significance of fox-stench storytelling. Lijiang's transformation from a centrally planned state economy to a mainly profit-based private economy relied less on the cultivation of labor than on the cultivation of the town itself: the marketing of the antiquity of the Old Town and, to some extent, the exoticism of Lijiang's people. New forms of labor—performed by taxi drivers, construction workers, prostitutes, entrepreneurs, and tourist industry employees—were the embodiments of the modern and made material the local experiences of capitalist privatization. But local people's views of these varied actors depended on their relationship to the new economy. Although they displayed widespread hostility toward the prostitutes and itinerant workers who were thought (with or without justification) to be associated with criminal activity, their attitudes toward entrepreneurs and taxi drivers were more varied.

Local people were, paradoxically, seeking a modern identity at the same time that they were seen as mirroring an ancient one. The images of matriarchal gender inversion and free sexuality that attracted outsiders, though at odds with local practices, were made present by the influx of outside prostitutes and migrant women taxi drivers, as well as by the marketing of love suicide as part of the mythic Naxi past. These images were as much a creation of UNESCO officials, foreign tourists, and Chinese pleasure seekers, whose desires had the power to attract flows of labor and capital within China, as of the enterprising local people, migrating entrepreneurs, and young prostitutes who sought to capitalize on Lijiang's growth as a center for tourism and pleasure (see Grewal and Kaplan 1994). Local people could not remain untouched by the imagery their own town projected, though they often had no part in creating it.

Prestige linked to the consumption of sex led to new constructions of masculinity and heightened community surveillance of local women, who needed to be differentiated from the imaginings and embodiments of female immorality. These perceived threats to the sexual purity and morality of local women were articulated in the widely circulating stories about taxi drivers who were in danger because they were women out of place. Stories of dismemberment and death warned young women who might be considering the possibility of gaining material rewards without taking into account the risk of bodily endangerment that might accompany it.

Elements of the taxi driver stories both criticized and promoted state campaigns to create modern subjects and a modern population. Allegations of one driver's ambiguous genitalia and another's inalterable "unhygienic" condition implicitly assailed constructions of the feminine body that emphasized appearance and physical alterability, thus attacking both the consumer culture and the ideological indoctrination promoted in state discourse. According to the logic of fox-stench stories, one cannot simply cloak one's body in the accoutrements of modernity; rather, bodies, as well as the categories of people who possess them, are different in their essence.

The false logic of essential difference has long played a role in local history. During the Maoist era, one's moral standing was determined by inherited class labels. In late imperial and Republican-era Lijiang, imperial and state civilizing projects linked class and sexual morality. Geographic origin—the town, rural basin, or mountains—marked distinctions as ethnic, and the adoption of Chinese courtship and marriage practices was equated with sexual morality. Urban centers and the rural areas closest to them were the first targets of governmental coercion and proselytizing. As the Naxi in those places adopted Chinese marriage practices, those at a greater distance came to be seen by their sinicized counterparts as backward, both economically and morally. These contingent distinctions between groups of Naxi were expressed as essential in local accusations of witchcraft that sought to police regional boundaries of hierarchy and difference. In both prerevolutionary civilizing projects and Lijiang's transformation by global capital, the cultural sensibilities of more powerful outsiders led to the alteration and transgression of boundaries. And, in both cases, local groups sought to preserve their class standing by stressing intra-ethnic differences (not of their making, but now key to their identities) as essential and inalterable, marginalizing those who were imagined to be purveyors of poison or afflicted with fox stench.

In the late 1990s, intellectuals and state-sector workers were most affected by the harmful effects of the privatization of Lijiang's economy. What these downwardly mobile town dwellers saw or smelled in female taxi drivers was the embodiment of danger, the violation of gender boundaries, and the power of artifice, all tied to the workings of capitalism. Taxi driver stories about women with fox stench and *yinyangren*, or a person who was neither man nor woman, enabled them to contest the ascendant social hierarchy in which material wealth was equated with modernity, and bodies and the categories of people who possessed them were alterable. The essential differences described by these stories echoed older, familiar notions of pollution—understood not as a lack of hygiene or as mundane dirtiness, but as something supernatural. These stories did not speak of witches and fox spirits, which in the late twentieth century would seem to be mere superstition. Instead, stories of fox stench evoked not only fox folklore but also the medical condition of abnormal body odor.

The state-sector workers and intellectuals thus saw themselves as articulating modern concerns and sensibilities, using the language of scientific-medical categories compatible with state discourse about population quality and the aims of national progress.

Those in the Republican era who described fox stench in racialized terms that focused on the number of sweat glands possessed by foreign races and those in the 1990s who demonized taxi drivers by invoking fox stench were alike in belonging to groups whose modern identity was threatened by the types of individuals they censured. In both cases, they targeted groups associated with the modern—foreign racial groups and taxi drivers—and thereby enabled modernity to be located elsewhere. In Lijiang, however, such displacement did not lead to the invention of new models of modernity. Rather, definitions of modernity already circulated by the state, which identified "modern womanhood" with childbearing and maternal nurture, came to the fore. Thus, in erecting boundaries against taxi drivers with fox stench, the storytellers invoked a higher standard of family and community reproduction.

Although fox-stench accusations challenged the notions of alterability underlying the discourse on population quality, they were compatible with other aspects of this discourse. In the post-Mao era, the state's birth-planning policy, which is central to the construction of modernity, naturalizes the female body as a site of feminine identity (Rofel 1999, 247). The female body is essential to this population policy because a modern state relies on high-quality procreative and maternal functions—"good birth, good nurturing" (Anagnost 1997, 127). Taxi driver stories resonated most strongly with contemporary models of femininity and the state's birth-planning policy. Female taxi drivers who were believed to present a danger to others were at odds with the high-quality female bodies required for the improvement of the nation. Their bodies questioned as abnormal, such women were portents of reproductive disaster. As women of dubious morality, they surely could not meet the higher state standards of maternal nurturing.

But the female taxi drivers described as "in danger" similarly failed to match the model of femaleness promoted by state discourse on improving the population. The goal of "good birth, good nurturing" could not be met by women whose bodies circulated in dangerous spaces or whose employment in private-sector work required long hours and irregular schedules. Although stories of women in danger did not overtly criticize the female drivers, their bodies presented a negative model. Female drivers stood in opposition to women whose bodies circulated in safer places, whose employment in the state sector suggested a higher standard of morality, and whose less demanding work schedules permitted greater commitment to the newly valued feminine tasks of wife and mother.[21] In the context of Lijiang's economic transformations, the taxi driver—associated with dangerous and sexualized space, private employment, and money—was the opposite of the model daughter who chose "the doctor's knife over the barber's" (i.e., the safety of state-sector employment over more profitable, but morally suspect, private employment). In this respect, state discourse on population improvement—which designates women's bodies as sites for surveillance in order to ensure population quality—converged with and reinforced new local perceptions of public space as sexualized and dangerous, thus requiring the increased policing of women in Lijiang. Through the lens of these new feminine ideals, work perceived as dangerous (and also most profitable)—as well as the women who sought to pursue professions with the potential of economic mobility and parity with men—were more likely to be perceived as falling short of the reform-era feminine ideal.

FOX-STENCH ADVERTISEMENTS IN 2011

In the summer of 2011, years after the research for this chapter was conducted, I was encouraged to find that many Lijiang women were still driving taxis. Like the women described in the fox-stench stories, the women I interviewed were all originally from the countryside. Urban acquaintances did not tell me any new fox-stench stories about taxi drivers, although there were several about less fortunate friends of friends who were afflicted with fox stench. Urban Lijiang residents said that the advertisements for fox-stench remedies were still common, although not as ubiquitous as they had been in the late 1990s and first decade of the twenty-first century, a period roughly corresponding to the beginning of the transformation of Lijiang's economy following the earthquake in 1996. It was in the late 1990s that the town changed significantly, and professions such as taxi driving were on the rise.

In the 1990s, advertisements for fox-stench remedies, largely offering secret herbal ingredients, were pasted to the walls of buildings. In 2011, cures for the stench were trumpeted in pamphlets advertising private hospital services.[22]

FIG. 4.2 Taxi driver in Lijiang, 2011

One advertisement reported that Aling, a twenty-three-year-old girl, had attempted suicide by adding poison to her instant noodles. After half an hour she was discovered by a family member and rushed to the hospital; she survived. The ad pamphlet asks: "Why did the young woman want to commit suicide? She was very beautiful, but had fox stench." In college, she had reportedly had an inferiority complex and was depressed. Thinking that there was no hope, she wanted to kill herself. The pamphlet goes on to describe fox stench as a condition that can be medically treated, and, although some people fear surgery, this operation is minor and relatively painless, with no significant scarring. Underarm hair and odor are eliminated. The pamphlet ends by exhorting reader to "come to our hospital to cure fox stench; there's no need for suicide."

The shaded insert of the advertisement tells another story: Wang Xiaoqing, a twenty-one-year-old woman, had fox stench for ten years, but she can now wear sleeveless tops. The advertisement reports that sweat and smell were problems that caused her endless inconvenience. When she took the bus, people would look askance at her. No one wanted to be close to her and she was very unhappy. But after one successful operation, her situation changed and her life changed. Others with this illness are encouraged to come to the hospital.

Both accounts of fox stench feature pictures of attractive young women. Although Aling is described as twenty-three and a current or former college student, the photograph depicts a smiling young girl of perhaps thirteen or slightly older, who is flanked by a nurse and doctor. The second photograph shows an attractive young woman, Wang Xiaoqing, wearing sleeveless attire, with her bare arms raised confidently. Wang's casual clothing suggests that she is not at her place of employment, and her glowing smile and surroundings allude to happiness in the context of her personal life. While people with fox stench can be male or female, these advertisements suggest that the target audience is women, particularly young girls and women who are close to marriage age. The advertisements promise that fox stench need not be a permanent condition and can be eliminated by medical means. In both cases, fox stench is equated with death. Aling's suicide attempt indicates that death is preferable to a life afflicted with fox stench; in the second case, Wang Xiaoqing's fox stench conferred a form of social death as she was shunned by strangers on the bus and in other social situations. The advertisements inform their audience that "there's no need for suicide," reasoning that creates

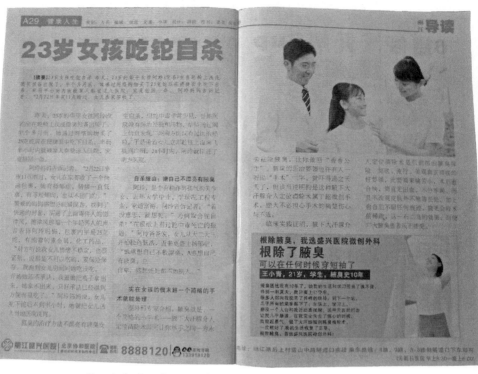

FIG. 4.3 Hospital advertisement for fox-stench surgery

154

an urgency in which fox-stench surgery becomes a matter of life or death. In the advertisements, achieving the feminine ideal necessitates consumption (by purchasing elective hospital services) that will create a high-quality female body, defined in terms of purity or eradicated impurity.

Fox-stench advertisements compete with taxi driver stories in attempting to define the feminine ideal. Taxi driver stories articulate claims of inalterable difference and deny that consumption and bodily alteration can result in feminine mobility, while fox-stench ads argue that the modern feminine ideal is available through consumption and scientific-medical intervention.[23] The disparity between these views is not about the contest between superstition and science. Both ads and stories are biopolitical narratives. They echo the postsocialist state's discourse on population improvements (renkou suzhi) and its idealization of the maternally nurturant feminine body whose opposite can be found in the varied representations of the polluted female body.

BIOPOLITICAL NARRATIVES AND GENDER INEQUALITY

Lijiang advertisements and taxi driver stories appear in the backdrop of cataclysmic changes in the organization of labor and the transformation of Lijiang by global, national, and local forces. The new hypervisibility of the female body throughout China narrates a particular history in which the market economy and commodification contribute to a new model of femininity obsessed with the quality of the female body. What is distinctive to areas largely populated by ethnic groups, like Lijiang, is the centrality of ethnic difference to the tourist economy and the way in which tourism is the path of economic development promoted by the state as appropriate for ethnic areas. Thus, in Lijiang the ethnicized and exoticized body bears a double burden in terms of signification. While both men and women experience the promotion of ethnicized consumption, it implicates minority women in a different way. According to Gail Hershatter, "Chinese businessmen in the eastern coastal regions were willing to pay as much as five times more for sex with exotic 'minority' women" than for their urban Chinese counterparts (cited in Makley 2007, 218). Although sex work employs only a small portion of Lijiang's population, the sexualization of the ethnic female body burdens most Lijiang women, compelling them to defend their sexual purity by drawing distinctions between themselves and immoral female others.

While fox-stench stories and advertisements may not be distinctive to Li-jiang, their articulation in Lijiang speaks to the gendered consequences of the ethnicization and exoticization of minority occupied areas (see Schein 2000; Makley 2007; Hyde 2007). These consequences are inseparable from both the market forces and the development plans that essentialize ethnic difference in order to promote China's economic development.

MARKETING DIFFERENCE
DOG MEAT, COURT CASES
AND ETHNOPRENEURS

At different times and places in Lijiang Prefecture, the term "dog meat" has variously referred to: an inexpensive cut of meat clandestinely substituted for lamb, an ethnic insult, an exotic culinary delicacy, a marker of cosmopolitanism, evidence of a depraved act, and the corporeal remains of a friend. These multiple meanings of "dog meat" index the layered subjectivities that narrate Lijiang's transformation from a borderland market town to a destination for national and international tourism.

OF DEFAMATION LAWSUITS AND DOG MEAT

"Dog meat" as a pejorative term featured prominently in a defamation lawsuit initiated by an acclaimed and notorious figure in the Lijiang arts scene.[1] The case involved a scholarly article by a Chinese musicologist, Wu Xueyuan, that appeared in the journal *Arts Criticism* (Yishu pinglun) (2003).[2] The article, "What Is This Thing Called Ancient Naxi Music?" (Naxi guyue shi shenme dongxi?), alleged that Ancient Naxi Music (Naxi guyue) was a cultural fraud (Wu Xueyuan 2003). Following publication of the article, Xuan Ke, impresario of the Ancient Naxi Music Association (Naxi Guyuehui), sued Wu and *Arts Criticism*'s editor for defamation. At the conclusion of the litigation, Xuan was awarded sizable monetary damages. Cited as key to the court's decision was Wu's sarcasm, particularly his use of the term "dog meat" to refer to Ancient Naxi Music.

This litigation regarding Ancient Naxi Music illustrates local government control over a new type of valued economic resource. The court's decision should not be mistaken for the persistence of Maoist-era governance, but it signifies what Foucault refers to as the neoliberal turn, in which "the market itself [becomes] the organizing and regulating principle underlying the state" (Comaroff and Comaroff 2009, 50). Postsocialist China has been characterized by economic development agendas informed by neoliberalism. Neoliberal governance philosophy is based on the idea that the market should reign and that state governments enable the economy to grow and thrive by removing obstacles to "natural" entrepreneurial activity. China's embrace of neoliberal philosophy marks a shift from a system of value that prioritizes the welfare of collectivities to one that prioritizes economic growth. The lawsuit demonstrates how, in the calculus of the market, ethnicity may be attached to commodifiable experiences, and how those experiences in turn are perceived as intellectual property. The marketing of Naxi ethnicity and cultural heritage was accompanied by substantial migration to Lijiang and a reorientation of Lijiang's economy toward tourism. In the late 1990s, migration and tourism in Lijiang were encouraged by central state policies for opening up southwest China (part of a broader initiative targeting various regions of China's interior, many of them ethnic, for development), as well as by policies and regulations implemented in 2001 by the China National Tourism Administration (Goodman 2004; Litzinger 2004).[3]

This chapter focuses on how China's global aspirations and global markets shape local experiences and local politics. The Ancient Naxi Music lawsuit provides glimpses of a submerged ethnic tension, resulting from migration, that found expression in the symbolism of food and those who consume it.

At the same time, Xuan's Ke's metamorphosis from outcast to respected entrepreneur enables us to track the transformation of value in the wake of neoliberal logic. These changes are manifest in the remaking of reputation, the emergence of a new form of masculinity, and the valorization of capitalist acumen.

HISTORICIZING ETHNICITY

Ethnic tension has been largely absent in Lijiang's history since 1949, but it has surfaced in the context of a postsocialist-era migration occurring from the mid-1990s onward. Articulations of ethnic tension cannot be understood apart from some discussion of ethnicity in postrevolutionary China. As previously discussed, the Naxi are one of the minority ethnic groups who were incorporated into the Chinese empire during the Ming and Qing dynasties. In the Republican era, only five ethnic groups were recognized as distinct (Han, Hui, Manchu, Mongol, and Tibetan),[4] and the Naxi defined themselves as descendants of Han, Tibetan, or Mongol groups. In the 1950s, the Naxi were given recognition as a distinct ethnic group, but opportunities to define that ethnic identity were short-lived due to an emphasis on national culture and the political limitations placed on the expression of ethnic identity during the Maoist era.

From the reform era, however, national history was re-narrated to prominently feature ethnic diversity. The reform era was characterized by ethnic groups seeking to articulate their ethnic distinctiveness as a means of securing political representation and the rights associated with status as a recognized ethnic group. As previously discussed, Naxi politicians and intellectuals during the reform era renamed pre-1949 *dongba* ritual practices and script as "*dongba* culture," a term used to secularize these practices in order to claim them as the primary source of Naxi heritage. However, a strong sense of Naxi ethnic identity based on *dongba* culture did not instantaneously take hold. After more than two and a half decades of the state stressing national identity, most Lijiang residents construed their identity in terms of place and not in terms of a newly imagined ethnicity. Many rural residents had no idea what *dongba* culture was during the 1970s and 1980s, but by the postsocialist era, two decades later, this had changed. A special emphasis on the city as a center of the distinctive Naxi ethnic group was key to its refashioning as a major tourist destination.

The identification of Lijiang with certain ethnic attributes by transglobal, national, and local actors during the postsocialist era had gone hand in hand with tourism development. Ethnic attractions and artifacts perceived as marketable became a primary focus of economic development plans. Commodity production and commodifiable experiences used to market tourism in Lijiang flowed from national and global tastes and desires. The global and local became indistinct "permeable constructs" in the sense that the former shaped the creation of the latter (Grewal and Kaplan 1994, 11).[5] Lijiang's growth as a destination for tourism attracted entrepreneurs and workers from other areas in China. Migration enabled development, in the sense of providing labor with which to expand the town into a city, but it also threatened to change the composition of Lijiang as a predominantly Naxi enclave. Tensions developed between established residents of Lijiang and the newcomers, many of whom were entrepreneurs seeking to profit from Lijiang's new success as a tourist destination. The reform-era ethnicization of Lijiang-as-a-place contributed to tensions that were articulated in ethnic terms. In the postsocialist era, the state-directed economy shifted to neoliberal protection of the market. Informed by market logic, Lijiang residents came to conceptualize ethnicity not as local heritage but as marketable property. At the same time, narratives about ethnicity came to express discomfort over the loss of an older place-based identity and the rising economic inequality between some residents and migrant outsiders, newcomers who were perceived as profiting from Lijiang's ethnic resources. The story of Xuan Ke and Ancient Naxi Music illustrates the way in which entrepreneurs were the greatest beneficiaries of Lijiang's ethnicization.

A DEBATE OVER MUSIC

Xuan Ke began marketing performances of what he claimed was distinctively "Ancient Naxi Music" to tourists visiting Lijiang in the late 1980s. These performances were presented by an ensemble of elderly musicians playing traditional instruments. By 2003, when the litigation took place, Xuan's Ancient Naxi Music performances had become one of the major tourist attractions of the Old Town, and he was considered to be a key player in Lijiang's tourist industry.

After attending musical performances presided over by Xuan, Wu Xueyuan, a Chinese ethnomusicologist and specialist on Daoist music, published an article questioning the authenticity of Ancient Naxi Music. Wu's allegations were made at a time when Xuan was seeking to have Naxi Ancient Music included in UNESCO's Intangible Cultural Heritage List under the category "Traditional Music." As defined by UNESCO, an intangible cultural heritage "consists of non-physical characteristics, practices, representations, expressions, as well as knowledge and skills that identify and define a group or civilization" (http://portal.unesco.org). The purpose of this designation is to promote global recognition of distinctive forms of music, dance, or other cultural practices. With designation as an intangible cultural heritage comes financial assistance for countries and ethnic groups within countries so that they can document and preserve these cultural practices.

Wu argued that Ancient Naxi Music is not "a living fossil of music" (*yinyue huohuashi*) because it is actually a combination of different musical genres and does not represent a "pure cultural form" (Wu Xueyuan 2003, 23). Chinese social scientists use the "living fossil" category to refer to forms of antiquity that persist with little or no modification. Wu's use of the term "living fossil" drew on nineteenth-century Western evolutionary anthropology, adopted by twentieth-century Chinese scholarly discourse on antiquity and applied to China's minority ethnic groups. According to this discourse, ethnic practices were *authentic* only if they were primordial (i.e., a part of the original practices of the group). The living-fossil metaphor implies that a particular cultural form could belong to only one ethnic group. The import of Wu's critique was that Ancient Naxi Music could not be authentic because it was originally Han music and was only later adopted by the Naxi.

Wu's article pointed out that, before 1995, Xuan's orchestra performed only *dongjing* music, a form of Chinese music surviving primarily in southwest China, and that Xuan later added *remeicuo*[6] and Baisha "lyrical music" (*xiyue*) songs in order to bolster the claim that his performances were distinctively Naxi. *Remeicuo* and lyrical music were performed in the Lijiang area, and a stronger case can be made that these forms originated in Lijiang.[7] In sum, Wu suggested that Ancient Naxi Music consists of nothing more than Xuan's mongrelization of genres in a strategic attempt to gain international recognition for Naxi music.

It can certainly be said that *dongjing* music performed in Lijiang is Naxi in the sense that it has been performed continuously for hundreds of years in the Lijiang Town and basin areas, where it has played an important role in the social and ritual practices of Naxi communities. In contrast to Wu, it might appear that Xuan—in his defense of Ancient Naxi Music—manifested a more porous understanding of ethnicity. During performances, Xuan explains that *dongjing* music is Han in origin but spread to the Lijiang area during the Ming dynasty and *became* Naxi over the next 622 years. But the debate between Wu and Xuan does not simply parallel the old debate between primordialist and constructivist understandings of ethnicity. For while Xuan asserts that Ancient Naxi Music became Naxi, he also states that it "belongs to the Naxi nationality" (Xuan cited in Barmé 2005). Upon closer examination, it is apparent that Xuan's argument treats *dongjing* music as ethnic property. His understanding of ethnicity might be better understood as instrumentalist or, more specifically, indicative of a new subjectivity that reflects the penetration of global capitalism during the postsocialist era.

GLOBALIZATION AND COMMODIFIED ETHNICITY

There is nothing particularly novel about Xuan's understanding of ethnicity. Ethnicity had begun to play a central role in how China represented itself during the reform era. According to Comaroff and Comaroff, coming to terms with heterogeneity has been a global phenomenon affecting nation-states since the turn of the twentieth century as a result of three factors: the reverse colonial flow of populations from center to periphery; the global indigenous peoples' movements (aimed at enhancing the rights of indigenous populations); and the transformative impact of neoliberalism since 1989, in which the market economically and "semiotically" affects all (2009, 46, 47). While the Comaroffs were not referring to China, their analysis fits well with the situation in Lijiang. Han migration to the peripheral areas occupied by China's ethnic minorities corresponds roughly to the Campaign to Open Up the West, which was implemented in 2000. There has not been an indigenous people's movement per se in Lijiang; through the efforts of nongovernmental organizations, however, citizens' groups from Lijiang have met with U.S. and Canadian indigenous groups and discussed their common experiences. Most significantly, the market in reform-era China has become the "principle underlying the state" (Comaroff and Comaroff 2009, 50). It is well known among scholars of China that, since the reform era, market expansion and success has been the primary motivation behind state policies. As part of this dynamic, local and national actors have seized upon ethnicity as a source of value, and ethnic practices and objects have consequently become fetishized as commodities.

The perception of ethnicity as reducible to market value is manifested by tourist attractions other than Ancient Naxi Music. In Lijiang, private-sector economic interests led to the reinvention of cultural practices for the purpose of fostering tourism. For instance, at the entrance of the Old Town, young women dressed in Naxi clothing sell paper lanterns to tourists. Tourists are told that, by purchasing a lantern and sending it afloat down the river, a wish can be granted or a difficulty resolved. Before the mid-1990s, people floated a lantern down a stream to light the path for a recently deceased person's soul, so that the soul could make its way to the land of the dead. This practice was originally part of a local funerary ritual in which relatives of the deceased were the sole participants. By isolating and decontextualizing this single element of the ritual, entrepreneurs created a commodified attraction and gave tourists an opportunity to simulate participation in local cultural customs. Marketers of the converted ritual element are well aware that most tourists who visit Lijiang come from urban China and overseas Chinese communities. The attraction expunges the practice of its association with death, which many Chinese perceive as polluting and inauspicious.[8] It provides an opportunity for tourists to improve their luck or fortune and acquire the symbolic capital accrued by becoming knowledgeable about cultural traditions beyond one's own, an experience associated with cosmopolitans. (Ironically, Naxi scholars have told me that the lantern-lighting ceremony was a local version of Chinese funerary practice, which was adopted in Lijiang's Old Town probably as part of the late imperial incorporation of minority ethnic groups into the Qing empire.)

Another example of reinvented tradition is Da Tiao, a form of line dance practiced in Four Corner Street (Sifangjie), the main square in Lijiang's Old Town. Tourists are told that performing the dance in the town square is a Naxi tradition. The dance has even been lauded by cultural geographers as an example of local residents resisting change and reclaiming local space from tourists (Su and Teo 2008). However, dancing in Four Corner Street dates from the late 1990s, when the square was converted from a vegetable market to a tourist attraction. The idea that town people are "reclaiming space" is curious because the Da Tiao dancers are not Old Town residents but predominantly elderly farmers bused from the countryside and paid to help create a cultural attraction for visiting tourists. It is not an accident that Da Tiao performances are held in the former main square of the Old Town. Tourists are invited to watch or join in the dancing as it takes place. While itself not a commodified attraction, Da Tiao draws tourists to this central location, which has the largest concentration of trinket shops and restaurants devoted to the tourist trade. Much as in Disneyland's Main Street parade, scheduled performances are intended to draw tourists to sites of consumption (see Harrell 2001). While many Lijiang Town residents are often sarcastic about these invented traditions, some maintain that as long as the participants are Naxi, these attractions may be considered ethnic and authentic.[9]

Xuan Ke's presentation of Ancient Naxi Music was one of the most significant reinvented traditions in Lijiang. His defamation suit and the ensuing decision by the Lijiang People's Court (Lijiang Zhongji Fayuan) raise a number of questions. What was really at stake in the court's decision? How can it be understood in terms of the broader transformations taking place in Lijiang and postsocialist China?

GLOBAL CULTURAL HERITAGE VERSUS ETHNIC OWNERSHIP

Wu was essentially making a point about ethnic origins and had no financial interest in cultural property, but for Xuan, the ethnic labeling of Lijiang music was inseparable from its marketability as a commodity. Moreover, the potential failure of Ancient Naxi Music to be considered a UNESCO intangible cultural heritage was clearly understood in economic terms. At issue was not only the loss of financial assistance to preserve Ancient Naxi Music as a cultural form but, more significantly, the prestige associated with the UNESCO designation and the expansion of tourism it would likely generate.

Unlike Wu or Xuan, UNESCO does not concern itself with the purity of ethnic forms. Its ethos is in tension with ideas of local and ethnic commodification and ownership. UNESCO's program is intended to recognize forms of cultural heritage that are of value and importance to a global collectivity. UNESCO's philosophy is that the mission to preserve global cultural heritage is the responsibility of all nations. This philosophy is predicated on the understanding that cultural heritage is globally owned. World Heritage sites "belong to all the peoples of the world, irrespective of the territory on which they are located."[10] The collective ownership of World Heritage sources (i.e., sites, cultural practices, etc.) is underscored by UNESCO's Memory of the World Program, through which the organization provides financial assistance for the documentation of designated sources so that they will be accessible to a global audience. UNESCO programs employ the logic of delocalization in order to create an understanding of heritage as "global." The logic of the UNESCO designation is that, once a cultural form is so designated, it is no longer local but becomes part of the world's cultural heritage. The Memory of the World Program works against local ownership by making images and texts digitally available without cost to users.

In a sense, UNESCO's philosophy of global ownership contradicts the logic of neoliberalism, in which the market reigns and cultural products and practices are assessed according to an "economic cost-benefit calculation" (cf. Comaroff and Comaroff 2009, 50). Neoliberalism fosters what the Comaroffs refer to as "ethno-preneurialism," the marketing of cultural and ethnic phenomena as "intellectual property" and "sources of value" (ibid., 51).[11] Commodifiable forms of heritage become indispensable for promoting tourism to a particular locality. In Lijiang, *dongba* script and Ancient Naxi Music are understood to "belong" to Lijiang and are perceived as property that can be marketed for the purpose of attracting tourists and capital to the area.

Wu's article dealt a blow to both private entrepreneurs and Lijiang's tourism development plans by claiming that Ancient Naxi Music was inappropriate for inclusion as a UNESCO intangible cultural heritage. Lijiang's government had hoped that the aura of international cultural prestige signified by the UNESCO label would give a substantial boost to the town's tourist industry. There was also concern that, if Ancient Naxi Music were denied UNESCO's designation, other ethnic groups might make similar bids for the status based on their *dongjing* music groups. The tourism potential of Ancient Naxi Music would be threatened if another group received the UNESCO designation for *dongjing* music and were able to claim it as an "ethno-commodity."[12]

DOG-MEAT DISCOURSE:
MEMORY, INSULTS, AND BOUNDARIES

Following publication of Wu's article, Xuan Ke brought the lawsuit against him and Tian Qing, editor of *Arts Criticism*, for damaging his reputation and the chance of Ancient Naxi Music to be awarded UNESCO's intangible cultural heritage designation. The Lijiang People's Court awarded Xuan ¥1.2 million ($161,649) in damages to be paid by Tian and ¥100,000 ($13,500) to be paid by Wu (Barmé 2005).[13] Curiously, the court declined to rule on the veracity of Wu's claims, refusing to admit "any intellectual arguments" as evidence. Rather, its judgment in favor of Xuan was based on "sarcastic phrases" in Wu's article. One of the phrases at issue was the question "What is this thing Ancient Naxi Music?" (*Naxi Guyue shi shenme dongxi?*). "What is this thing?" may be read as insulting or sarcastic, or simply as a question, depending on the tone and context.

The section of Wu's article that received the most severe criticism from the court was his use of an expression in standard Chinese that conveys the concept of someone selling or representing one thing as another, literally, "to hang a sheep's head to sell dog meat" (*gua yangtou mai gou rou*). The phrase conjures the image of a butcher professing to sell mutton while actually giving customers dog meat. The court's opinion chastised Wu for using this expression. The court undoubtedly assumed Wu's use of the phrase was not meant simply to convey that Ancient Naxi Music is something other than what it represents itself to be and that he was familiar with the local meaning of "dog meat." Use of the term "dog meat" to refer to anything Naxi, particularly if one is Han, is likely to have outraged most Naxi audiences.

The dog-meat metaphor plays a significant role in the mnemonics of ethnic boundary construction in Lijiang, where "dog meat" is metonymically associated with Han culture. The popular association comes from the Naxi saying "Han eat dog meat" (*Happa kurshi zi*), a common insult historically used by town-dwelling Naxi. The insult essentializes the Han people as dog eaters, a characterization used by many Naxi who find the consumption of dog meat repulsive. Pastoralism had been a key component of subsistence in the mountainous regions of Lijiang, and dogs were essential to the maintenance of goat and sheep herds—and still are today. As a reflection of their high regard for dogs, mountain-dwelling rural Naxi families mourned and held funerals for their dogs. Many urban Naxi households, and virtually every rural household in the Lijiang basin, have fierce guard dogs. Younger people now raise dogs not so much for protection but as pampered pets. Cooking and eating a dog are repugnant acts, and Naxi considered their abstinence from this practice as a reflection of their superiority to the Han. In the Lijiang basin, and particularly in Lijiang Town, the saying "Han eat dog meat" is not simply a statement of differentiation but an outright rebuke—a moral condemnation of the Han. Before the reform era, the basin and mountain villages where I conducted fieldwork were fairly ethnically homogeneous, populated primarily by Naxi. This was not the case with Lijiang Town, however, where there has been a history of sporadic Han migration and some intermarriage. The use of "dog-meat eating" as a form of insult is more common in Lijiang Town, where the numerically dominant Naxi have lived in constant contact with a smaller Han population and Han travelers.

Wu's phrase "hang a sheep's head to sell dog meat" used in reference to music suggests that something Han ("dog meat," a Lijiang metonym for Chineseness) was being marketed as something other than what it is. In other words, Han *dongjing* music was being deceptively sold as Ancient Naxi Music. Wu's criticism also invoked the Naxi slur about Han eating dog and countered that insult by likening the Naxi to something even worse: dog butchers and dog-meat vendors. His comment may be interpreted as opining that the Naxi are hypocritical and worse than the Han, whom they denigrate as dog eaters. The Lijiang People's Court's emphasis on "sarcastic phrases" indicates that it interpreted Wu's statement as a double entendre, a cutting reference to the Naxi caricature of the Han as dog eaters and an accusation that the Naxi fraudulently market Han music as their own.

The anger likely to be generated among Naxi by the dog-meat insult must be understood in the context of politics and ethnic boundary construction. At the level of overt representation, the justification for Naxi denigration of the Han appears to be culinary. As Mary Douglas has insightfully explained, however, the classification of food into categories of pure and polluted carries strong moral valences. What an individual eats must be pure; conversely, what she or he rejects lies outside the boundary of purity and is considered to be polluted. Symbolically, that which may be incorporated into the self and the social body furnishes guidelines for social interaction (Douglas 1966, 115). What is eaten becomes incorporated into the self. With dog meat, it is not the dog itself that is polluting but the immoral act of treating the dog, an animal worthy of funerary veneration, as merely unslaughtered meat. It is a polluting act because it constitutes the categorical violation of consuming the inedible. Hence, Naxi concern with the Han consumption of dog meat is less about an inventory of eating patterns than about moral boundaries and ethnic opposition indexed by culinary practices. At a meta-interpretive level, since dog meat is ethnically marked as "Han," rejection of its incorporation into the body parallels the Naxi ethnic group's rejection of the incorporation of Han people into the body politic of Lijiang. Wu's dog-meat insult may have represented only his individual ethnic bias, but it revealed an enmity between the Han and Naxi ethnic groups. However, ethnic insults and tensions over cultural difference provide no explanations in and of themselves. Ethnic and cultural markers are part of a system that categorizes difference. Tensions and insults are indicators of a shift in relations between groups that must be contextualized in the remaking of Lijiang as a tourist destination and the material consequences of this change.

In the early 1990s, Lijiang was a town frequented only by small groups of backpacking tourists, mostly from Europe or the United States. It was not a destination for national or significant international tourism. The transformation of Lijiang into a major tourist destination involved a process of place-making whereby it was invented as a site of antiquity, an ethnic enclave, and a site for touristic leisure and consumption. As Gupta and Ferguson suggest, place-making always "involves construction, rather than merely a discovery, of difference" (1997, 13; Notar 2006).

During the post-Mao era, Lijiang's identity was based on its productive and not its culinary reputation. The town was known for the production of leather and silver goods and wood products. It was a center for the manufacture of leather shoes and belts, silver jewelry, and wood crafts and was a regional source for lumber. There was very little restaurant culture in Lijiang, and what there was catered to local people and regional traders. Lijiang had a limited number of culinary specialties: Lijiang flat bread (baba), fried bean gelatin (liangfen), and yak butter tea (suyou cha). During the Republican era, Lijiang was a regional market town and its flat bread, being both dense and portable, was prized because it could provision one for months without spoiling. Flat bread and fried bean gelatin were foods of Naxi origin. Yak butter tea was Tibetan in origin but was widely consumed among the Naxi as well. Lijiang was known for hot pot (huoguo), which is also prepared in other parts of China. Dog-meat dishes were the only cuisine distinctly marked as Han, and they were widely regarded as inedible by Lijiang residents.

When I began my fieldwork in Lijiang in 1990, Professor Guo Dalie, a Naxi scholar from Lijiang, invited me to his home for a meal. His wife, who is Han, prepared a special dish of dog meat as a tribute to my arrival. There was no slight intended by Professor Guo when he enthusiastically intoned "Han eat dog meat." The menu, informed by the essentialization of my Han difference, was intended to please. Having been categorized as Han, rather than American, my hosts assumed that I ate dog meat.

The reference to Han as dog eaters, however, is more commonly used as an insult or as a barbed form of joking. The negativity of the association requires some historical and contemporary contextualization. In Lijiang, understandings of ethnic difference are inseparable from the state's hierarchical categorization of minority groups. Many sinicized Naxi have internalized these ideas and refer to the rural Naxi as backward compared to the Han, although more advanced than other ethnic groups. Yet sometimes the same actors undercut Han superiority by adding that Chinese eat dog meat. The invocation of dog meat to denigrate the Han is widespread in Lijiang town and reflects Naxi criticism of "Han chauvinism" (da Hanzuzhuyi).

However, the dog-meat insult does not reflect a timeless or unchallenged persistence of ethnic boundaries or even culinary boundaries. Even when the consumption of dog meat elicited widespread revulsion among the Naxi, ethnic boundaries were not absolute. As early as the Ming dynasty, the ruling Mu family invited Han tradesmen to settle in Lijiang Town. These families intermarried with the Naxi. Their descendants, though marked by Han surnames, adopted the Naxi language and Naxi cultural practices. There was some intermarriage during the Republican era, though intra-ethnic marriage was more common in rural and semi-urban areas of Lijiang. In the rural areas, marriage across ethnic groups occurred only rarely.[14]

Today, the Naxi remain the largest ethnic group in Lijiang and hold most of the positions of authority in local government. As discussed, Lijiang has, since the late 1990s, embraced national directives advocating economic development and this has transformed the town into a tourist center. As a result, Lijiang has attracted a substantial number of economic migrants from a variety of ethnic groups, straining what was formerly a predominantly Naxi ethnic enclave. Significantly, this migration has led to the erosion of culinary boundaries.

A minority of older Naxi have sampled dog meat as a medicinal remedy for "rheumatism" (fengshi bing), although this practice is far from widespread. The interest in consuming new types of food is somewhat generational. Young people have been attracted to the new teashops and coffee shops, as well as to the Western and regional Chinese restaurants. The first restaurants serving Western food opened in the late 1980s and targeted the small number of backpackers who visited the area. More restaurants opened to cater to Chinese and international tourism after the Lijiang airport opened in 1995.

Lijiang's transformation into a center for tourism has wrought substantial change in the lives of its residents. Many Naxi moved out of the Old Town and put their architecturally distinctive houses up for rent. Depending on the size of a house in the Old Town, former residents could make between ¥20,000–30,000 (approximately three to five thousand dollars) a year, the equivalent of an annual salary for most residents. The local government encouraged other Old Town residents to move, and they relocated to new suburbs. In the meantime, Lijiang has grown into a city. Leaving the Old Town became attractive after the earthquake because residents could purchase government land on which to build a house for about ¥7,000 (a little more than $1,000). The plots of land, which were all the same size, were sufficient for a house and a tiny garden, but not large enough for replicating the architecture of Old Town houses, which had been built around courtyards. Many residents shared courtyards with other families in the Old Town and were able to have living spaces that were more private in the suburbs. Some residents were pleased to inhabit new houses with modern fixtures; houses in this old part of Lijiang could not accommodate plumbed toilets, so residents had to dump their nightsoil in neighborhood outhouses in the early 1990s.[15] But there remained some ambivalence about relocation. Old Town, with its elegant tile-roofed buildings and gated courtyards, was associated with prestige and was a residential ideal. Several former residents told me they had not wanted to move, but that ultimately they did to escape the noise created by the restaurants and bars, which are open late into the evening.

Beginning in the early 2000s, with the development of Lijiang as a site for national and international tourism, Han migrants from Jiangnan, Dongbei (Northeast China), and Sichuan have flooded into the town. Many ethnic Bai merchants were the first to open businesses in the Old Town. By 2005, more than 70 percent of the shops in Lijiang were run by outsiders (Su and Teo 2009, 128), and by 2011, about 90 percent of the homes in Lijiang's Old Town had been turned into guesthouses or businesses run by outsiders.[16] According to former residents, less than 10 percent of the Old Town's houses are inhabited by pre-tourism Lijiang residents. And while Lijiang (both the new and the old city) continues to be predominantly Naxi, infusions of Han and other ethnic groups threaten to alter what was once a largely Naxi cultural and political region.

Since the advent of tourism, the most popular professions for Naxi have included landlords, tour guides, and restaurant owners. Naxi restaurants have sold Western food, Chinese-style dishes, and Naxi cuisine. One conspicuous change has been culinary, with the opening of a variety of Chinese restaurants catering to tourists. (By the late 1990s, there were more than a hundred restaurants in Lijiang catering to tourists; in 1992, there had been only about a dozen.) Many Lijiang residents consider the opening of restaurants selling Beijing-style roasted duck or Sichuanese cuisine emblematic of the city's new sophistication and cosmopolitanism, but restaurants selling dog meat have aroused indignation.

A resident complained, "It's one thing to tolerate Guizhou Huajiang Gourou [a restaurant that offers dog-meat dishes as a specialty of the Huajiang region of Guizhou], but it's quite another thing when dog-meat restaurants pretend to sell Naxi cuisine." Apparently, a Han proprietor who had settled in Lijiang named his restaurant Dongba's Dog-Meat Restaurant (Dongba Gourou Dian). As discussed in chapter 2, dongba culture became officially fused with Naxi culture in the 1980s. It was broadly embraced throughout the Lijiang region after the town's transformation in the late 1990s into a national tourism site. This was largely because dongba script, the script of Naxi ritual practitioners, is identified as a form of writing distinctive to the Naxi. With the development of tourism in Lijiang, the addition of the modifier "dongba" to attractions or commodities is understood locally as a way of branding them as ethnically Naxi. The name Dongba's Dog-Meat Restaurant caused a furor after an elderly dongba from the Dongba Cultural Research Institute let it be known that such a restaurant was a grave insult to dongba culture and the Naxi. The term "dongba culture" refers to the historical cultural practices of the Naxi, which are believed to survive only in mountain regions. These practices include the veneration of sheep dogs and revulsion at eating dog meat. The restaurant's sign was perceived as oxymoronic and deeply offensive; it would be comparable to a sign reading "Rabbi's Pork Eatery." As the dongba complained, "The words 'dog meat' and 'dongba' cannot appear together! I have no complaints about any of the other restaurants, but Dongba's Dog-Meat Restaurant, this goes too far!" The dongba's complaint circulated throughout the Old Town, and within days the offending sign had been removed. His criticism was effective because it gave voice to Lijiang residents' growing concerns that their town had lost its ethnic distinctiveness and that Naxi culture was becoming indistinguishable from formerly reviled Han practices.

Dog-meat discourse has a history of usage based on moments when Naxi actors have sought to invert the ever-lurking Han hierarchy of difference. It may be understood as asserting an oppositional identity in which the Naxi lay claim to moral and territorial superiority at times of ethnic imperilment. Dog-meat discourse attempts to privilege forms of difference associated with place, particularly Naxi culinary practice. The dog-meat restaurant represents three distinct phenomena: culinary heterogeneity, mimetic alterity, and in-

FIG. 5.1 Dog-meat restaurant

strumental marketing. Culinary heterogeneity was unleashed by national and global demand, in which centers of tourism offer a variety of cuisines in order to cater to cosmopolitan tastes. It also draws on non-local symbols of perceived "otherness" that exoticize local food. One of the earliest restaurants catering to tourists in Lijiang was named "Ali Baba" and appeared to draw on one form of exotic imagery in its attempt to market another.[17] For tourists interested in the consumption of difference, dog meat or other regional cuisines contribute to Lijiang's exoticization. There are also a number of restaurants that simply label their cuisine as Naxi for the purpose of capitalizing on the allure of the ethnic.

From the vantage point of some Lijiang residents, anti-dog-meat discourse attempts to essentialize difference by reestablishing older boundaries. Such boundaries are drawn against migrant restaurateurs who are attempting to profit from ethnic resources. In this case, dongba—read as interchangeable with Naxi—is used to create an ethno-commodity perceived to be part of Naxi heritage. There are many shops in Lijiang selling Naxi ethno-commodities, but unlike those commodities, dog meat is the quintessential non-Naxi marker, representing an earlier, but still persisting, ethnic boundary. As one informant put it: "When tourists want dog meat, they know where to get it—Guizhou," referring either to the Guizhou restaurant (which features Huajiang dog meat, a regional specialty of Huajiang City) or to the neighboring province. The offense taken by local residents may also be understood as echoing concern about more than commodities. If Lijiang were to become a place associated with another ethnic group (through their cuisine), then it would implicitly be diminished as a distinctively Naxi ethnic town and site for ethnic tourism, a dynamic already threatened by the migration of entrepreneurs of other ethnic groups in the wake of the town's tourist development.

By symbolically equating Ancient Naxi Music with dog meat, Wu Xueyuan—knowingly or unknowingly—converted a dispute over musical authenticity and origins into a contest over ethnic hierarchy, heritage, and property. Faced with evaluating Wu's assertion of Han superiority, the Lijiang People's Court's resolution of the lawsuit was obvious. In a city populated and governed by Naxi, a city that markets itself as Naxi, how could this insult to what Xuan claimed was Ancient Naxi music be separated from an insult to the Naxi themselves?

The actions of the court may be understood as the "judicialization of politics" in the sense that the court acted to protect what it perceived as a collective Naxi resource (Comaroff and Comaroff 2009, 58). It also reflects the perception of ethnic phenomena fetishized as "owned property" that is, therefore, appropriately under jural regulation (ibid.). The litigant, Xuan Ke, may have been awarded damages not because Wu's article was an attack on his reputation but because it was an insult to the Naxi and to Lijiang's newly important heritage. The court's decision also questions the right of outsiders, their scholarly musical expertise notwithstanding, to define Naxi culture and potentially affect the economic welfare of Lijiang and its people. By awarding damages, the court in effect legitimized Xuan's claim that his music was uniquely Naxi. But how could this happen? How did Xuan Ke's identity become fused with Lijiang? And how could he be awarded such substantial damages merely for being slighted in a scholarly article?

TOURISM PLANNING AND THE WOOING OF UNESCO

The court's ruling needs to be understood in the broader context of Lijiang's development as a center for tourism. This development predates but is relevant to the Campaign to Open Up the West, a national initiative intended to foster economic development in western China through tourism. In 1994, the Yunnan Provincial Government implemented the Lijiang Town Preservation Five-Four-Three-Two-One Project as part of its application to become a UNESCO World Heritage site (Wai 2001). Preparation for tourism development began with changes in infrastructure, such as the construction of Lijiang's airport, which was completed in 1995. Following the earthquake of 1996, Lijiang's Old Town underwent major structural changes: the removal of modern buildings, restoration of historic structures, burial of electrical wires, and modification of the water and sewage system. In addition, a number of new buildings, constructed in the style of Ming and Qing architecture, were added to the Old Town. Residents were encouraged to move out of town in order to decrease population density, and measures were taken to improve air quality (Wai 2001, 4).[18] In 1998, the Dali-Lijiang Highway was completed, and 2009 saw the completion of a Dali-Lijiang Railroad. In 1997, two million tourists were visiting Lijiang annually, and in 1999, the figure had grown to three million, with fifteen thousand visitors a day during the Spring Festival (McKhann 1999, 2). By 2006, the annual figure had reached 4 million, and it grew to 5.3 million in 2007 (Lijiang Bureau of Statistics cited in Su and Teo 2009). In order to create the necessary infrastructure to support this tourism, the Lijiang County government had spent ¥3 billion (more than $400 million) and closed thirty factories. The closings were aimed at redirecting the timber used by these factories to construction and restoration, but more significantly, they marked a shift from a state to a private-sector economy. Specifically, they marked a change for residents from an economy based on the sale of labor to an economy based on the sale of culture.

The elimination of state-sector industry resulted in serious revenue losses to the local government. Development created a prospering private sector but also a tourism-dependent city with a local government heavily in debt. In 2002, Lijiang County was carrying a debt of more than ¥252 million (more than $34 million) (Duang 2000, 16; H. Zhang 2004, 5). In 2000, when the Campaign to Open Up the West was launched, Lijiang was arguably already opened up. While the campaign did not initiate Lijiang development, it articulated and reaffirmed development strategy as a course of economic change, which the Lijiang government had begun two years before. But in 2000, the strain of maintaining a city flooded with tourists was causing tension between state laws and local regulations (Wai 2001). There was a lack of "harmony" among the national, provincial, and county government officials charged with heritage management (Duang 2000, 10; Wai 2001, 7). Despite this, Lijiang embraced a tourism implementation plan with the goal of even more development as the solution.

Lijiang's tourism implementation plan identified several key elements of the city's historic culture for future development, one of which was Ancient Naxi Music. The new historic essence of Lijiang was determined largely by marketability and international recognition. There were hopes and expectations for Lijiang that the 1997 UNESCO World Heritage Site recognition and the 2003 UNESCO Memory of the World Register recognition given to *Dongba* Pictographic Script might be followed by UNESCO's recognition of Ancient Naxi Music as part of the world's intangible cultural heritage. In the year 2000, "Ancient Naxi Music" appeared in a Lijiang Heritage document presented to UNESCO as a resource for tourism development which, according to Lijiang authorities, had a proven global record of success (Duang 2000, 13, 25). By 2003, when Xuan Ke was awarded damages by the Lijiang People's Court, Ancient Naxi Music was already fairly entrenched as a key attraction in the local government's marketing of the city as a tourist center. The UNESCO intangible cultural heritage designation figured prominently in the litigation against Wu and *Arts Criticism*. The court must have been aware that Wu's allegations would harm Lijiang's bid to secure intangible cultural heritage status and that their punitive ruling could discredit Wu's and *Arts Criticism*'s claim. At stake in the verdict was Lijiang's reputation and the future of its tourist economy.

OLD STORIES AND A REPUTATION REMADE

Xuan Ke's personal story provides a means of scrutinizing how prestige and ethnicity were reconfigured by imbricated projects of tourism development and heritage commodification. In Lijiang in the 1990s, many Lijiang residents treated Xuan with derision and disdain. His bad reputation appeared to be based on his affectation of Western ways, his criminal history, and his zealous approach to marketing musical performances to the few tourists who visited Lijiang.[19] Xuan was known to comb the streets, accosting tourists and attempting to organize impromptu concerts.

In a city populated predominantly by Naxi, local residents described Xuan as Han or Tibetan, not as Naxi (Xuan described himself to me as Tibetan). He had some Naxi relatives, but he was considered an outsider. Xuan was from one of a handful of stigmatized families that had converted to Christianity during the Republican era and learned English from missionaries. In Lijiang, the few converts to Christianity were not Naxi but members of poorer ethnic groups.

Many of the prominent Lijiang families avoided Xuan because he was seen as a charlatan selling *dongjing* music as "Naxi." It was common knowledge among Lijiang intellectuals that *dongjing* music was originally Han. During the Republican era, local *dongjing* music was associated with Confucian and Daoist practices, particularly with the worship of Wenchang, the god of literature, and Guandi, the god of war. Ethnomusicologist Helen Rees describes early Republican-era *dongjing* music in Lijiang as the province of elites and concludes that it "suggests a traditional Confucian, Han-oriented cultural mindset" with "no hint of any specific Naxi input" (2000, 191). Ironically, *dongjing* music was considered prestigious in Lijiang not because it was perceived as Naxi but because it was Han. Models of prestige could not be disaggregated from Han political dominance at the national level or from the

Maoist-era evolutionary discourse that ranked minorities according to their similarity to the Han.

These negative portrayals of Xuan were informed by an earlier, more politicized socialist system of prestige in which association with religion, entrepreneurship, or things foreign marked one as morally problematic. In the late 1980s and early 1990s, state-sector employment was identified with prestige and morality, and only those, like Xuan, who had no other options worked in the private sector. Xuan was among the first entrepreneurs in Lijiang. He was also distinctive in that his work involved cultural representation. In the 1980s and early 1990s, intellectuals working at state-funded universities or in research institutes were the ones who defined Naxi culture. Earlier essentializations of "Naxi" had been created for the purpose of political representation and scholarship. When Xuan's musical group traveled with other Lijiang attractions, some Naxi refused to appear in public with him. In 1991, when Xuan was permitted to join a group of dignitaries for a presentation on Naxi culture at the Guangzhou Ethnic Village, he was required to sign a statement promising that he would "not talk nonsense or engage in problematic activities." Yet, as tourism became an increasingly important part of the Lijiang economy, Xuan's reputation underwent gradual improvement. Some intellectuals still shunned him, and residents with older relatives in his orchestra sometimes complained that he pocketed the lion's share of the profits and paid the elderly musicians very little. But it was also acknowledged that Xuan's English-speaking skills and his ability to sell the music to tourists had made him increasingly prosperous and brought recognition to Lijiang.

By 1993, Xuan and his orchestra had traveled to Beijing on a concert tour funded by the Yunnan Province Propaganda Department, the Yunnan Ethnic Culture Arts Exchange Company, and the governments of Lijiang Prefecture, Lijiang County, and Dayanzhen (Rees 2000, 186). These successful events, which were part of early attempts by officials in Yunnan and Lijiang to promote tourism, were followed by concert tours to Hong Kong, England, and other countries. They also marked a transition from the academic representation of culture and ethnicity to its articulation by government officials based on marketability. In the twenty-first century, agents like Xuan Ke began replacing the very intellectuals who had criticized him a decade earlier.

Xuan's popularity was also tied to a shift in values. After the mid-1990s, entrepreneurs had become increasingly acceptable, if not envied. Earlier, Xuan's sartorial choices were criticized. Town dwellers made fun of him, a middle-aged man who wore the blue jeans identified with "teenagers or very young adults" (qingnianren). It was scandalous that Xuan had a young wife between twenty and thirty years his junior. But by the twenty-first century, tastes in Lijiang reflected a larger shift in values taking place across China. As commodities flooded into the town, their consumption narrated the modernity of their consumers. The mooring of local identity had changed, particularly among the younger generation. Xuan's blue jeans, still derided by some, now marked him as fashionable and a trendsetter. In contrast to the valuation of labor and productivity during the Maoist era, the postsocialist era placed emphasis on gender-based identity. In this context, men with substantially younger wives or mistresses, who would have been morally derided for such behavior in the 1990s, were praised as exceptional, potent, and possessed of remarkable masculine vigor. Xuan purchased several acres of farmland at the foot of Huangshan and built a luxurious mansion there. He was indisputably one of the wealthiest residents of Lijiang. Now a philanthropist, Xuan is known as a benefactor of civic and charitable affairs. He has referred to himself as *guicai*, a person possessing *demonic* talent.

Xuan's meteoric rise, from reviled social outcast to pillar of Lijiang society, is more than a tale of ambition and persistence. By riding the wave of ethnic re-essentialization, he had succeeded in marketing *dongjing* music as authentically Naxi and profited handsomely from the state's embrace of neoliberalism and the market economy. In 2009, China Central Television broadcast a program entitled "Xuan Ke: Defender of Naxi Culture." With the transformation of Lijiang into a tourism hot spot in the mid-1990s, Xuan's "Ancient Naxi Music" was a key ethnic attraction, an emblem of local authenticity that had become eponymous with Lijiang. Perhaps more important, in the minds of many of the town's officials, the success of Ancient Naxi Music had become associated with the future success of tourism in Lijiang.

After 2000, Lijiang Town, bursting with tourists and facing severe management and waste problems, was seeking ways to further develop tourism while preserving key attractions. It could not afford to lose Ancient Naxi Music, which had both international acclaim and a history of marketability. Having lost the name "Shangri-la" to Zhongdian County,[20] Lijiang could not afford to lose *dongjing* music to Dali or Kunming, or other places in Yunnan where it was performed, or to scholars like Wu who claimed it as part of Han antiquity.

Xuan's legal victory and new social standing illustrate how tourism and development reshape social hierarchies and local understandings of what may be represented as "ethnic" heritage. When the Lijiang economy changed, so did the fortunes of private entrepreneurs and cultural experts. In the Lijiang of the early 1990s, state-sector intellectuals were the arbiters of cultural authenticity, but little more than a decade later they had been supplanted by government officials and entrepreneurs like Xuan. By awarding damages to Xuan, the Lijiang People's Court signaled a shift in local constructions of prestige. Its affirmation of entrepreneurship over scholarship could easily be mistaken to suggest that the Lijiang court system now upheld individual property rights in a manner consistent with the promotion of neoliberal values resulting from this shift in the economic system. Proponents of neoliberalism have argued that the market economy will enable economic growth accompanied by an increase in individual rights for citizens, eventually leading to democratic reform.[21]

The rise of Xuan Ke to become a pillar of the community demonstrates that the market economy has fostered new values and new forms of agency that would have been disparaged during the Maoist era or even the early reform era. In this respect, Xuan does fit the profile of the new neoliberal subject. His agency is not without limit, however, and it is less clear that the court's decision indicates advocacy of individual agents so much as the rights of entrepreneurial actors tied to economic development in Lijiang. Xuan's victory signified a championing of individual rights only to the extent that such rights were compatible with the perceived collective economic interests of Lijiang residents. At least in Lijiang, it was neither socialist values nor possessive individualism that the Lijiang People's Court upheld. Rather, the outcome of the lawsuit demonstrates that the court system was malleable to Lijiang political agendas in conformity with the neoliberal policies promoting tourism development. The large monetary award may have been aimed more at punishing those who might challenge the collective interests of the Lijiang government and Lijiang's perceived economic interests than at protecting the financial interests of Xuan Ke in particular. Xuan's meteoric rise suggests that the formerly stigmatized may succeed at reinventing themselves as entrepreneurs if their interests are consistent with local political and economic initiatives as framed by the market. And while this court case may be interpreted as a triumph of local power, the exercise of local power cannot be abstracted from either the larger national plan to promote economic development in the southwest or the neoliberal logic that leads to the creation of ethno-commodities. The Lijiang government's faith in tourism as the sole path to prosperity is an indicator of the success of central state policies, such as the Campaign to Open Up the West, which have been enthusiastically embraced at the local level despite the debt and mixed results such policies have engendered.

As if to demonstrate that it was, ultimately, perceived collective interests as opposed to individual rights that prevailed in the judgment handed down by the Lijiang People's Court, a subsequent lawsuit initiated by Xuan Ke had a very different result. Xuan recently brought legal action against Liang Wei, Lijiang's retired director of the Department of Foreign Affairs, who had formed his own Ancient Naxi Music group, which also performs for tourists. Xuan sued for theft of intellectual property, arguing that Liang Wei was encroaching on his domain, Ancient Naxi Music. He dropped the suit after local officials intervened and subjected both parties to "ideological work" (*sixiang gongzuo*). Communist Party officials persuaded Xuan that such a lawsuit would hurt tourism in Lijiang and the city's reputation. As a Party official recounted, Xuan and Liang were told that they were both important to Lijiang's future and should not be fighting with each other. Given the success of his first lawsuit, Xuan may have thought his right to financial damages, as the "inventor" of Ancient Naxi Music, would be upheld by the court, but Party intervention in the second lawsuit suggests that the enforcement of individual rights is secondary to the hegemony of the market in the postsocialist era.

CONCLUSION
FORGETTING THE MADMAN AND
REMEMBERING THE ANCIENT TEA HORSE
ROAD

Since the 1990s, policies instituted by the Chinese state have shaped how Lijiang actors interpret and craft their identities and practices. A decade after the dismantling of collectivized agriculture, residents of East Wind Village still puzzle over who or what was responsible for the madness and welfare of their most impoverished fellow villager.

Throughout reform-era China, urban and rural populations had come to be differentiated in terms of quality, or *suzhi*, a characteristic largely imagined to be absent in rural populations and present in urban ones. In Lijiang Town, the state's promotion of ethnic categories inspired local leaders and intellectuals to essentialize the Naxi in terms of *dongba* culture. The creators of *dongba* culture reinterpreted geographic residence (mountain, basin, and town) to represent gradations of ethnic authenticity based on historical and reform-era differentiations. *Dongba* culture imagined urban Naxi as sinicized and modern, and viewed rural mountain Naxi as backward—yet eligible for praise as ethnically authentic. The category "*dongba* culture" was initially ignored by rural Lijiang residents, but in East Wind Village during the early to mid-1990s, the category was appropriated by a prominent Lijiang official and some indigent households in defense of elopement, whose largely underage practitioners were in violation of China's marriage law. In East Wind Village and other regions largely occupied by minorities, marriage practices linked with poverty were reclassified as "ethnic."

The Asian financial crisis and the Campaign to Open Up the West accelerated the local promotion of ethnic identity beginning in the mid-1990s. The extraction of western China's rich natural resources and the utilization of its diverse ethnic populations as a resource for tourism development were seen as beneficial to the national economy in several ways. Resource extraction could provide the power and water needed in China's developed east (Goodman 2004; Oakes 2007). The expansion of tourism created destinations for domestic consumption and economic growth. Additionally, this growth would ensure political stability in comparatively impoverished western China, which is populated largely by minority ethnic groups (ibid.). The shift in Lijiang's economy from the production of goods to tourism (hotels, souvenir shops, tourist attractions and services) dates from the devastating earthquake in the mid-1990s. Lijiang's rebuilding could be understood as "disaster capitalism," in which a catastrophic event was used to transform an old economic regime and introduce an economy guided by neoliberal principles (Klein 2007). This resulted in local reliance on a private-sector economy for the development of a tourist industry, with the hope that it would bring widespread prosperity. The transformation of Lijiang into a tourist destination required the creation not only of infrastructure for providing the transportation, accommodations, food, goods, and activities needed to facilitate opportunities for consumption; it also required the creation of a desire to consume on the part of Han tourists from urban centers as well as the willingness of local officials to reinvent Lijiang as a place and Lijiang people as a population that would play host to that consumption.

Throughout China, urbanization (chengshihua)—the expansion and concentration of economic development in cities—changed the lives of both farmers and city dwellers. Lijiang was no exception. It welcomed investors and attracted economic migrants from China's southwest (Yunnan and Sichuan), Jiangnan, Dongbei, and south China. Surrounding rural land was repurposed for hotels, tourist attractions, and luxury homes. Farmland was purchased and developed, often with only meager compensation paid to the farmers, while developers and unscrupulous officials reaped huge profits. Upward economic mobility for rural residents who had received Lijiang City residence permits, and for rural migrants without permits, usually meant either spending long hours driving a taxi or performing morally stigmatized labor as bar hostesses, massage parlor attendants, or sex workers. Most rural Naxi worked in town as low-paid maids, construction workers, menial laborers, entertainers, itinerant peddlers, cooks, or nannies. Along with rural migrants from Yunnan and Sichuan, they became an urban underclass. Tourism development disproportionately created low-paying jobs for young rural women, whose youth and exoticized ethnic bodies became a magnet for prosperous Han men from China's cosmopolitan centers (see Makley 2002; Hyde 2001; Schein 2000; Walsh 2005).

Meanwhile, rural Lijiang villages, like rural villages throughout China, were emptied of young people, leaving the elderly and middle-aged with the burden of farming without the labor of young people and caring for grandchildren whose parents had neither the time nor the resources to care for them in the urban centers where they worked.[1] Most of the younger villagers who remained either had young children, were disabled, or had insufficient education (primary school or less) and lacked the language skills necessary for finding jobs outside the village.

As entrepreneurs from other regions established businesses within Lijiang's Old Town, most of its former inhabitants sold their properties or became landlords and built houses on newly cleared farmland set aside for suburbs by the Lijiang government. Although a minority of Lijiang residents opened restaurants, or in some cases guesthouses, they complained that they could not compete with outside entrepreneurs. It was those with capital and resources to invest, such as the owners of hotels and expensive tourist attractions, who reaped the greatest economic benefits from the marketing of ethnicity and tourism in Lijiang (Young and Yang 2005). The wealthiest investors do not live in Lijiang but have homes in other parts of China or abroad, and their Lijiang businesses are often only one of many ventures.[2] Unlike the Lijiang officials connected with tourism and the local entrepreneurs who have prospered, the largest beneficiaries of Lijiang's new economy were already wealthy. Hence the new postsocialist economy, rather than creating prosperity for a broad section of the population, has facilitated the upward movement of wealth (see Harvey 1989).

The development of Lijiang into a center for tourism left residents ambivalent. Social and economic fluidity led to the reordering of prestige in Lijiang Town. The old distinctions between the remaining urban state-sector workers and upwardly mobile workers with rural origins began to blur. Taxi driver stories warning of bodily pollution, circulated by downwardly mobile urbanites, sought to reestablish older forms of prestige that had been eroded by the new economy. Narratives of bodily essence were articulated in a national arena in which analogous ideas about ethnic kinds and (urban and rural) body quality explained reform-era hierarchies.

In the twenty-first century, Lijiang's Old Town has ceased to be a residential community of primarily Naxi residents and is now essentially a hub of tourist activity populated largely by outsiders and merchants who run most of the shops and hotels. The prevalence of outsiders capitalizing on Naxi ethnic tourism created tensions in Lijiang. Former residents of Old Town complained bitterly that outside entrepreneurs are often rude to local Naxi or Lijiang residents despite profiting from the marketing of Naxi culture. The commodification of culture informed local views that Naxi and Lijiang culture should be treated like property; in one instance, a Lijiang court ruled that a scholarly critique that diminished the market value of Naxi music warranted financial compensation. In order to address complaints that local people were being excluded from the economic benefits of tourism, an initiative establishing a minimum quota of businesses owned by Lijiang residents was proposed but was ultimately rejected (Su and Teo 2009).[3]

Despite the growing dissatisfaction among many urban residents, the neoliberal discourse reigns.[4] Questioning the virtues of the market economy is unimaginable because economic development is envisioned as the means of connecting Lijiang with the "grid of modernity."[5] Consistent with Dengist-era rhetoric, the prosperity of developers and entrepreneurs is embraced by many as a model for future local prosperity. Neoliberal logic assumes that any problems created by the market economy can be solved only by more market expansion.

The extent to which local understandings are informed by the hegemony of neoliberalism was apparent during a meeting of the International Advisory Committee of UNESCO's Memory of the World Program in 2005. After *dongba* script was selected for the Memory of the World Register, Lijiang was asked to host the meeting's delegates (i.e., cover the costs of lodging, conference, and entertainment). The Memory of the World Program consists primarily of librarians charged with the identification of textual sources for preservation and global access. During the final day of the meeting, Lijiang officials asked the UNESCO delegation for guidance in the use of *dongba* text for economic development. A lengthy exchange took place during which frustrated UNESCO delegates reiterated that the Memory of the World Program was not concerned with the potential economic uses of *dongba* texts and that they could not provide funds beyond those already granted for recording and digitizing the texts. It was abundantly clear that the Lijiang government envisioned *dongba* script primarily as a vehicle for the profitable accumulation of capital.[6] This misunderstanding illustrates how, in the postsocialist era, the value of cultural resources is structured by market logic, and the promotion of heritage and capitalist development have been one and the same.[7]

While the putative aim of development has been to benefit Lijiang residents, the result has been extremely uneven. For Lijiang's poorest and most vulnerable residents, development has actually lowered the standard of living and increased the gap between these primarily rural residents and their more prosperous urban neighbors. In evaluating how tourism has benefited Lijiang's residents, it is also important to include the effects of urban development on rural Lijiang.[8] Luxury golf courses and five-star resorts were built on land that was once rural, and the former inhabitants have not benefitted from the wealth generated by the new projects. As the countryside is increasingly converted to luxury homes and residential suburbs, proponents of development imagine that young rural migrants now performing the lowest-paid jobs on the lowest rungs of the urban economic ladder are somehow the beneficiaries of development. The negative effects of Lijiang's new economy are perhaps most conspicuously demonstrated in places like East Wind, the basin village in which the madman lived and died.

THE MADMAN YEARS LATER

People from outside think this is a rich village. This village is like a squash with a thick skin. On the outside it looks good, but the interior is rotten—infested with bugs.
—Elderly East Wind Man

The madman of East Wind Village died in 2003. After the shaman's ritual, villagers would occasionally give the madman a couple of "steamed buns" (*mantou*), which enabled him to get by. Zheng, a village intellectual, insisted that the madman wasn't completely mad but rather emotionally fragile, with moments of lucidity. He recalled that the madman's condition had improved after the ritual, but then a number of incidents led to his further deterioration.

Two of the village's "old bachelors" (*lao er tou*) began hassling the madman. Zheng recounted: "They were bored, and it was a form of entertainment for them. . . . They would throw sand on the madman's house at night, and this terrified him. His fear turned to craziness, and he wasn't able to farm." Fu, one of the madman's relatives and also the village leader, claimed that the madman was dangerous to others and locked him in his own courtyard. The madman, his wrists and ankles bound, criticized his relatives by loudly singing an aria performed by the imprisoned hero in *The Red Lantern* (a well-known Cultural Revolution opera). Hearing this song of complaint day after day prompted some villagers to take action. They liberated the madman and circulated criticism about his relatives throughout the village. Afterward, with care from a few friends in the village, the madman appeared to recover and began farming again.

But his house was damaged by the 1996 earthquake, and an inspection determined that it was uninhabitable. The local government assessed the damage, and the madman was supposed to receive ¥5,000 (about $760) to rebuild his house. Given the madman's fragile condition, Fu agreed to rebuild the house, but instead, he took the money and did nothing. The madman slept on bedding outside his condemned house, his condition worsened, and he intermittently expressed himself through operatic complaint. He survived like this for years, working and not working, sometimes better and sometimes worse. In the end, he lived by scavenging out of the village trash heap, which consisted largely of rotting vegetables. Ultimately, he became sick and was found dead in his courtyard in 2003. During his last months, he regaled the village with a Beijing Opera aria in which the hero rages against injustice in the kingdom.

Not all the villagers felt the same way about the madman. In 2007, many East Wind Village residents, particularly the younger ones, described the madman as "honest, simpleminded, stupid" (tai laoshi). Describing his situation as pitiful, other villagers explained that it was not their responsibility to care for him, that they had their own households and families to care for. These attitudes articulated a shift from the socialist to the postsocialist era, in which new ideas about sociality and subjectivity delineated the domains of the public and the private.

In the early 1990s, villagers still conceived of themselves as members of a moral community, a collectivity responsible for the welfare of its members. The madman's situation—his behavior, his poverty, his exploitation by his relatives, and his helplessness—was perceived as a public dilemma. When villagers mobilized the madman's relatives to hold the ritual for him, their actions were informed by a notion of what constituted the public domain. The madman's problem was considered not a private matter to be ceded to his kin but a situation that righteously demanded collective public action. The dismantling of state-sector agriculture that began in Lijiang in the 1980s did not immediately correspond to the termination of a social subjectivity in which villagers imagined themselves as part of a collective community. This was evident in the very words that the villagers used: for example, in the 1990s, they still referred to "production teams" (sheng chan dui), even though production teams had not existed for a decade.

But in the next two decades, the postsocialist economy destabilized ideas of what constituted "the public." Tending to one's own household articulated

FIG. C.1 The madman's grave in East Wind Village

a new hegemonic model of subjectivity. Even after the madman's death, the villagers' representation of his misfortune continued to change. A championing of self-sufficiency could be discerned in new characterizations in which the madman's problem was no longer thought of as a demon-induced madness but portrayed as some sort of personal defect. He was seen as a victim of his own "honesty," a notion bound up with naïveté and simplemindedness and, more recently, equated with stupidity. The madman had been "stupid" for trusting Fu, whose self-serving behavior was viewed not as morally aberrant but as in some sense consistent with a different construction of human nature. In this model of human nature, a person devoted to the maximization of his own material advantage was not problematic but clever and enterprising. Fu had played the part of a responsible kinsman by having the madman cremated, and therefore most villagers did not question his right to claim his relative's property: his damaged house, his land, and his money. Villagers who had fed the madman were locally understood as having acted as individuals based on their personal or household relationship with him rather than as people sharing a village responsibility.

The perception of Fu's behavior as unproblematic extended to his actions toward other villagers as well. Fu was the former village leader of East Wind. Han, an elderly villager, recounted how "the government wanted capitalism to come," so they were told to rent out one hundred mu (16.5 acres) of their best land far below market price instead of planting plum trees on it. Fu talked the villagers into renting this land to an entrepreneur who wanted to build a brick factory. Most of the young people did not want to farm, and Fu persuaded the villagers that building a brick factory would enable the young people to have paid jobs and allow the village to prosper. But his plan didn't work out that way. The village's best agricultural land ended up being used for a brick factory that employed only a few villagers at low pay. The money the villagers had been promised for handing over their land disappeared, and there was no record of the transaction. Villagers were angry, but they felt helpless. As Han put it, "People are angry, but people still can't speak up. This is a problem of Chinese law." He said that only the former village leader "knows the law; it is useless to speak up." More than a decade passed, and none of the villagers had been compensated for their shares of the land that had been used for the brick factory. The remaining farmland is not suitable for growing rice, and the villagers worry about the safety of their irrigation water, which they believe has been polluted by the factory. Meanwhile, Fu left East Wind

Village and moved to Lijiang Town. When recounting the story of the factory venture, most villagers were reluctant to blame Fu or even say he was in any way responsible. A sense of exploitation informed some accounts of what had happened, but taking action as a village or as individuals was unthinkable.

Zheng, a middle-aged man who had once been close friends with Fu, had a different interpretation of the madman's death:

Every place has a person who seems innocent or "stupid" but is actually gifted in another way. Those who knew his history could see that he was unusual; he had met and learned from exceptional people. When the madman was a young shepherd, he met a military officer who had studied Russian, and he learned from him. Then he met a college graduate from Jilin University who taught him Beijing Opera. When the madman was young, books fed him. Once he sang, he wasn't thirsty. Once he read, he wasn't hungry. He was talented; he could sing anything after hearing it only once!

. . . He married a beautiful girl, but they were poor, and his mother did not let her have enough to eat. When his wife was hungry, he sang a song about her hunger from the Cultural Revolution opera *White-Haired Girl* [Baimao nü]. It is said that if you endure eighty-one disasters, after having so suffered, one's future should be good. He suffered so much, but this did not happen. Good things died with him. When will we [the villagers] recover these good things, humanity [ren dao] and justice [tian dao]? The village should think about this question. The madman was a generous person who taught others about farming as well as about culture—songs and history. He was good to others and had a deep understanding of people. A person like this lived the life of an ant or a fly. From his spirit, could we not see good things? Every house has its ancestors [apuzi]. His house had them, too. What kind of world is this that the good are vanquished and the bad succeed? We should not forget him.

Zheng appeared to be chastising the village, criticizing what it had allowed to happen and what it had become. His criticism implied that the village, which was once a social body capable of collective public action, had lost its ability to provide for the welfare of its members. For Zheng, the madman's life was both tragic and charmed; he magically overcame thirst and hunger by singing and reading. Zheng's account of the madman combined frag-

FIG. C.2 East Wind brick factory

mented frames of reference: Cultural Revolution opera; a genre of folktales about magical beings and injustice dating from antiquity; and prerevolutionary practices associated with household fertility and reproduction that were reintroduced by *dongba* who performed marriages in the village in the early 1990s.[9] In Zheng's interpretation, the madman presented a pastiche of different ways of being and sociality. The madman might have been respected in another community or in the same community during the 1990s. But in the twenty-first century, he was a person out of time and place; he was "stupid" and had been forced to live the life of an insect.

In Zheng's view, the village community was responsible for having failed to save the madman. Having forgotten older conceptions of value, the village had ceased to exist as a cohesive social body. Yet Zheng's references to other valued ways of being did not engage in the idealization of any particular past. Martyrs of the Cultural Revolution and the gifted heroes of ancient folk legends also lived in worlds fraught with conflict and injustice. Was the story of the madman a critical commentary on the history of all humankind, or only a village tragedy?

Zheng's remarks about Fu and the brick factory struck a similar chord of ambivalence. Zheng, too, had lost land in the factory scheme, and, like the others, he had never been compensated for his land as promised. Yet he insisted that he would not seek compensation. He felt that Fu should pay the villagers for their land, but if this didn't happen, he—like the villagers—would do nothing about it. Zheng denied that his inaction was due to fear and insisted he had no desire to maintain social connections with Fu, since they no longer spoke to each other. Why then did Zheng and the villagers tolerate this situation?

The villagers' accounts, taken in sequence, suggest that they may be understood as related parables. The madman was considered responsible for his own livelihood, so the injustices he suffered at the hands of his relatives were perceived as his own fault. By the same logic, villagers who lost land to the former village leader's factory scheme were responsible for allowing Fu (the same person who had exploited the madman) to exploit them. For some villagers, the "stupidity" of the madman bitterly echoed their own experiences at Fu's hands.[10]

As in Lijiang Town, state discourse had identified privatization and entrepreneurship as the new forces and models of change for East Wind Village. But these ideas were in tension with the experiences of villagers. They did not prosper, nor would they seek to emulate Fu. Some villagers had made a pragmatic calculation and concluded that "Chinese law" would not permit them to successfully challenge someone like Fu and recuperate their losses. Perhaps most influential in creating resignation, however, was their internalization of the postsocialist model of self-responsibility, which argued that the villagers had only themselves to blame, rather than the village leader who had defrauded them of their land.[11]

WHAT DOES THE FUTURE HOLD?

Although the state has developed plans for market expansion in the twenty-first century, it has—to use Li Zhang and Aiwa Ong's phrase—governed "from afar" (2008). The hegemony of neoliberal discourse fuels the local conviction to embrace the market economy. In places like Lijiang, the local government, interpreting central state directives, facilitated economic restructuring by welcoming entrepreneurs and subsidizing them in the project of developing a privatized economy and economic ventures that were not subject to regulation or oversight. The extent to which the welfare of Lijiang's inhabitants, including its rural inhabitants, has been negatively affected by such ventures is not relevant to the neoliberal measure of success, which takes into account only the accumulation of profits and regional economic growth. Instead, neoliberal economic policies in China, as elsewhere, have further contributed to the "polarization of wealth" (see Ortner 2011).

The phenomenon of disproportionate poverty in ethnic minority regions has been used as justification for further development. Government white papers have outlined poverty alleviation plans. The solutions proposed in these documents identify the lack of infrastructure and the need for more economic development. This economic development has entailed preferential policies for foreign investors in minority-occupied regions much as the Campaign to Open Up the West advocated Han migration to minority areas as beneficial for ethnic groups. Oddly absent in these white papers are any incentives that will provide advantages to members of minority ethnic groups as investors or leaders in local economic development. The white papers indicate that the government will provide subsidies for the production of ethnic goods for everyday use. It is unclear, however, who will profit from these subsidies and if these items of everyday use will also make their way into the circuit of ethnic artifacts marketable to tourists. Is the subsidization of everyday ethnic-minority goods intended simply to produce more visible markers of ethnic group difference in terms of clothing and material culture? Or will subsidies guarantee lower prices for local customers? In any case, the white papers appear to suggest that the proper role for ethnic groups is to use more ethnic goods, whereas leadership in creating a privatized economy will come from overseas investors or migrating Han entrepreneurs.

What then is the state hoping to achieve for China's ethnic groups in these plans outlined in government white papers and development initiatives? Where do ethnic groups fit in? An understanding of the larger framework informing state strategies may be gained by examining the recent promotion of the Ancient Tea Horse Road.[12]

THE ANCIENT TEA HORSE ROAD AS NEW ANTIQUITY

The Ancient Tea Horse Road (Chamagudao) is one of the newest forms of antiquity being marketed in Lijiang and Yunnan. The road intersects with Lijiang's history as a market town because Naxi muleteers once used this road to transport goods from China to as far away as Lhasa and Kalimpong, India.

The sale of tea and the Ancient Tea Horse Road have recently been a focus of tourism in Lijiang. In the past five or so years, teashops and stores selling Pu'er tea have appeared on virtually every street in the heart of Lijiang's tourist trade. The Road's importance is recited by practically every tea merchant and tourist guide in Lijiang. In the Old Town, saddled horses and horse-driven carts provide rides for tourists, giving them the opportunity to simulate the experience of traveling the Ancient Tea Horse Road. In fact, the Ancient Tea Horse Road had little to do with exclusively equestrian traffic. While horses may have used the trail, caravans generally consisted of mule trains bearing trade goods. "Horse road" was the idiom used for all roads. The act of walking across the street, expressed as "cross a horse road" (guo ma lu), does not imply that the pedestrian always has a horse in tow. Certainly trade had been central to the economy and culture of Lijiang during the Sino-Japanese War and long before that. But why should the historicization of the road be seen as so essential now, in the twenty-first century?

The discursive trail of the Ancient Tea Horse Road is perhaps easier to follow. In 1994, Tian Zhuangzhuang, the acclaimed fifth-generation film direc-

FIG. C.3 Monument to the Ancient Tea Horse Road

tor, made *Tea Horse Road Series: Peace Angel* (Chamagudao xilie: Delamu). The mid-1990s marked the beginning of state projects designed to encourage domestic tourism in China. In the early twenty-first century, Pu'er tea, the brick tea made in the Pu'er region, became a major tourist good in Lijiang. Pu'er tea was a caravan trade good transported on the Ancient Tea Horse Road. It has been consumed in Lijiang because the Naxi, like the Tibetans, use it to make yak butter tea.

In 2004, a Tea Horse Road Museum opened in Suhe, a former rural village that had been converted into a tourist town. The fairly large museum houses only a sparse collection of artifacts and is devoted mainly to historical exhibits narrating the importance of the Ancient Tea Horse Road from the time of the Tang dynasty.[13] Several pictures of Communist Party officials and government dignitaries bear captions extolling the road's historical importance. In other exhibits, scholars liken the importance of the Ancient Tea Horse Road to the Silk Road. The museum features displays of Pu'er tea and offers opportunities to sample and purchase the tea. More than the museum's contents, however, its size (incorporating several buildings, courtyards, and a former school) suggests the political significance of the Ancient Tea Horse Road to the museum's goal of public education and the recrafting of local and national memory. Interestingly, 2004 was also the year stock market shares in Pu'er tea began skyrocketing, which led to a hoarding of shares that continued until prices finally dropped in 2007 (Chung 2007; Jacobs 2009). The inflated value of these shares appears to suggest that there was the expectation in China that Pu'er tea could become an "instrument of economic speculation" (see Harvey 1989 and 2005). The Pu'er tea bubble is consistent with what David Harvey has referred to as the "financialization" associated with neoliberalism (Harvey 2005, 161).

In 2007, the Ancient Tea Horse Road Culture Institute was established at Yunnan University to study "Tea Horse Road Culture." That same year, the Simao District, the name of the region since 1950, changed its name back to its original name, Pu'er, which dated from 1729. The name change concretized the region's ties with both Pu'er tea and the Ancient Tea Horse Road.

The concept of a road possessing culture is, in and of itself, interesting. It is particularly interesting given that the road traverses China, Tibet, Nepal, and India. Establishing ties to new territory often begins with the assertion of a common cultural heritage in a geographic region.[14] The State Administration for Cultural Heritage generously funded Mu Jihong, a Yunnan University literature professor (who is, incidentally, Naxi), to conduct a large-scale research project on the cultural heritage of the Ancient Tea Horse Road. On June 2–4, 2010, the National Bureau of Cultural Relics and the People's Government of Yunnan held the Ancient Tea Horse Road Heritage Protection conference in Pu'er. The conference concluded with the ratification of the Pu'er Declaration, which called for all levels of government and society to work toward preservation of the Ancient Tea Horse Road. It is unclear what the potential ramifications of the declaration will be for Lijiang and Yunnan residents living along the soon-to-be-preserved route. The so-called "preservation" of Lijiang's Old Town resulted in its being emptied of the majority of its original Naxi inhabitants and transformed from a vibrant community into a tourist hub.

Thus far, sites along the Tea Horse Road have not been developed and in Lijiang people have no idea where the road is. However, on July 6–8, 2010, a similar Ancient Tea Horse Road Culture Symposium was held in Lijiang. Ning'er County, the road's trailhead, has planned to hold an annual Ancient Tea Horse Festival in order to promote tourism and an understanding of the road's significance. In 2009, a Sichuan University scholar published an article on Tea Horse Road architectural relics that details specifically how the road meets specific UNESCO World Heritage criteria (Darragon 2009). In addition, the Tea and Horse Road Institute has submitted an application to UNESCO for selection as a World Heritage site.

There is no doubt that the Ancient Tea Horse Road was a historic trade corridor between southwest China, Tibet, and south Asia, but is the project to preserve the road as a UNESCO World Heritage site simply about history and heritage? What is at stake in preservation and memorialization?[15] Will such projects have the effect of empowering local governments to require citizens to vacate new heritage sites in the interests of preserving or developing collective cultural heritage or fostering economic development?

In a *People's Daily* article dated October 8, 2010, Wang Junzheng, Lijiang Communist Party Secretary and mayor of Lijiang, described "opening up" as having enabled Lijiang to shake off "poverty and backwardness." By "opening up," Wang was referring explicitly to two state projects: the Campaign to Open Up the West and the Bridgehead Strategy Plan. The metaphors used in both projects are redolent of the language of earlier times. "Opening up" of the west echoes the discourse of Qing expansion, which was articulated as the "opening of land" (*kai di*), which suggested the seemingly benign commencement of agricultural cultivation as the motivation behind imperial expansion.[16] The name Bridgehead Strategy is less veiled. The term "bridgehead," defined as a defended area extended into hostile territory or a foothold for operational maneuvering, is more blatant about the potential conflict of political interests involved in China's economic expansion, via Yunnan, into south and southeast Asia.

This focus on the memorialization of the Ancient Tea Horse Road, coming at a time when Yunnan is seeking to develop more tourism sites and China is seeking to make market inroads into south Asia, is not accidental. The designation of the Tea Horse Road as a UNESCO World Heritage site has the potential to give visibility to towns situated along the road, enabling the development of their economies through tourism. But it is uncertain if it will be the inhabitants of these areas who will profit. Moreover, the international recognition of the Ancient Tea Horse Road as a World Heritage site may be driven by more than local economic development. Its development would enhance the narrative of a rich shared history and cultural interchange—among China's border regions, Nepal, and India—at a historical moment when China needs good will in order to expand trade and political influence in those areas. Scholars of politics refer to the sort of cultural initiatives meant to forward the construction of political relationships as "soft power."

In a speech delivered in July 2010, Hu Jintao, the current paramount leader of the People's Republic of China,[17] stated that the Bridgehead Strategy Plan would take advantage of Yunnan's location to connect China with south and southeast Asia. Hu described the plan as seeking to promote "friendly relations with [China's] southern neighbors" but ultimately to "extend China's economic and political reach beyond the region toward the Indian Ocean, the Middle East, and even Africa" (Lu and Chong 2010, 2). Recently, Chinese trade and market expansion into southeast Asia has been facilitated by rail and air connections from Yunnan, but attempts to connect south Asia with southwest China have proceeded more tentatively due to a history of tensions dating back to the Sino-Indian border war of 1962 and the Cold War. In 2006, China and India reopened the Nathu La, the China-India border crossing through Tibet. The recent interest in the Ancient Tea Horse Road cannot be understood apart from China's desires to reestablish trade connections between Yunnan and south Asia. In July 2011, in a two-page advertisement taken out by the Chinese government in the *New York Times*, Yunnan's governor Qin Guangrong is quoted as stating that Lijiang, Dali, Xishuangbanna, and Shangrila have all been targeted for tourism expansion based on their "ethnic cultures." Qin refers to plans that stress expanding international tourism to Yunnan and creating transportation infrastructure that will connect Yunnan via highway with China's coastal cities and south Asia. Official recognition of the Ancient Tea Horse Road, the trade route that once connected China, Tibet, Nepal, and India, provides opportunities for accentuating a history of cultural connection for the purposes of current and future Chinese interests in the south Asian region. The memorialization and cultural preservation of Ancient Tea Horse Road sites serve to celebrate a road with shared historical significance to China, Nepal, and India. Privileging a road that bisects a common cultural space blurs, and potentially extends, the boundaries of both south Asia and southwest China in ways that create possibilities for the extension of China's economic and geopolitical influence.

This book has sought to interrogate biopolitical projects of ethnic essentialization by locating them in the larger discursive arenas where they have been promoted. What is perceived as "ethnic" is embraced as an element of identity and a means of advancing the economies and rights of groups who participate in these projects. The sincere motivations behind projects of ethnic essentialization undertaken by groups that seek to improve the livelihoods of those they represent are not in question.[18] Rather, I hope to make visible, in these stories of people and places, the logic and unforeseen consequences of biopolitical categorization. While market models of development carry the promise of prosperity and poverty alleviation, ethnic tourism and development often fail to deliver benefits to a broad cross-section of the population.

A fuller understanding of what is at stake in the creation of "the ethnic" requires us to locate these projects in the state's representational order and postsocialist market economy (informed by a neoliberal ideology that privileges privatization and capital growth), and to understand how they fit with China's strategic aims in the twenty-first century.

NOTES

Introduction

1 Throughout this book I refer to Lijiang as Lijiang Town. Technically, Lijiang is administratively classified as a city, composed of an Old Town (Dayanzhen) and a new city (*xincheng*), a newer urban section with more modern architecture. That said, when Lijiang residents use the term Dayanzhen they may be referring to either the Old Town alone or the entire city. Despite the administrative classification, urban and rural Lijiang residents rarely use the name "Lijiang City."

2 The second Mao cult of the late 1980s to early 1990s was fueled in part by the Chinese Communist Party's seventieth birthday (Barmé 1996).

3 With its graceful Song dynasty architecture, willow-lined streams, and cobblestone streets, Lijiang's Old Town has become a major tourist destination in China.

4 Not all stores treated Red Culture in the same way. One store sold notebooks, matches, aprons, and mugs decorated with images from the Cultural Revolution but coupled these images with satirical comments. A notebook cover featured Barack Obama dressed as a PLA soldier and the slogan "Serve the people!" A man's apron was decorated with the image of a young Cultural Revolution zealot and the implicitly sexist message "I serve my wife."

5 Colin Mackerras attributes the rise in ethnic identity to a reaction against forced assimilation during the Cultural Revolution and links the phenomenon to "pride in one's culture" and resentment of Han chauvinism (1995, 214). David Wu, alternatively, explains the intensification of ethnic expression as having been stimulated by official state promotion (1990, 9).

6 I have made the similar observation that the attribution of a particular practice to an ethnic group may cloud our ability to recognize that such practices might be common to an entire region (Chao 1996).

7 Recent historical works address this absence (see Crossley, Siu, and Sutton 2006; Perdue 2005).

8 In terms of rural and ethnic coding, I refer to the discursive power of these categories and do not claim that they negated all forms of mobility for those categorized as "rural" or "ethnic." In addition, it should be noted that ethnicity has also been disembodied or detached from ethnic others and deployed as a "sign" in marketing.

9 Su Xiaokang's *River Elegy* (Heshang), a television series shown nationally in 1988, illustrates what could be called a biopolitical differentiation of urban and rural Chinese populations.

10 Naomi Klein (2007) describes "disaster capitalism" in the wake of the Asian financial crisis although largely in reference to Southeast Asia and South Korea. China reacted quickly to the crisis and was the only country in Asia not ravaged by it (Klein 2007, 269).

1. The Maoist Shaman and the Madman

1 All village names and most proper names are pseudonyms. The names of public figures have not been changed.

2 While the Naxi nationality officially includes the Mosuo, a subgroup that contests its categorization as "Naxi," I conducted my research among informants who identify themselves as Naxi. The Mosuo areas are adjacent to, but geographically distinct and separate from, Naxi-populated areas. The designation Autonomous Prefecture is based on the demographic dominance of a particular ethnic group in that region. Autonomous areas were established in 1949 in order to both cultivate the expression of ethnic characteristics and integrate ethnic groups into national culture. The Chinese borrowed this system of autonomous areas from Soviet practice, but, unlike the former Soviet republics, the Chinese autonomous areas have no implied right to secede and are considered an inalienable part of China (Dreyer 1976, 262). These designations do not imply juridical autonomy and are simply the state governmental structures used in minority areas.

3 The post-liberation era was divided into the collective period (collectives were the administrative units under which the state merged all agricultural holdings in 1955 and organized all agricultural labor until 1980), roughly corresponding to the Maoist era (1949–76), and decollectivization, roughly corresponding to the post-Mao era (1976 onward).

4 Just as particular villagers who rejected Maoism had once been true believers and some villagers who had resisted a national identity later accepted it, subjects may be understood as having pluralized subjectivity, that is, stratigraphic layers of subjectivity as they live through history.

5 According to Spence, "the Lei Feng spirit is the Communist spirit, the spirit of serving the people wholeheartedly, and the spirit of warmly loving the Party wholeheartedly, the spirit of warmly loving the motherland and socialism, of studying painstakingly, of waging arduous struggle, of being selfless, and of taking pleasure in helping others . . . as defined for the PLA Political Department senior CCP [Chinese Communist Party] leaders during the Lei Feng Spirit Forum" (1990, 727). Patricia Ebrey describes Lei Feng as "a PLA icon of socialist sacrifice whose narrative is redolent of tales of virtuous exemplars dating from the imperial and pre-1949 eras" (1993, 382).

6 Residents of East Wind Village referred to the shaman as a *sanba*, a type of ritual practitioner dating from the prerevolutionary era. According to Rock (1959), who lived in the Lijiang basin but traveled widely in the Lijiang area, there were no longer any female shamans when he arrived in 1922 or when he left in 1949.

7 Isabel Wong has pointed out that many songs composed during the Sino-Japanese War were later used as a medium for expressing modern Chinese nationalism (1984, 142).

8 The Nationalists were the ruling party and government of the Republic of China, from 1911 to 1949. In 1949, Nationalist leaders fled to Taiwan, which continues to be called the Republic of China.

9 I do not know if the Bai have a similar history of resisting conscription during the 1930s and 1940s. Hsu, who studied the Bai in the 1930s, refers to a spirit tablet at a Bai temple erected in memory of brave Bai residents who died fighting the Japanese (1967, 168). This may support speculation that the Bai supported anti-Japanese efforts.

10 According to Yang Fuquan, the lyrics of the "Lawei" song recount the suffering of the Naxi during the Sino-Japanese War (Yang 1991, personal communication). "Lawei" is a archaic phonetic translation from Naxi to Chinese. In Chinese "lawei" has no meaning.

11 Cult followers were often sent to labor-education camps. Some were also forced to act as "death escorts" (*peisha*) and were made to stand on a platform in public holding the hand of a cult leader (*tou*) while the leader was shot in the head.

12 Generally speaking, the term "religion" should be prefaced by some discussion of the problematics associated with its use as a category and the ethnographic topography in which it is articulated. Asad (1993) has illustrated how elements of medieval Christianity were disavowed when an Enlightenment doctrine of critical reason redefined certain practices as "uncivilized" and outside the pale of Christianity as a "religion." David Scott similarly demonstrates that the distinction between Buddhism and spirit religion does not issue from Sinhala practices but, rather, is an artifact of colonial British preoccupations with marking such distinctions (1994). A similar case can be made for the distinction between practices labeled "religion" and those labeled "feudal superstition" in postrevolutionary China. In the construction of religion as a category, the Chinese state actually extends its authority to arbitrarily defining what constitutes "Buddhism," "Daoism," and the like. Local agents, however, had the last word in the struggle over categorizations. The tourist pamphlets describing Lijiang and the Naxi, dating from the late 1980s when the area opened to foreign travel, translated *dongba jiao* as the "*dongba* religious sect" (Tang and Jin 1988; Huang 1988). However, with the escalation in ethnic tourism in the 1990s, a number of glossy books on the customs and cultures of China's ethnic minorities were published (Lijiang Naxi Autonomous Prefecture 1990; Wanbao He 1992; Duanqi He 1993). These more extensive publications identify a key attribute of the Naxi ethnic group as *dongba* culture.

13 Generally, national and local projects asserting the boundedness of cultural categories must identify objective characteristics and historical narratives in order to support their existence. Thus, a category such as "*dongba* culture," once created, presents the illusion of historical depth around which to imagine "Naxi" identities and promote claims to ethnic autonomy and rights. As the substantial literature on the social construction of ethnic categories demonstrates, such categories are problematically treated as a priori entities and are more productively understood as the end points of the political processes that have led to their construction (Anderson 1983; Handler 1988; J. Jackson 1995; Chao 1996).

14 The Dongba Cultural Research Institute, located in Lijiang, is a government-funded research institute and branch of the Yunnan Academy of Social Sciences devoted to the task of translating and preserving *dongba* texts. While translation is the primary task of the institute, the resident scholars also conduct ethnological research and publish articles on Naxi cultural practices. The institute was founded by He Wanbao in 1981. Its scholars are considered some of the foremost authorities on Naxi culture.

15 For more on the concept of magical power, see Sangren 1987; Weller 1995; J. Watson 1988; and Duara 1988.

16 It could be argued that Mao's first apotheosis took place during the Cultural Revolution. His second apotheosis, in the 1990s, is referred to as "Mao fever" or the "Mao craze" (*Maore*) (Barmé 1996). Mao fever began with taxi talismans, continued with the development of Mao's hometown as a tourist attraction, and eventually took hold among avant-garde urban Chinese artists and their overseas Chinese counterparts. The second Mao cult began in Shenzhen, a free-trade zone and "the laboratory of post-Mao capitalist reforms" (Barmé 1996, 23).

17　When I returned to Lijiang town in 1995, Mao memorabilia, or "Maorabilia," in the form of taxi amulets, Mao buttons, and commemorative Mao fountain pens were being sold at both the open market, which caters to national and international tourists, and the government department store, where customers are local people. The presence of such items and their local buyers illustrates the continued association between Mao and magical power. As a testament to the prescient powers of the shaman, in 1997, six years after her ritual, many Lijiang taxis were sporting talismans with Deng's picture, some with Deng on one side and Mao on the other.

18　In order to control migration to urban areas, the state implemented the hukou system in 1958, whereby each citizen received a residence permit that assigned a residence in a rural area or in a particular town or city. Those without residence permits for towns and cities were not permitted to reside there, and people without residence permits were forced to buy grain at inflated prices and usually had no access to permanent housing. As Potter and Potter (1990) have noted, the residence system created a castelike hierarchy with rural residents on the bottom and an urban elite at the top. This system was still in effect during 1990–91, the time frame this chapter addresses. After the late 1990s, however, barriers to rural people working in cities began to erode, and the residence permit became less indicative of where one actually lived and worked. This is particularly the case for migratory rural workers who live in urban centers and constitute sizable "floating populations" (liudong renkou).

19　It should be noted that while both cases involve madmen, we cannot assume these men were marked by their madness in the same way. For many Naxi, madness does not exist as a distinct category. In these two cases, the reactions of villagers to "madness" resonate with differences between Western and Chinese medicine. A frequently made distinction between Western and Chinese medicine is that the former relies on "giant disease classes that lump syndromes together" while the latter attends to the peculiarities of "time, place, and person" (Farquhar 1996, 249). Some villagers described madness as an omen and not an affliction. When someone goes mad, it may not be a case of demonic interference but rather a sign that the afflicted is about to become a shaman, is on the verge of death, or is simply acting out of sorts. For these villagers, madness is not necessarily perceived as problematic in and of itself. In other cases, however, madness is interpreted as a secondary indication or symptom of a larger affliction, one that may not be contained within the parameters of an individual.

20　Although a daughter's fertility usually leaves the household when she marries, this would probably not have been true in this case. It is quite common for Naxi families to find men to contract uxorilocal marriages with their daughters. In the madman's household, because there was an infertile daughter-in-law (women are blamed for infertility) married to the only son, if the family's own daughter had lived, the parents probably would have found a husband willing to marry into their family as a means of ensuring their line of descent.

21　Since decollectivization, the low status of Communist Party officials was evident in such local sayings as "With the household responsibility system, who wants cadres?" and "With the household responsibility system, we don't want cadres" (Anagnost 1985, 94).

22　The shaman's ritual may still be evaluated as successful in the future. Her line of reasoning was consistent with that of other local shamans who have appeared in the Lijiang area since her ritual performance. In 1995, I visited another shaman who incorporated political slogans into her ritual exhortations and learned of the similar practices of two other such shamans. One of these women was regarded as mad, but the other was reported to be popular.

Chapter 2. *Dongba* Culture and the Authenticization of Marginality

1 Older *dongba* from mountain villages recalled that *dongba* religion came to a standstill during the Cultural Revolution, although the practices were permitted again in the late 1980s.

2 By 2011, most of the *dongba* who had practiced before the revolution had died. There are a handful of farmers practicing as *dongba* in the mountain districts, but the *dongba* in Lijiang Town are largely rural men holding tourism-related jobs. For many of these young men, learning *dongba* practices provided a way of leaving the countryside and making a living in an urban area. Some of them occasionally return to the countryside to visit their families and perform at funerals, but their employment is in Lijiang Town.

3 It should be noted that before Chinese contact, the Naxi cremated their dead and that contemporary *dongba* funerary rituals, which entail burials, suggest syncretism with Han ritual forms. The transition from cremation to burial took place at different times in different villages. During the Maoist era, cremation was encouraged, but in the post-Mao era, burials have once again become standard practice in most areas.

4 Chas McKhann, Li Ying, Li Lifen, and He Pingzhen (2007, personal communications) and Yang Fuquan (2003, 482) have conducted research in Baidi and in Muli, Sichuan. Their research will provide a fuller regional picture of contemporary *dongba* practice in these areas.

5 He Wanbao's college degree was from the Chinese department at Yunnan University. He was one of the few Naxi of his generation to receive a college degree.

6 *Wenhua* may be translated as "culture" or "civilization" depending on its context. I have translated the term as "civilization" here because it invokes the prestige associated with learning. Naxi scholars refer to the Naxi ethnic group both as having a "high cultural level" (*wenhua shuiping bijiao gao*) and as being a "civilized ethnic group" (*wenming minzu*) in comparison to ethnic groups without a written language.

7 The pictographic script was a regionally specific form of writing known only to *dongba* in the western and northwestern parts of Naxi territory, whereas the phonetic script was used by all *dongba*.

8 During the late imperial era, Naxi rulers were literate in Chinese, as were many urban elites in Lijiang Town, which had a number of Chinese schools.

9 A state minorities language project undertaken in the 1950s developed Naxi pinyin, a romanized script. According to White (1993, 37, 323), this script was used in the 1980s as part of an experimental program for elementary school children in rural areas but has been discontinued. Very few Naxi became literate in Naxi pinyin.

10 Rock's work was criticized during the Maoist era, but it has been acknowledged as a valuable source of documentation by Chinese and Naxi scholars since the post-Mao era. Like the founders of the Dongba Cultural Research Institute, Rock was attracted to *dongba* because they had their own form of writing, which set the Naxi apart from most other indigenous groups in Yunnan.

11 While Rock gave his collection of Naxi manuscripts to the Harvard-Yenching Library,

he was affiliated with the University of Hawaii, where he founded the herbarium, served as its curator, and was awarded an honorary doctorate.

12 In the 1980s, mountain villages were also told that it was again permissible to hold *dongba* rituals.

13 Male *sanba* continue to outnumber female *sanba* in the mountain areas. On rare occasions, shamans of other ethnic groups serve lowland Naxi communities. Local Bai and Han shamans tend to be female, which may explain why the feminized portrayal of the *sanba* is persuasive to the basin and adjacent town-dwelling Naxi.

14 Naxi scholars, however, have reported that there were female *sanba* practicing during Rock's time, though they were substantially outnumbered by male *sanba* (Yang Fuquan, personal communication, 1991).

15 The dictionary uses the phrase "does not use books" as opposed to using the label "illiterate," but in practice they were the same thing. *Dongba* were usually the only Naxi capable of reading indigenous script.

16 The dictionary was part of the resumption of social scientific studies of minorities that coincided with the national promotion of ethnic difference and specific post-Mao-era Naxi efforts to essentialize and articulate Naxi ethnicity.

17 The dictionary authors Fang Guoyu and He Zhiwu are, respectively, Chinese and Naxi, but as scholars trained in Chinese universities, their criteria for differentiation likely privilege Han scholarly values.

18 This distinction was a discursive creation. In a mountain village where I conducted research, one *dongba* claimed his wife could read almost as many *dongba* characters as he could.

19 See Makley (2002 and 2007) for a fascinating account of how the gendered essentialization of Tibetans during the reform era valorized particular aspects of masculinity that negatively impinged on Tibetan women.

20 Sydney White has similarly noted that in Lijiang Town, women are associated with "authentic" Naxi culture, whereas Naxi men mimic Chinese literati by "affecting the manner and habits of the Confucian gentleman scholar . . . tending one's flowers, drinking one's tea and/or grain alcohol, growing out the fingernail of one's little finger, and generally leading a life of leisure" (1993, 297, 300–301). She suggests that these constructions of gender and ethnicity indicate that individual Naxi men and women have appropriated state discourses of hierarchy and authenticity. Her interpretation with respect to Naxi men is persuasive in part because it elevates the urban Naxi men she describes with respect to the broader Chinese prestige system. There is less evidence, however, that Naxi women identify themselves as more authentically Naxi than Naxi men. I suggest that state and local constructions are both contemporary and rooted in imperial distinctions and creations.

21 It should be acknowledged that the Yuan dynasty was Mongol and the Qing dynasty was Manchu, and the two empires were separated by the Ming dynasty, which was a Chinese empire. I refer to the Yuan, Ming, and Qing dynasties with the term "Chinese empire" because these periods marked the beginning of imperial expansion and the sinicization of the southwestern ethnic groups. Although little is known about interactions between the Mu rulers (from whom the Naxi are descended) and the Yuan empire, during the Ming and Qing dynasties the Mu rulers were encouraged to adopt Chinese, not Manchu, marriage and burial rituals and to learn the Chinese language. The term

"Han" is not used to describe the Qing, because they were not Han, although they required Naxi rulers and later Naxi subjects to adopt Chinese practices.

22 The term "Naxi" is anachronistic but is used here for simplicity. The Naxi claim to be descendants of the Mu rulers who had tributary relations with the Yuan, Ming, and Qing empires. Imperial documents list the Mu as Mosuo, a group that has included the Naxi. Since the 1950s, this relationship has been reversed, and the Mosuo are considered part of the larger, officially recognized Naxi ethnic group.

23 It is unlikely, however, that the four schools opened in Naxi territory managed to attain this goal.

24 While the incorporation of Han practices varied across Naxi territory, it should not be assumed that all Naxi who adopted Han ways did so without coercion and to the exclusion of Naxi practices, or that the process did not yield new syncretic forms or subjectivities (Chao 1990; X. Zhao 1993).

25 After the development of tourism in Lijiang Town, more girls in rural areas have been attending school for more years, enabling them to emigrate to urban areas.

26 This is a point frequently made by Naxi scholars and officials.

27 Dongba religion appears closer to Daoism, which is accepted as a legitimate religious practice by the state. Sanba shamanism would be categorized as feudal superstition.

28 Access to dongba texts changed after they were recognized as a source of documentary heritage by UNESCO and placed on the Memory of the World Register in 2003. Now many texts are digitally available to all scholars, although this was not the case in the 1990s.

29 Swain (1990), Schein (2000), and Cheung (1995) discuss the link between the promotion of ethnicity and state and local efforts to develop tourism.

30 The house was later moved to another site in Heilongtan Park and is no longer associated with the institute.

31 I am grateful to Lisa Handwerker for calling this article to my attention.

32 The Lulu assert that they are the descendants of a union between a Naxi father and a Lisu mother. This origin story, however, does not account for their distinct language. Although the Lulu have dongba, their funerary ritual differs from that of the Naxi in the placement of the coffin.

33 Therefore, once a minority such as the Naxi has claimed the dongba, the Prmi cannot. The Prmi may, however, differentiate themselves by invoking the Hangui religion as different from dongba culture (Chao 1996; Harrell 1995). The cultivation of difference where common practices existed is clearly demonstrated in Wellens's new research on Premi in Ninglang and their counterparts (categorized as Tibetans) in Muli (2012, 209). The Premi (Prmi) have revived hangui/anji religious practices as key to their official minzu status as Premi, whereas the same group in Muli—classified as Tibetan—adheres to Tibetan Gelag Buddhism as the cornerstone of their minzu identity (Wellens 2010). These Muli and Ninglang groups share a common religious past in which both Tibetan Buddhism and Hangui ritual practices were important. However, what ethnic elites could articulate as their distinctiveness in the post-Mao era was determined not by this shared religious history but by the necessity of narrating distinct ethnic histories

34 The spatialized conceptions of authenticity among Naxi scholars corresponded to spatialized notions of "difference" in popular Naxi discourse. Sydney White (1993, 71) points out that the Naxi envision progress in terms of a geographic or spatial model

radiating out from Lijiang Town. The identification of town and basin Naxi as progressive and civilized (read "sinicized") and mountain Naxi as "backward" and "authentic" (i.e., not sinicized) corresponded to a similar distinction between plains and mountain aborigines in Taiwan (see Brown 1996). In the early 1990s, attempts by town and basin Naxi to represent themselves as somehow outside the category Naxi were part of a larger pattern among sinicized ethnic minorities throughout China of contesting their categorization as non-Chinese (Hsu [1948] 1967, 19; Moseley 1973, 41). This pattern may reflect the early hegemony of the Chinese prestige system. Earlier disavowals of Naxi authenticity among town dwellers have been reversed since the late 1990s and the growth of the tourist economy.

35 Sydney White also suggests that there is a paradoxical representation of the remote mountain areas as a romanticized zone of untouched indigenous Naxi authenticity and simultaneously a site of backwardness (1993, 71). Bulag (2003), Han (1995), and Upton (1995) make parallel arguments about the Mongolian and Tibetan grasslands being symbols of ethnic identity and sites of nostalgic return.

36 The Republican government established schools only in Lijiang Town and the surrounding villages, which were basin areas. In the 1933 census, 132,582 Naxi were registered in Lijiang District; 5,340 of the 68,216 males were literate in Chinese compared to 170 out of 64,366 females (cited in Rock 1963a, 29).

37 Only in the 1980s, with the rise of *dongba* culture, did literacy in Naxi become associated with status in limited scholarly circles. It was not uncommon to find elderly rural men capable of reading some *dongba* script, but this ability did not translate into a higher social standing in Naxi villages. An elderly *dongba* told me that his wife could read and write as well as he could but that this did not mean anything because, as a woman, she could never be a *dongba*. In other words, literacy was not a socially recognized ability separable from *dongba* practice.

38 Rock observed that even the plains between mountain peaks were occupied by Chinese except where the altitude prohibited agriculture (cited in Sutton 1974, 55).

39 I am not suggesting that all mountain Naxi were once basin inhabitants who were driven into the mountains as a result of imperial expansion. In one mountain village I visited, however, the inhabitants' ancestors had settled there only eight generations ago.

40 This characterization represents the situated view of imperial colonizers and the state, which shapes popular understandings of local history. Anyone who threatened the control of the state was subject to being labeled a bandit. Contrary to popular conceptions, Rock observed in the 1920s that the poor tribal areas located in the mountains were actually the safest, owing to the lack of anything to steal (cited in Sutton 1988, 94).

41 The association between minority-inhabited mountainous areas in Yunnan and banditry was still prevalent in official reports of the early 1950s (Moseley 1973, 43). While the mountains are no longer linked with banditry, they are still associated with danger, lack of civilization, backwardness, and poverty in both Han and Naxi popular discourse. According to popular perceptions in Lijiang Town and the basin, the mountain Naxi are backward, an assessment based on their relative poverty in comparison to other Naxi and visually confirmed by their dress. A young Naxi farmer from a Lijiang basin village told me that a common insult used to denigrate a peer is to call him *Nanshanren*, someone from Nanshan, meaning that he is backward. Nanshan is the mountain district closest to Lijiang Town and the basin villages that surround it.

42 Naxi scholars explain that the mountain Naxi have changed at a much slower rate than the town and basin Naxi, who have historically had more contact with the Han and are now sinicized (*hanhua*), and that the mountain Naxi have been able to preserve (*bao liu*) some Naxi practices in the same form as in ancient times. This explanation appears to suggest that relative isolation has sustained cultural differences. Yet the mountain Naxi have not lived in isolation. Their periodic appearances in the Lijiang Town marketplace are not a new phenomenon but part of a historical pattern of trade with and dependence on market centers such as Lijiang Town. As Fredrik Barth (1969, 9–10) has argued, the attribution of difference to isolation is not supportable because boundaries persist despite the flow of people across them.

43 Chen Kaige's *Yellow Earth* (Huang tudi) and Tian Zhuangzhuang's *Girl from Hunan* (Xiangnu xiao xiao) are two such films that present Chinese rural culture as an obstacle to change and progress. A clip from *Yellow Earth* was featured in *River Elegy*.

44 This may appear to conflict with evidence of ethnic boosterism among the Naxi. Naxi in Lijiang Town and Naxi scholars frequently extol the greatness of the Naxi relative to other groups and even the Han (see S. White 1993). In the 1990s, however, a sense of being inferior to the economically and politically dominant Han prevailed among the broader Naxi population. Moreover, the Naxi discourse of greatness and nostalgia reveals ambivalence on the part of its promoters. When Naxi scholars and officials residing in Kunming, the capital of Yunnan, or residents of Lijiang Town wax poetic about the Naxi past and the idyllic (authentically Naxi) life in the mountains, we should not assume that they would willingly trade places with their mountain counterparts.

45 For a discussion of the permeability of boundaries of difference during the late imperial era, see Dikötter 1992. During the imperial era as well as the Republican era (despite the division of the population into five "racial categories" [*zhongzu*]), notions of difference were popularly constructed along lines of religious practice and place and were mutable.

46 In Lijiang Town and in the rural basin in the early 1990s, Naxi men considered themselves "just like the Chinese" (comparatively sinicized and civilized). However, older women and mountain people, both of whom are associated with extreme difference and backwardness, were perceived as the true Naxi (Chao 1996; S. White 1997).

47 Ethnic essentialization created hierarchy at a discursive rather than an intentional level.

48 Many of these men were motivated to learn *dongba* practices because they were interested in making a living in urban Lijiang rather than remaining in their home villages and serving as ritual practitioners.

3. Ethnicizing Myth, Bride Abduction, and Elopement

1 It is significant that Coqsseililee's mentor is a rat. In Lijiang, "The Rat's Marriage" (Laoshu qu qing), the story of how the rat finds affinal kin, is well known and was embroidered on clothing during the Republican era.

2 In terms of *dongba* text, the Coqbbersa story is divided into two parts: "Coqbbertv," the search for a bride, and "Coqbbersa," learning to worship heaven.

3 Although the creation of *dongba* culture dates to the post-Mao era, it draws on the epistemology of evolutionary anthropology that reigned in China from the 1950s. Like the conclusions of nineteenth-century sociocultural evolutionary theorists, the most mar-

ginalized peoples were identified as living representatives of antiquity and valorized as living fossils.

4 Harrell was the first to critically represent the conquest and incorporation of non-Han groups into southwest China as a "civilizing project" (1995, 3). It is in the same sense that I use the term "civilizing."

5 Historians believe that the ancestors of the contemporary Naxi were part of a larger group identified in historical documents as the Mosuo, dating from the Ming and Qing dynasties (Chao 1996).

6 Apparently the Ming chronicles singled out the Mu chiefs for their mastery of Confucian classics (Zhang Daqun cited in Hansen 1999, 30).

7 Local officials faced punishment if they failed to educate their sons in Chinese schools, and they were charged with requiring commoners to attend these schools as well (Yang Qichang 1987, 29, cited in Hansen 1999, 31).

8 Bridewealth is also referred to as "bride-price." It consists of goods or money given by a groom's family to the bride's family as part of a marriage agreement.

9 By "Lijiang region" I refer to Naxi-occupied areas (including Lijiang Town, Lijiang basin villages and rural mountain villages)—what is now Lijiang Naxi Autonomous Prefecture. During the late imperial era, the term "Naxi" was not used in official documents, and the Naxi were identified as part of the Mosuo.

10 Group suicide by young women resisting marriage was practiced in southern China (specifically Guangdong) among Han as well (Peplow and Barker 1931, cited in Stockard 1989, 119, 120; also Chao 1990).

11 In some versions, the three groups are Tibetans, Naxi, and Bai.

12 Based on sixty household interviews, there were eleven cases of bride abduction in East Wind Village before 1949.

13 Bride abduction was considered youthful male activity. Informants told me that married (adult) men could not participate because abduction was associated with a recklessness attributable to, and only excusable in, boys who had not reached adulthood.

14 I was given three different explanations for this act. First, an outmarrying daughter is likened to water being poured from a basin. Once she leaves, there is no way to retrieve her, and pouring water on the abducted woman symbolically conveys this message. Second, one of the last tasks a daughter does before leaving her parents' courtyard to be the bride of another family is to wash her hair; hence, in bride abduction, the abducted woman is having her hair washed for her, signifying the end of her role as a member of her natal household. Third, in rural areas, touching water is symbolically associated with cooking and the role of the daughter-in-law, so when a strange woman touches the water of a new household, it suggests that she is destined to become its daughter-in-law. The symbolism associated with the first two explanations is identical with and appears to be derived from Han marriage practices (E. Ahern 1981).

15 In rural areas many abducted women described being locked up and left alone.

16 For much of the Republican era until the institution of the 1930 marriage law, marriage was governed essentially by Qing dynasty law, which meant that it was a contractual relationship between families. As Ocko (1991) notes, the 1930 law stated that coercion or sale of a daughter or daughter-in-law was forbidden but the acceptance of betrothal gifts did not constitute a sale. It appears that the Naxi seized on the difference between sales and marriage and the importance of betrothal gifts to the ratification of unions as

marriage. Practices such as bride abduction, which place emphasis on betrothal gifts, reflect local interpretations of the state's definition of marriage.

17 In some cases, the bride's family might send some sort of dowry, usually a set of clothes for their daughter, after accepting bridewealth from the groom's family.

18 It was virtually impossible to reverse child betrothal agreements. Other accounts of bride abduction during the Republican era among the southern Han and the Bai minority group similarly note the intractable nature of such agreements (cited in Stockard 1989, 124, 125; Hsu 1967, 91, 92). Such agreements were perceived as so permanent that one young Bai woman, aided by her sister, murdered her fiancé so that she could marry another man, because this was the only way the obligation could be nullified (Hsu 1967, 92).

19 In Lijiang Town, a portion of this bridewealth was customarily converted into "private money" (sifanqian) (lit., "private room money") and was used to teach a girl how to run a business. This was considered her money, but it was returned with the bride to her husband's home—albeit under her control—along with the remainder of the bridewealth that had been converted into dowry consisting of household goods that she brings to her new home (jiazhuang). Depending on their financial situation, the bride's family might have paid for the dowry with bridewealth, and more prosperous families may have substantially supplemented it. A larger dowry reflected positively on the prestige of the bride and her family. Dowries were displayed in the bride's natal courtyard during the days preceding the wedding and then transported to the groom's house in a procession with much fanfare. The public spectacle of the bridal procession underscores the importance of marriage ritual to household prestige.

20 When recounting the negative aspects of the old society, elderly informants often stressed child betrothal, whereas engagements frequently took place as late as sixteen years of age or older. In Lijiang Town, early engagements usually meant more bridewealth, suggesting that child betrothal may have been a strategy used by more prosperous families. In the basin village where I did fieldwork, many of the older women had been engaged at fifteen or even twenty, in contrast to engagements in Lijiang Town.

21 In Lijiang Town, widows were not abducted by unmarried men, who could always resort to marrying a woman from the countryside. In rural areas, widows tended to be abducted by widowers, but a young widow might be abducted by an unmarried man from an exceptionally poor family.

22 Naxi households were organized along the same lines as Han households. This meant that a corporate family, consisting of parents, married sons and their spouses, and unmarried children, might live together as a single economic unit with shared resources and housing. The exception to this rule was the dowry brought to the household by a married son's wife and her private money. Private money was completely controlled by the wife and became the property of the couple and their children after the household's assets were divided (cf. Cohen 1976; R. Watson 1991). The custom of private money was common among the Han during Republican-era China. In rural areas, large corporate families were rare, but in Lijiang Town, such families were not uncommon. There, many divided households shared a single courtyard, whereas in rural areas a son's marriage was often followed by property division and creation of a new household for the married son and his wife.

23 Families in Pagoda Hill Village practiced the levirate (in which a brother marries his deceased brother's widow), but it was considered a low-status form of marriage.

24 While this sort of bride abduction is not associated with the Han, the Han in Yunnan employed this strategy for the remarriage of widows (Osgood 1963, 285), and it was common among the neighboring Minjia (Bai) of Dali (Fitzgerald 1949, 76). Several authors have noted other instances of bride abduction among the Han (Gates 1996; Honig and Hershatter 1988; Mann 1997; McLaren 2001).

25 During the Republican era, marriage ceremonies in Pagoda Hill Village also included male and female go-betweens. Families invited a *dongba* to perform *siku*. During *siku*, the *dongba* would make offerings to the house god, symbolized by a "life basket" (*ssudu* in Naxi) representing the household's prosperity. The *dongba* would then dot the foreheads of the bride and groom with yak butter and read the *dongba* texts for the ceremony.

26 The go-between, symbolically portrayed as a crane that flies between heaven and earth, was a central figure in this form of social reproduction in which heaven and earth were literally united in marriage.

27 With regard to households facing financial hardship, see Ahearn 2001, 105; Bates 1974, 277; Brukman 1974, 312; Chao 1996, 216; Conant 1974, 322; Honig and Hershatter 1988, 359n13; Kudat 1974, 289; Lockwood 1974, 262; McLaren 2001, 957; Stross 1974, 340; and Werner 2009, 326; for disabled or otherwise stigmatized males, see Ahearn 2001, 106; Chao 1996; and Stross 1974, 342.

28 See Ayres 1974, 239; Bates 1974, 276; Brukman 1974, 308; Chao 1996; Conant 1974, 322; Fitzgerald 1941, 76; Lockwood 1974, 265; Stross 1974, 339. Many of these authors problematically conflate bride abduction and elopement. Such an interpretation is often based on the anthropologist's acceptance of the household's or the young man's point of view. Such analyses are often blind to important distinctions based on the woman's perspective.

29 According to the elders' account, farmers were required to feed the former Mu soldiers as they traveled through the Mu kingdom. Pagoda Hill was formerly a forest, but the soldiers found the land suitable for hunting and herding. They were also impressed with how quickly their seeds sprouted in the region, and thus they settled there.

30 Such contingencies, however, excluded families with physically or mentally disabled sons. I was told that the families of such men often resorted to trickery in which they enlisted a kinsman to represent himself as the potential groom during negotiations. In such cases, the hapless bride would discover the truth too late—after arriving at her new home—and her family had no recourse.

31 As Rock (1963a, 40) noted: "[T]he male population was always in excess of the female and not every boy was assured a wife."

32 In 1990, forty-one households identified sons or daughters as having married by elopement in a village consisting of sixty-five households. Girls were under the legal marriage age in eighteen cases and had reached the legal marriage age in seventeen. In the six remaining elopements, the age of the eloping wife was unknown but presumed by other villagers to have been under the legal marriage age.

33 The verb *pao* suggests agency, but it is the agency of someone in a position of weakness who must run, flee, or escape, in contrast to *ling*, which implies a position of superiority over someone who, like a child, is subject to being led, piloted, or guided.

34　For groups of young age-mates who congregated in Lijiang Town on Friday and Saturday nights near department stores, movie theaters, and outdoor ballrooms, courtship and romance were imbued with an aura of the modern. Pleasurable rendezvous in town broke the tedium of rural life but also provided opportunities for the refashioning and display of new, generationally based rural identities.

35　In the early 1990s, the Taiwanese pop tune "Go with Your Feelings" (Genzhe ganjue zou) was being played on basin village boom boxes everywhere and appeared to set the stage for the elopement craze. Young men claimed elopement was "new and modern" and complained that girls' parents "only look at money and not the person." Young women placed emphasis on the importance of a young man's "honesty, good looks, and ability to talk" and his "feelings for the girl."

36　New motivations for women were also pragmatic. In another case, a young woman visited one of her closest female age-mates who had eloped to a nearby village. During the visit, she was introduced to the eligible village men and selected one to marry. Then, so that her age-mate would not be blamed, she waited until the next festival before eloping so that no connection could be made between her elopement and her visit to her age-mate. Thus, preserving the friendship between village sisters played a significant role in one woman's marriage choice.

37　This was exemplified by an intravillage elopement in 1975, one of the earliest cases in East Wind Village. The young woman went home every day to check on her father. She eventually became the "village women's representative" (funü zhuren).

38　The hazing consists of much teasing, with pointed sexual innuendo, aimed at forcing the bride and groom to "become acquainted" with each other, and was derived from a model of matrimony in which bride and groom would meet each other for the first time on their wedding day. Though clearly not virgins (Wen was two months pregnant), the couple was nevertheless obliged to undergo this part of the marriage ritual.

39　Some in East Wind Village speculated that the Naxi had adopted the practice from the neighboring Bai ethnic group, with whom there was occasional intermarriage. East Wind is part of a region composed of Naxi and Bai villages. Male informants favorably compared Naxi to Bai elopement, which they characterized as greedy and money-oriented. Bai girls were described as particularly cunning about elopement; they were said to have bank accounts and to demand large sums of money (¥200–300) as a betrothal gift before entering a man's family courtyard. In the 1990s, it was common for Bai families to want an additional ¥1,000–2,000 to consent to the elopement. Young men and their families favorably characterized Naxi elopement because Naxi women and their families were not as demanding about money. The demonization of Bai girls as cunning was consistent with the national trend of blaming the high price of betrothal on women's greed (Honig and Hershatter 1988, 148). This comparison of Bai and Naxi elopements, based on the ultimate cost to a man's family, supports the theory that elopement was motivated by financial concerns.

40　Much of courtship for young people from the basin took place in town. Young girls disclosed that, when cruising the streets looking for potential "sweethearts" (duixiang), they considered only boys with bicycles (who were from the basin) and rejected boys from the mountains (identifiable by their lack of bicycles, since the mountains were so far away that they had to ride the bus).

41　Davis has noted that between 1989 and 1995, income inequality in China increased more quickly than in any other country tracked by the World Bank since the end of the Second World War (2005, 694).

42 While the Five Good Families Campaign began in the 1950s, it was emphasized on and off through the late 1990s. The Civilized Village Campaign dates from the post-Mao era and continued through 1992 in Lijiang.

43 According to Anagnost, the Civilized Village Campaign promoted "socialist morality" in order to harmonize tensions arising from growing material inequalities in rural areas since decollectivization and the return to a household-based economy. The Five Good Families Campaign, addressed at public forums such as village meetings and meetings for the elderly, sought to reinforce family relationships based on rank, age, and gender (1985, 81, 83).

44 A daughter who had "run off with a man" could only be perceived as illegitimate. Elopement was female agency that stood in opposition to the prestigious form of marriage, an institution historically requiring parental control or at least consent. At the same time, it was equated with romantic liaisons, desire, and sex detached from marriage. In terms of the symbolism of local gender and ritual discourse, the opposition of female : male corresponded to the parallel oppositions of sexuality : fertility (social reproduction) and illegitimate : legitimate (Bloch and Perry 1982, 19; Martin 1988, 165).

45 These guidelines were themselves vague: one should listen to parents and the state, register marriages, engage in courtship only when of legal age, and act in a civilized manner (i.e., not engage in premarital sex).

46 In contrast to the freedom of young people in Pagoda Hill, basin courtships took place with some degree of freedom in town, but girls feared parental disapproval and did not bring young men to their homes or openly engage in courtship in the village. In the 1990s, parents were the ultimate arbiters of potential husbands, and the only way to bypass parental disapproval was to elope.

47 The poorest households often did little more than apologize for elopements, while households with more economic resources (such as that of Wen and Jiao) went to great lengths to ritualize elopement by adding bridewealth, negotiation, fetching the bride, hazing, banquets, and the like.

48 This might have been the case because even the most well-to-do households simply lacked the expendable resources for such displays.

49 The 2001 marriage law allowed exemptions based on the ethnic practices of recognized ethnic minorities.

50 For instance, impoverished Han areas where similar strategies were practiced could not apply for these exemptions.

51 If the seeds that Ceiheeqbbubbeqmil and Coqsseililee obtained from Ceiheeqbbub-beqmil's parents are any indication, the soldiers received agricultural assistance from their in-laws.

52 After the 1949 revolution and throughout the Maoist era, marriage in Lijiang was still largely parentally arranged, with varying levels of consent on the part of sons (usually more) and daughters (usually less). The 1950 marriage law guaranteed freedom of marriage and proscribed parentally arranged marriages. Bridewealth, explicitly associated with purchasing women, was illegal. In keeping with state policy, Maoist era marriages were characterized by simplicity, if not austerity, and modest betrothal gifts. Economic differences between rural households were not significant, nor did

marriage expenditures factor into the production of prestige. In most cases, marriage was parentally arranged, with a few rare instances of "free marriage" (*ziyou*) involving couples who met while working in temporary jobs outside the village (on road crews or in urban factories), with the men then bringing their brides back to East Wind.

53 The marriage laws of 2001 and of 2003 make no provision for exemptions for Han communities based on ethnic practices.

54 Many of those involved in kidnapping rings are simply criminals, but at the receiving end, the households that purchase brides in this way are similar to those of the households of bride abductors.

4. Biopolitics

1 At the time of my last visit in the summer of 2011, there was no longer a charge for using the toilets.

2 Visitors in 1999 reached nearly three million, including fifteen thousand a day during the Spring Festival (McKhann 1999, 2).

3 The romanticism associated with Naxi love suicides was not invented solely by tourists. Since 1949, isolated incidents have persisted in both Lijiang Town and the countryside, and age-mates of those who committed suicide often place flowers on their graves. Many Naxi intellectuals and young people in Lijiang sympathize with the dead, whom they see as having acted to avoid arranged marriages.

4 The term "prostitute" is used here not to denigrate sex workers but to translate local terminology. The judgment-free term "sex worker" does not convey the local disdain for these women.

5 Many Naxi, informed by Confucian and residual Maoist-era sensibilities, valued education and government service over employment in business. In Lijiang, the presumed connection between state-sector employment and education was reflected in the popular use of the term "teacher" as a respectful form of address for state-sector administrators. In the 1990s, it seemed to me that almost a quarter of Lijiang's population was called "teacher," despite their playing no role in the education system.

6 In standard Chinese, the phrase is *buyong zijide qian, buyong zijide liangshi, buyong zijide laopo*. The last part of the saying is a double entendre, meaning both "not having sex with one's own wife" and "having sex with someone else's wife."

7 This was true primarily for taxi drivers, entrepreneurs, and hotel hostesses. For urbanites, it was unthinkable to marry a rural laborer.

8 Men who continued to work in low-paying, state-sector jobs were seen as lacking initiative and going nowhere. In 1997, old friends who fit this description told of their plans to leave such positions. Some middle-aged men lamented that they had no option but to wait for retirement.

9 The high-paying, private-sector jobs available to young, beautiful women—such as, in Lijiang, tour guides, hotel hostesses, and beauticians—were a new phenomenon, part of a national trend in urban employment fostered by the rise of consumer culture. Women eating from the "rice bowl of youth" and associated with glamour and fragility were set against the state-sector employees who ate from the iron rice bowl associated with job security and low pay (Zhen 2000, 94, 98).

10 Despite popular construction of state- and private-sector labor as distinct realms, these categories became increasingly porous. As state work units were required to make a

profit, many turned to operating businesses. Both the Lijiang Forestry and Public Security Bureaus ran hotels, and the Ministry of Culture opened a nightclub featuring dancing and karaoke.

11 According to news reports, women rescued from such abductions may be suicidal and face considerable stigma after returning to their communities.

12 Lijiang folk healers began advertising their "secret inherited method" (*zhuchuanmifang*) for treating fox stench in the 1980s. I was not able to establish when treatments in hospitals first became available.

13 Most cases of witchcraft I learned about involved in-marrying women from mountain villages. The one exception was a man who had a uxorilocal marriage, which is associated with male hypergamy. The marriages of all the accused entailed upward mobility, and the resulting witchcraft accusations sought to exclude those perceived as polluted and inferior from community membership.

14 Although the fox spirit is typically portrayed as evil in the fox-spirit genre, some tales from the Qing dynasty do not fall into this pattern. In a story by Pu Songling, a benevolent fox spirit marries and bears human children for her husband. However, as Monschein (1988, 415) has argued, even such a spirit is an outsider whose behavior would not be tolerated by the societies in which the tales were told.

15 Sex and death are associated with extreme pollution in Lijiang (Rock 1972) and throughout China (see J. Watson 1988, 109).

16 The persistence of the fox as a symbol of female evil, deception, and illicit sexuality is visible in Ang Lee's film *Crouching Tiger, Hidden Dragon* (2000). The film's villain, who has killed the hero's master, is named Jade Fox. Viewers learn that Jade Fox was the master's lover and that she poisoned him because he was unwilling to share his knowledge of Chinese martial arts (*wushu*) with her. In classic foxlike fashion, Jade Fox eludes capture by disguising herself as a young woman's governess; from that position, she deceives her enemies and can corrupt her charge by providing a dangerous model of female agency. The film was very popular in the United States, but Ang Lee has said that it was intended for Chinese audiences, for whom the villain's name is extremely evocative.

17 Stories in the femme fatale genre range from "The Story of the White Snake" (Baishezhuan), in which a demon poses as a seductive woman and brings ruin to her lovers (McLaren 1994, 11), to hand-copied fiction from the Cultural Revolution featuring Black Peony and other seductresses who lure men to their deaths (Link 1989, 28). In the 1990s, "The Story of the White Snake" was standard reading for Lijiang elementary school students.

18 I refer here to definitions of fox stench that describe it as incurable, the dominant strain in popular discourse. However, as noted above, in the late 1990s medical and folk treatments for fox stench continued to be marketed.

19 As Unschuld (1985, 234) has shown, during the Republican era the Chinese absorbed models of "Western" medicine, notions of cause and therapy whose values and structures reflected Western industrial society of the nineteenth and twentieth centuries. Chen Yinke ([1937] 1980) explicitly distanced his understanding of fox stench from beliefs in "traditional" Chinese medicine that attribute bodily conditions to "blood" (*xue*) and environment (*qi*). He presented fox stench as hereditary, implying that his understanding was consistent with a Western scientific-medical approach.

20 The male entrepreneur with a wife and mistress is not marked by an exceptional body; rather, it is his consumption of sex that gives him an aura of masculine prestige. Masculinity is tied to character (to traits such as risk taking), not bodily attributes.

21 Ironically, women employed in the state sector, who narrated many of these taxi driver stories, did not emerge as the new model of feminine labor. Although their positions were implicitly idealized, their prestige as workers was not enhanced. Rather, these less demanding, lower-paying, and lower-status jobs in the state sector were simply "naturalized" as "more feminine" and compatible with the "modern priorities" of women as wives and mothers that were being promoted by the contemporary socialist state.

22 This was a sixty-six page booklet with colored advertisements marketing products and services to Lijiang residents. Stacks of this booklet were given away at the local supermarket.

23 These interventions may be likened to cosmetic surgery in a global context.

5. Marketing Difference

1 The June 2005 issue of the Australian National University's *Chinese Heritage Quarterly* featured an article about this litigation surrounding Naxi Ancient Music. The litigation explicitly concerned cultural heritage.

2 The Chinese musicologist, Wu Xueyuan, began studying ethnic music in Yunnan in 1961. He is an expert on *dong jing* music in Yunnan. He is currently senior editor of Yunnan Art Research Institute (Yunnan Yishu Yanjiusuo) and associate director of the Chinese Traditional Music Association (Zhongguo Chuantong Yinyue Xuehui). Wu is the author of *Instrumental Ethnic Folk Music of Yunnan, China* (Yunnan zhongguo minzu minjian qiyou).

3 More information on how tourism is promoted by the central government may be found on the China National Tourism Administration (CNTA) website.

4 Recent research by Tom Mullaney indicates that the categories were subsequently redefined to include the Miao and Yao. During the Republican era, however, the Naxi defined their ancestry only in relation to Mongol, Tibetan, and Han groups.

5 UNESCO played an advisory role in Lijiang's development, and UNESCO's notions of authenticity led to the removal of neon signs and Nike shoe stores from Lijiang's Old Town.

6 *Remeicuo* is a form of Naxi vocal music originally performed in Tacheng and the fifth district (He Wenguang, personal communication, 2011).

7 According to ethnomusicologist Helen Rees, it is not clear that *xiyue* is Naxi because there are contradictory explanations of its origin as Mongolian or Han (2000, 66, 67). *Remeicuo*, while a distinctly local form, is also shaped by strong "inter-ethnic influences" (ibid., 59), a point Wu also made by noting that similar forms are practiced by ethnic groups in other parts of Yunnan (Wu 2005). According to Rees, *remeicuo* was originally performed at funerals "before and after 1949," and *xiyue* dates back to the mid-eighteenth century (2000, 59, 67).

8 I spoke with a middle-aged Chinese couple, originally from Jiangxi, whose grandson had purchased one of the lanterns for this purpose. The couple, intellectuals who live in Pasadena, California, told me they would never have permitted their grandson to purchase the lantern had they known that the origin of the practice was funerary.

9 If the dancers were not Naxi, presumably the performance would have been deemed in-authentic, even if the dancing was faithful to Naxi practice. Town residents' perception of Da Tiao equates its authenticity with the genealogical essence of the dancers them-selves. The dance resembles the fusion of biology and performance, in which biology signifies ownership.

10 United Nations Educational, Scientific and Cultural Organization, About World Heri-tage, http://whc.unesco.org/en/about.

11 While ideas of ethnic ownership predate the neoliberal era, the logic of neoliberalism, in which ethnic phenomena are linked to inherent rights, is a recent arrival in Lijiang and in China.

12 The term "ethno-commodity" was coined by Comaroff and Comaroff (2009, 20).

13 The Lijiang People's Court is a "mid-level court" (zhongji fayuan). The case was later appealed to the provincial level, and the Yunnan High Court (Yunnan Gaoji Fayuan) upheld the verdict, although it reduced the awards to ¥50,000 ($7,733) against *Arts Criticism* and ¥10,000 ($1,547) against Wu. According to a performer in the Lijiang mu-sic scene who is familiar with this case, as of the summer of 2011 not a cent of the award had been collected.

14 The phenomenon of interethnic marriage mentioned in chapter 3 is largely a post-1949 practice.

15 There are now toilets at the entrance of the Old Town. These were initially pay toilets but are now free.

16 Some Lijiang residents complained that it was difficult for them to own or operate a business in the Old Town due to "black hands," or criminal networks, that demanded various types of payoffs. Others noted that while there were many Lijiang people with property in the Old Town, they lacked the connections to open a guesthouse and had to resort to renting out their property. According to their estimates, a guesthouse with fif-teen rooms might clear a profit of $200,000 or $300,000 per year, while owners of such property would share $15,000 annually if renting out a space that could be renovated to create a guesthouse of that size. Most Old Town homes might have between a half and a third of such a space.

17 In a similar vein, new furnished condominiums (marketed to foreigners) located at the base of Jade Dragon Mountain are decorated with carved teak woodwork and artifacts from Thailand. Shops in Lijiang's Old Town sell artifacts that are represented as being from Lijiang but are actually imported from Tibet and Nepal.

18 Three thousand workers lost their jobs because of the ensuing factory closings. By 1996, eight thousand households (twelve thousand people) had been persuaded to move out of the Old Town so that it could be developed as a tourist site (Wai 2001, 8, 9).

19 Xuan has discussed the time he spent in prison in a radio interview. Although he de-picts himself as a former political prisoner, other Lijiang residents have contested that description. (April 7, 2008, www.radio.86.co.uk.)

20 Based on Rock's description of Lijiang, Lijiang County attempted to change its name to "Shangri-la" as a means of promoting tourism. However, Zhongdian County did it first and has been profiting handsomely from the name change ever since (Hillman 2003; Hillman and Henfry 2006, 257).

21 While critical of these developments, scholars such as Rofel (2007) have suggested that recent court cases in other parts of China involving intellectual property and fraud

illustrate the legal privileging of the individual over the collective and reveal new constructions of morality corresponding to the ascension of neoliberal over socialist-era values.

Conclusion. Forgetting the Madman and Remembering the Ancient Tea Horse Road

1 Young men from the Lijiang basin have migrated to other urban centers to work as laborers. In Lijiang's mountain villages this was also the case, but a number of rural men in mountain villages who were unable to find jobs remained behind. Many of these young men face difficulties finding wives due to their poor financial situations. In Pagoda Hill Village, there is a small group of aging bachelors in their thirties and forties who are considered too old and too poor to attract wives.

2 The owner of one of the most lavish recently built hotels in Lijiang, which cost more than ¥1 billion to construct, lives in Kunming and owns several other hotels and businesses.

3 The information about quotas came from an Old Town shop owner. According to Su and Teo, the Committee of World Heritage Management and Conservation of Lijiang Ancient Town (CWHMC) sought to raise local participation in the Old Town tourist economy by stipulating that, after 2003, only locals could apply for business licenses to sell souvenirs or provide tourist services there (2009, 158). It is not clear how effective this strategy has been because outside business people who make arrangements with local residents are able to sidestep this regulation.

4 Dissatisfaction runs in both directions. Migrant shopkeepers complain that they will be fined ¥300 per day if they fail to wear ethnic clothing or hang signs that do not conform to regulations requiring Chinese, English, and *dongba* characters to be written on wooden signs with yellow paint. Other merchants complained of local corruption and claimed that officials and police could be paid off if one failed to observe these regulations.

5 Here I borrow Ferguson's phrase to describe the discourse of modernization (2002, 139).

6 Lijiang officials understand the prestige associated with the Memory of the World Register as contributing to the aggrandizement of the Naxi and beneficial for tourism in Lijiang.

7 The state's promotion of scholarship is also part of this mission. The state-funded Yunnan Academy of Social Sciences (YASS) established an institute, the Centre of World Heritage Studies, devoted to the research and documentation in support of the creation of new forms of World Heritage. According to their website, one of their current projects concerns Pu'er tea.

8 Su and Teo have argued that, on balance, Lijiang's urban residents have profited from the tourist economy, but this assessment takes account only of urban residents who owned homes in Old Town or property in Beimenpo, the adjacent Lion Hill neighborhood also graced with traditional architecture. Many of Lijiang's urban residents lived in the new town before the development of tourism and have not benefited from the new economy. According to informants, most Old Town residents owned homes in shared courtyards. Hence, they did not have sufficient space to open their own guesthouses. It was common for one or two families to rent their homes to an entrepreneur

with the financial resources to remodel a courtyard (two or three homes) and pay each household the equivalent of a year's local income (¥6,000–8,000) for the rental.

9 Zheng told me many times, however, that he did not subscribe to the beliefs associated with *dongba* culture.

10 One of the villagers, Old Dong, recounted with irritation how the village had originally selected Fu as village leader. Fu had brought a large container of beer to the election; the young village men drank it and then elected him village leader. Old Dong complained that the villagers should not have chosen so capriciously, that Fu was a "beer village leader" (*pijiu cunzhang*) who had bought the election with alcohol. Old Dong described the position of village leader as important, one that should have been filled by someone who would use this authority properly.

11 By the summer of 2010, five years after my interviews about the madman and the brick factory, residents of East Wind Village reported receiving a few thousand *yuan* per household (equivalent to one or two months' salary for an urban worker) for ten years of rent for the first brick factory. The village leader is reported to have made a substantial profit on the deal. Villagers complained that the young people spent the money in a couple of months, and then more land was rented to create a second brick factory. The lease for the first factory expires soon, but the land has been destroyed (paved over in places and the soil polluted in others) and cannot be used for farming.

12 The Ancient Tea Horse Road is also known simply as the Tea Horse Road.

13 The museum features enlarged reproductions of photos taken by Joseph Rock, a small assortment of pottery, a few tools, and a wooden saddle, with few artifacts on display despite its commodious premises.

14 Bulag has noted that the claim that the Han are indigenous to Inner Mongolia was used to bolster justifications for political representation and power in Inner Mongolia (Bulag 2003).

15 As Hevia (2001) has illustrated, cultural heritage projects, like that in Chengde, engage in a re-narration of regional ethnic and national history. Communities embrace calls for preservation, such as the Pu'er Declaration, based on promises of economic development and the alleviation of poverty.

16 The apparently neutral concept of "opening" land for agriculture might involve the migration of sedentary agriculturalists to a region previously used for herding, displacing groups who subsist by raising livestock (Bulag 2003).

17 Hu has been the general secretary of the Chinese Communist Party since 2002, president of the People's Republic of China since 2003, and chairman of the Central Military Commission since 2004.

18 I do not intend to suggest, however, that such groups do not include individuals or collectivities guided by entrepreneurial motivations.

REFERENCES

ENGLISH-LANGUAGE SOURCES

Adams, Vincanne. 1992. "The Production of Self and the Body in Sherpa-Tibetan Society." In *Anthropological Approaches to the Study of Ethnomedicine*, edited by M. Nichter, 149–89. Philadelphia: Gordon and Breach Science Publishers.

———. 1996a. "Karoake as Modern Lhasa, Tibet: Western Encounters with Cultural Politic." *Cultural Anthropology* 11 (4): 51–146.

———. 1996b. *Tigers of the Snow and Other Virtual Sherpas*. Princeton, NJ: Princeton University Press.

Ahearn, Laura. 2001. *Invitations to Love: Literacy, Love Letters, and Social Change in Nepal*. Ann Arbor: University of Michigan Press.

Ahern, Emily. 1975. "The Power and Pollution of Chinese Women." In *Women in Chinese Society*, edited by M. Wolf and R. Witke, 193–214. Stanford, CA: Stanford University Press.

———. 1981. *Chinese Ritual and Politics*. Cambridge, U.K.: Cambridge University Press.

Anagnost, Ann. 1985. "The Beginning and End of an Emperor." *Modern China* 11 (2): 147–76.

———. 1988. "Politics and Magic in Contemporary China." *Modern China* 13 (1): 40–61.

———. 1989. "Prosperity and Counter-Prosperity: The Moral Discourse on Wealth in Post-Mao China." In *Marxism and the Chinese Experience*, edited by A. Dirlik and M. Meisner, 210-34. Armonk, NY: M. E. Sharpe.

———. 1992. "Socialist Ethics and the Legal System." In *Popular Protest and Political Culture in Modern China*, edited by J. Wasserstrom and E. Perry, 177–205. Boulder, CO: Westview Press.

———. 1993. "The Nationscape: Movement in the Field of Vision." *Positions* 1 (3): 585–606.

———. 1997. *National Past-times: Narrative, Representation, and Power in Modern China*. Durham, NC: Duke University Press.

———. 2004. "The Corporeal Politics of Quality (Suzhi)." *Public Culture* 16 (2): 189–208.

Anderson, Benedict. 1983. *Imagined Communities: Reflections on the Origin and Spread of Nationalism*. London: Verso.

Appadurai, Arjun. 1990. "Disjuncture and Difference in the Global Cultural Economy." *Public Culture* 2 (2) (Spring): 1-24.

Asad, Talal. 1975. *Anthropology and the Colonial Encounter*. London: Ithaca Press.

———. 1993. *Genealogies of Religion: Discipline and Reason of Power in Christianity and Islam*. Baltimore, MD: Johns Hopkins University Press.

Ayres, Barbara. 1974. "Bride Theft and Raiding for Wives in Cross-cultural Perspective." *Anthropological Quarterly* 47 (3): 238–52.

Barlow, Tani. 1991. "Theorizing Woman: Funu, Guojia, Jiating (Chinese Woman, Chinese State, Chinese Family)." *Genders* 10 (1): 132–60.

Barmé, Geremie. 1996. *Shades of Mao: The Posthumous Cult of the Great Leader*. Armonk, NY: M. E. Sharpe.

———. 2005. "Litigation Surrounding Nakhi Ancient Music." *China Heritage Quarterly* (The Australian National University) 2 (June).

———. 2008. "Painting over Mao." *China Beat* (August 12).

Barth, Fredrik, ed. 1969. *Ethnic Groups and Boundaries*. Boston: Little, Brown and Company.

Bates, Daniel. 1974. "Normative and Alternative Systems of Marriage among the Yoruk of Southeastern Turkey." *Anthropological Quarterly* 47 (3): 270–87.

Bates, Daniel, Francis Conant, and Ayse Kudat. 1974. "Introduction: Kidnapping and Elopement as Alternative Systems of Marriage." *Anthropological Quarterly* 47 (3): 233–37.

Bell, Catherine. 1992. *Ritual Theory, Ritual Practice*. New York: Oxford University Press.

Blekinge. 2010. *Investment and Trade Promotion in Kunming*. Kunming, China: Blekinge Investment and Trade Promotion Office.

Bloch, M., and J. Perry. 1982. *Death and the Regeneration of Life*. Cambridge, U.K.: Cambridge University Press.

Blum, Susan. 1992. "Ethnic Diversity in Southwest China: Perceptions of Self and Other." *Ethnic Groups* 9: 267–79.

———. 2001. *Portraits of Primitives*. Lanham, MD: Rowan & Littlefield.

Blumenfield Kedar, Tami. 2010. "Scenes from Yongning: Media Creation in China's Na Villages." PhD diss., University of Hawai'i.

Bockman, Harald. 1987. "Naxi Studies in China: A Research Report." Manuscript. University of Norway, Oslo.

Boon, James. 1990. *Affinities and Extremes: Crisscrossing the Bittersweet Ethnology of East Indies History, Hindu-Balinese Culture and Indo-European Allure*. Chicago: University of Chicago Press.

Bossen, Laurel. 1992. "Chinese Rural Women: What Keeps Them Down on the Farm?" Paper presented at the Harvard University and Wellesley College Conference "Engendering China," February 7–9.

Bourdieu, Pierre. 1984. *Distinction: A Social Critique of the Judgment of Taste*. Cambridge, U.K.: Cambridge University Press.

Brown, Melissa. 1996. "On Becoming Chinese." In *Negotiating Ethnicities in China and Taiwan*. Berkeley, CA: Institute of East Asian Studies.

Brownell, Susan. 2009. "The Beijing Olympics as a Turning Point? China's First Olympics in East Asian Perspective." *Asia-Pacific Journal Japan Focus* 23 (4).

Brukman, Jan. 1974. "Stealing Women among the Koya of South India." *Anthropological Quarterly* 47 (3): 304–13.

Bulag, Uradyn. 1998. *Nationalism and Hybridity in Mongolia*. Oxford, U.K.: Oxford University Press.

———. 2000. "Ethnic Resistance with Socialist Characteristics." In *Chinese Society: Change, Conflict and Resistance*, edited by E. Perry and M. Selden, 178–97. New York: Routledge.

Carlitz, Katherine. 1994. "Desire, Danger and the Body." In *Engendering China*, edited by C. Gilmartin, G. Hershatter, L. Rofel, and T. White, 101–24. Cambridge, MA: Harvard University Press.

Cattelino, Jessica. 2010. "The Double Bind of American Indian Need-Based Sovereignty." *Cultural Anthropology* 25 (2): 235–62.

Chan, A., R. Madsen, and J. Unger. 2009. *Chen Village: Revolution to Globalization*. Berkeley: University of California Press.

Chao, Emily. 1990. "Suicide, Ritual and Gender Transformation among the Naxi." *Michigan Discussions in Anthropology* 9 (Spring): 61–74.

———. 1995. "Depictions of Difference." PhD diss., University of Michigan.

———. 1996. "Hegemony, Agency and Re-presenting the Past." In *Negotiating Ethnicities in China and Taiwan*, edited by M. Brown. Berkeley, CA: Institute of East Asian Studies.

———. 2003. "Dangerous Work: Women in Traffic." *Modern China* 29 (1): 71–107.

———. 2005. "Cautionary Tales: Marriage Strategies, State Discourse and Women's Agency in a Naxi Village in Southwestern China." In *Cross-Border Marriages: Gender and Mobility in Transnational Asia*, edited by N. Constable, 34-52. Philadelphia: University of Pennsylvania Press.

Chau, Adam. 2005. "The Politics of Legitimization and the Revival of Popular Religion in Shaanbei, North Central China." *Modern China* 31: 236–78.

Cheung, Siu-woo. 1995. "Representation and Negotiation of Miao/Ge Identities in Southeast Guizhou: A Preliminary Report." In *Negotiating Identities in China and Taiwan*, edited by M. Brown. Berkeley: University of California Press.

Chio, Jenny. 2010. "China's Campaign for Civilized Tourism: What to Do When Tourists Behave Badly?" *Anthropology Newsletter* (November 30): 14–15.

Chow, Rey. 1995. *Primitive Passions: Visuality, Sexuality, Ethnography, and Contemporary Chinese Cinema*. New York: Columbia University Press.

Chung, Olivia. 2007. "The Bubble Bursts for Pu'er Tea." *Asia Times*. Asia Times online LDT.

Clifford, James, and George Marcus. 1986. *Writing Culture: The Poetics and Politics of Ethnography*. Berkeley: University of California Press.

Cohen, Myron L. 1976. *House United, House Divided: The Chinese Family in Taiwan*. New York: Columbia University Press.

———. 1988. "Souls and Salvation: Conflicting Themes in Chinese Popular Religion." In *Death Ritual in Late Imperial and Modern China*, edited by J. Watson and E. Rawski, 180–202. Berkeley: University of California Press.

———. 1993. "Cultural and Political Inventions in Modern China: The Case of the Chinese 'Peasant.'" *Daedalus* 122 (2): 151–70.

Comaroff, Jean. 1981. "Healing and Cultural Transformation: The Tswana of Southern Africa." *Social Science and Medicine* 15 (B): 367–78.

———. 1985. *Body, Power, Spirit of Resistance*. Chicago: University of Chicago Press.

Comaroff, John. 1987. "Sui Genderis: Feminism, Kinship Theory and Structural Domains." In *Gender and Kinship: Essays toward a Unified Analysis*, edited by J. Collier and S. Yanagisako, 53–85. Stanford, CA: Stanford University Press.

———. 1996. "Ethnicity, Nationalism, and the Politics of Difference in an Age of Revolution." In *The Politics of Difference: Ethnic Premises in a World of Power*, edited by E. Wilmsen and P. McAllister, 162–83. Chicago: University of Chicago Press.

Comaroff, J., and J. Comaroff. 2009. *Ethnicity, Inc.* Chicago: University of Chicago Press.

Conant, Francis. 1974. "Frustration, Marriage Alternatives and Subsistence Risks among the Pokot of East Africa: Impressions of Co-variance." *Anthropological Quarterly* 47 (3): 314–26.

Constable, Nicole. 2005. *Cross-Border Marriages: Gender and Mobility in Transnational Asia*. Philadelphia: University of Pennsylvania Press.

Cowie, A. P., and A. Evison. 1988. *Concise English-Chinese, Chinese-English Dictionary*. Oxford, U.K.: Oxford University Press.

Croll, Elizabeth. 1983. *Chinese Women since Mao*. New York: M. E. Sharpe.

Crossley, Pamela K. 1990. "Thinking about Ethnicity in Early Modern China." *Late Imperial China* 11 (1): 1–34.

Crossley, P., H. Siu, and D. Sutton. 2006. *Empire at the Margins: Culture, Ethnicity and Frontier in Early Modern China*. Berkeley: University of California Press.

Darragon, Frederique. 2009. "The Star-Shaped Towers of the Tribal Corridor of Southwest China." *Journal of Cambridge Studies* 4 (2): 67–83.

Davis, Deborah. 2005. "Urban Consumer Culture." *China Quarterly* 183: 692–709.

Davis, Sara. 2005. *Song and Silence: Ethnic Revival on China's Southwest Borders*. New York: Columbia University Press.

De Groot, J. J. M. 1907. *The Religious System of China*. Vol. 5. Leiden: E. J. Brill.

Diamond, Norma. 1988. "The Miao and Poison: Interactions on China's Southwest Frontier." *Ethnology* 27 (1): 1–25.

Dikötter, Frank. 1992. *The Discourse of Race in Modern China*. Stanford, CA: Stanford University Press.

———. 1995. *Sex, Culture, and Modernity in China: Medical Science and the Construction of Sexual Identities in the Early Republican Period*. Honolulu: University of Hawai'i Press.

Doré, Henri. 1918. *Researches into Chinese Superstitions*. Vol. 5. Translated by M Kennelly. Shanghai: T'usewei Printing Press.

Douglas, Mary. 1966. *Purity and Danger: An Analysis of Concepts of Pollution and Taboo*. London: Routledge and Kegan Paul.

Dreyer, June. 1976. *China's Forty Millions*. Cambridge, MA: Harvard University Press.

Duang, Songting. 2000. "A Heritage Protection and Tourism Development Case Study of Lijiang Ancient Town China." Report submitted to UNESCO Office of the Regional Advisor for Culture in Asia and the Pacific, Bhaktaphur.

Duara, Prasenjit. 1988. "Superscribing Symbols." *Journal of Asian Studies* 47 (4): 778–95.

———. 1995. *Rescuing History from the Nation*. Chicago: University of Chicago Press.

Ebrey, Patricia. 1981. "Introduction." In *Marriage and Inequality in Chinese Society*, edited by R. Watson and P. Ebrey, 1–24. Berkeley: University of California Press.

———, ed. 1993. *Chinese Civilization: A Source Book*. New York: The Free Press.

Eliade, Mircea. 1964. *Shamanism*. Princeton, NJ: Princeton University Press.

Elvin, Mark. 1984. "Female Virtue and the State in China." *Past and Present* 104: 111–52.

———. 1989. "Tales of Shen and Xin: Body-Person and Heart-Mind in China during the Last 150 Years." In *Fragments for a History of the Human Body*, vol. 2, edited by Michel Feher. New York: Zone.

Evans, H. 2002. "Past, Perfect, or Imperfect: Changing Images of the Ideal Chinese Wife." In *Chinese Femininities and Chinese Masculinities*, edited by S. Brownell and J. Wasserstrom. Berkeley: University of California Press.

Fairbank, J., and S. Teng. 1941–42. "On Ch'ing Tributary System." *Harvard Journal of Asiatic Studies* 6: 135.

Farquhar, Judith. 1996. "Market Magic: Getting Rich and Getting Personal in Medicine after Mao." *American Ethnologist* 23 (2): 239–57.

———. 2005. "Biopolotical Beijing: Pleasure, Sovereignty, and Self-Cutltivation in China's Capital." *Cultural Anthropology* 20 (3): 303–27.

Fei, Xiaotong. (1947) 1992. *From the Soil: The Foundations of Chinese Society*. Berkeley: University of California Press.

Feng, H. Y., and J. K. Shyrock. 1935. "The Black Magic in China Known as Ku." *Journal of the American Oriental Society* 55: 1–30.

Ferguson, James. 2002. "Global Disconnect: Abjection and the Aftermath of Modernism." In *The Anthropology of Globalization*, edited by J. Inda and R. Rosaldo, 136–53. Malden, MA: Blackwell.

Fitzgerald, C. P. 1949. *The Tower of Five Glories*. London: Cresset Press.

Foucault, Michel. 1977. *Discipline and Punish: The Birth of a Prison*. New York: New Pantheon Books.

———. 1980. *The History of Sexuality*. New York: Vintage.

Friedman, Edward. 1994. "Reconstructing China's National Identity: A Southern Alternative to Mao-Era Anti-Imperialist Nationalism." *Journal of Asian Studies* 53 (1): 67–91.

Garver, J. W. 2006. "The Development of China's Overland Transportation Links." *China Quarterly* 185: 1–22.

Gates, Hill. 1996. *China's Motor: A Thousand Years of Petty Capitalism*. Ithaca, NY: Cornell University Press.

Gilroy, Paul. 1987. *There Ain't No Black in the Union Jack*. Chicago: University of Chicago Press.

Gladney, Dru C. 1994. "Representing Nationality in China." *Journal of Asian Studies* 53 (1): 93–123.

Gong, Qian. 1993. "Findings in Dongba Study." *China Daily* (September 24): 5.

Goodman, David. 2004. "The Campaign to 'Open Up the West': National, Provincial-Level and Local Perspectives." *China Quarterly* 178: 317–34..

Goullart, Peter. 1955. *Forgotten Kingdom*. London: John Murray.

Graham, David C. 1928. "Religion in Szechuan Province, China." *Smithsonian Miscellaneous Collections* 80 (4). Washington, DC: Smithsonian Institution.

Grewal, Inderpawl, and Caren Kaplan, eds. 1994. "Introduction." In *Scattered Hegemonies: Postmodernity and Transnational Feminist Practices*. Minneapolis: University of Minnesota Press.

Grunfeld, A. Tom. 1985. "In Search of Equality: Relations between China's Ethnic Minorities and the Majority Han." *Bulletin of Concerned Asian Scholars* 17 (1): 54–67.

Guha, Ranijit, and Gayatri Spivak, eds. 1988. *Selected Subaltern Studies*. New York: Oxford University Press.

Guldin, Gregory E. 1987. "Anthropology in the People's Republic of China: The Winds of Change." *Social Research* 54 (4): 757–78.

———. 1990. *Anthropology in China*. Armonk, NY: M. E. Sharpe.

Gupta, Akhil, and James Ferguson, eds. 1997. *Culture, Power, Place: Explorations in Critical Anthropology*. Durham, NC: Duke University Press.

Han, Almaz. 1995. "Who Are the Mongols? Ethnicity, Authenticity, and the Politics of Representation in Inner Mongolia, People's Republic of China." In *Negotiating Ethnicities in China and Taiwan*, edited by M. Brown. Berkeley, CA: Institute of East Asian Studies.

Handler, Richard. 1988. *Nationalism and the Politics of Culture in Quebec*. Madison: University of Wisconsin Press.

Handlin, Joanna. 1975. "Lü K'un's New Audience: The Influence of Women's Literacy on Seventeenth-Century Thought." In *Women in Chinese Society*, edited by M. Wolf and R. Witke. Stanford, CA: Stanford University Press.

Hansen, Mette. 1999. *Lessons in Being Chinese: Minority Education and Ethnic Identity in Southwestern China*. Seattle: University of Washington Press.

Harrell, Stevan. 1990. "Ethnicity, Local Interests, and the State: Yi Communities in Southwest China." *Comparative Studies in Society and History* 32 (3): 515–48.

———. 1995. "Introduction: Civilizing Projects and the Reaction to Them." In *Cultural Encounters on China's Ethnic Frontiers*. Seattle: University of Washington Press.

———. 2001. "The Anthropology of Reform and the Reform of Anthropology: Anthropological Narratives of Recovery and Progress in China." *Annual Review of Anthropology* 30: 139–61.

Harvey, David. 1989. *The Condition of Postmodernity: An Enquiry into the Origins of Cultural Change*. Cambridge, MA: Blackwell Publishers.

———. 2005. *A Brief History of Neoliberalism*. Oxford, U.K.: Oxford University Press.

He, Duanqi, ed. 1993. *Lijiang Natural Scenery and Customs*. Kunming, China: Yunnan Art Publishers.

He, Wanbao, ed. 1992. *The Art of Naxi Dongba Culture*. Kunming, China: Yunnan Art Publishers.

Heberer, Thomas. 1989. *China and Its National Minorities: Autonomy or Assimilation?* Armonk, NY: M. E. Sharpe.

Hershatter, Gail. 1993. "The Subaltern Talks Back: Reflections on Subaltern Theory and Chinese History." *Positions* 1 (1): 103–30.

Hevia, James. 2001. "World Heritage, National Culture and the Restoration of Chengde." *Positions* 9 (1): 219–43.

Hillman, Ben. 2003. "Paradise under Construction: Minorities, Myths and Modernity in Northwest Yunnan." *Asian Ethnicity* 4 (2): 175–88.

Hillman, Ben, and Lee-Anne Henfry. 2006. "Macho Minority: Masculinity and Ethnicity on the Edge of Tibet." *Modern China* 32: 251–72.

Hobsbawm, Eric. 1983. *The Invention of Tradition*. Cambridge, U.K.: Cambridge University Press.

Hoffman, Lisa. 2008. "Post-Mao Professionalism: Self-enterprise and Patriotism." In *Privatizing China Socialism from Afar*, edited by L. Zhang and A. Ong. Ithaca, NY: Cornell University Press.

Honig, Emily. 1996. "Native Place and the Making of Chinese Ethnicity." In *Remapping China*, edited by G. Hershatter, E. Honig, and R. Stross. Stanford, CA: Stanford University Press.

Honig, E., and G. Hershatter. 1988. *Personal Voices: Chinese Women in the 1980's*. Stanford, CA: Stanford University Press.

Hsieh, Andrew, and Jonathan Spence. 1980. "Suicide and the Family in Pre-modern Chinese Society." In *Normal and Abnormal Behavior in Chinese Culture*, edited by A. Kleinman and T. Lin, 29–94. Hingham, MA: D. Reidel Publishing Company.

Hsu, Francis. 1967. *Under the Ancestor's Shadow*. Stanford, CA: Stanford University Press.

Huang, Yunsong. 1988. *Lijiang*. Kunming, China: Yunnan People's Publishers.

Hyde, Sandra. 2001. "Sex Tourism Practices on the Periphery: Eroticizing Ethnicity and Pathologizing Sex on the Lacang." In *China Urban: Ethnographies of Contemporary Culture*, edited by N. Chen, C. D. Clark, S. Z. Gottschang, and L. Jeffrey, 143–64. Durham, NC: Duke University Press.

————. 2007. *Eating Spring Rice: The Cultural Politics of AIDS in Southwest China*. Berkeley: University of California Press.

Information Office of the State Council of the People's Republic of China. 1999. "Ethnic Minorities Policy in China." White Paper. New York: Permanent Mission of the People's Republic of China to the UN.

Jacka, Tamara. 2005. "Finding a Place: Negotiations of Modernization and Globalization among Rural Women in Beijing." *Critical Asian Studies* 37 (1): 51–71.

Jacobs, Andrew. 2009. "A County in China Sees Its Fortune in Tea Leaves until a Bubble Bursts." *New York Times* (January 16).

Jackson, Anthony. 1971. "Kinship, Suicide, and Pictographs among the Nakhi." *Ethnos* 36 (1): 52–93.

————. 1979. *Na-Khi Religion: An Analytical Appraisal of the Na-Khi Ritual Texts*. The Hague: Mouton Publishers.

Jackson, Jean. 1995. "Culture, Genuine and Spurious." *American Ethnologist* 22 (1): 3–27.

Johnson, Chalmers. 1962. *Peasant Nationalism and Communist Power*. Stanford, CA: Stanford University Press.

Judd, Ellen. 1989. "Niangjia: Chinese Women and Their Natal Families." *Journal of Asian Studies* 48: 525–44.

————. 1994. *Gender and Power in Rural North China*. Stanford, CA: Stanford University Press.

Kammerer, Cornelia. 1988. "Territorial Imperatives: Akha Ethnic Identity and Thailand's National Integration." In *Ethnicities and Nations*, edited by R. Guideri, F. Pellizzi, and S. Tambiah, 259–92. Houston: University of Texas Press.

Keene, Donald. 1961. "Introduction." In *Four Major Plays of Chikamatsu*, 1-38. Translated by D. Keene. New York: Columbia University Press.

————. 1984. "Characteristic Responses to Confucianism in Tokugawa Literature." In *Confucianism and Tokugawa Culture*, edited by P. Nosco, 120–37. Princeton, NJ: Princeton University Press.

Klein, Naomi. 2007. *The Shock Doctrine: The Rise of Disaster Capitalism*. New York: Metropolitan Books.

Kristof, Nicholas. 1992. "China's Newest God: The Godless Mao." *New York Times*, June 2.

Kudat, Ayse. 1974. "Institutional Rigidity and Individual Initiative in Marriages of Turkish Peasants." *Anthropological Quarterly* 47 (3): 288–301.

Lamely, Harry. 1981. "Subethnic Rivalry in the Ch'ing Period." In *The Anthropology of Taiwanese Society*, edited by E. Martin and H. Gates, 182–318. Stanford, CA: Stanford University Press.

Lattimore, Owen. 1962. *Studies in Frontier History: Collected Papers, 1928–1958*. London: Oxford University Press.

Lavely, William. 1991. "Marriage and Mobility under Rural Collectivism." In *Marriage and Inequality in Chinese Society*, edited by R. Watson and P. Ebrey, 286–312. Berkeley: University of California Press.

Leach, Edmund. 1954. *Political Systems of Highland Burma: A Study of Kachin Social Structure*. Cambridge, MA: Harvard University Press.

Lee, Robert H. 1979. "Frontier Politics in the Southwestern Sino-Tibetan Borderlands during the Ch'ing Dynasty." In *Perspectives on a Changing China*, edited by J. Fogel and W. Rowe, 35–68. Boulder, CO: Westview Press.

———. 1982. "Food Supply and Population Growth in Southwest China, 1250–1850." *Journal of Asian Studies* 41 (4): 711–46.

Lee, S., and A. Kleinman. 2000. "Suicide as Resistance in Chinese Society" In *Chinese Society: Change, Conflict and Resistance*, edited by E. Perry and M. Selden, 221–40. London and New York: Routledge.

Levine, Marilyn. 1987. "Caste, State, and Ethnic Boundaries in Nepal." *Journal of Asian Studies* 46 (1): 71–88.

Lévi-Strauss, Claude. 1966. *The Savage Mind*. Chicago: University of Chicago Press..

Liechty, Mark. 2005. "Carnal Economies: The Commodification of Food and Sex in Kathmandu." *Cultural Anthropology* 20 (1): 1–38.

Lijiang Naxi Autonomous Prefecture. 1990. *Dongba Culture of the Ethnic Naxi in Brief*. Lijiang, China: Lijiang Naxi Autonomous Prefecture.

Link, Perry. 1989. "Hand-Copied Entertainment Fiction from the Cultural Revolution." In *Unofficial China*, edited by R. Madsen and P. Pickowicz. Boulder, CO: Westview Press.

Litzinger, Ralph. 2000. *Other Chinas*. Durham, NC: Duke University Press.

———. 2004. "The Mobilization of Nature: Perspectives from Northwest Yunnan." *China Quarterly* 178: 448–504.

Lockwood, William. 1974. "Bride Theft and Social Maneuverability in Western Bosnia." *Anthropological Quarterly* 47 (3): 253–68.

Lu Guang Sheng and Katherine Chong Siewkeng. 2010. *Yunnan—GMS (Greater Mekong Subregion): Economic Cooperation in the Context of "Bridgehead Strategy."* Singapore: East Asian Institute, National University of Singapore.

Lu, Xun. 1981. "The New-Year Sacrifice." In *The Complete Stories of Lu Xun*, edited by X. Yang and G. Yang, 153–71. Bloomington: Indiana University Press.

Mackerras, Colin. 1995. *China's Minority Cultures*. New York: St Martin's Press.

MacInnis, Donald. 1989. *Religion in China Today: Policy and Practice*. New York: Orbis Books.

Makley, Charlene. 2002. "On the Edge of Respectability: Sexual Politics in China's Tibet." *Positions: East Asia Cultures Critique* 10 (3): 575–630.

———. 2007. *The Violence of Liberation*. Berkeley: University of California Press.

Mallee, H. 2000. "Migration, Hukou and Resistance in Reform China." In *Chinese Society: Change, Conflict and Resistance*, edited by E. Perry and M. Seldon, 83–101 London: Routledge.

Mao Tse-tung. 1969. *Quotations from Chairman Mao Tse-tung*. Beijing: Foreign Language Press.

Mann, Susan. 1987. "Widows in the Kinship, Class and Community Structures of Qing Dynasty China." *Journal of Asian Studies* 46 (1): 37–56.

———. 1991. "Grooming a Daughter for Marriage: Brides and Wives in the Mid-Ch'ing Period." In *Marriage and Inequality in Chinese Society*, edited by R. Watson and P. Ebrey, 204–30. Berkeley: University of California Press.

———. 1994. "Learned Women in the Eighteenth Century." In *Engendering China*, edited by C. Gilmartin, G. Hershatter, L. Rofel, and T. White, 27–46. Cambridge, MA: Harvard University Press.

———. 1997. *Precious Records: Women in China's Long Eighteenth Century*. Stanford, CA: Stanford University Press.

Martin, Emily. 1988. "Gender and Ideological Differences in Representations of Life and Death." In *Death Ritual in Late Imperial and Modern China*, edited by J. Watson and E. Rawski, 164–79. Berkeley: University of California Press.

Mathews, R. H. 1931. *A Chinese-English Dictionary*. Shanghai: China Inland Mission and Presbyterian Mission Press.

McKhann, Charles. 1989. "Fleshing Out the Bones: The Cosmic and Social Dimensions of Space in Naxi Architecture." In *Ethnicity and Ethnic Groups in China*, edited by C. Chiao and N. Tapp. New Asia Academic Bulletin 8. The Chinese University, Hong Kong.

———. 1995. "The Naxi and the Nationalities Question." In *Cultural Encounters on China's Ethnic Frontiers*, edited by S. Harrell. Seattle: University of Washington Press.

———. 1999. "The Good, the Bad, and the Ugly: Observations and Reflections on Tourism Development in Lijiang, China." Paper presented at the International Conference on Anthropology, Chinese Society, and Tourism, Kunming, China.

McLaren, Anne. 1994. "The Chinese Femme Fatale: Stories from the Ming Period." *East Asian Studies Series No. 8*. Sydney, Aus.: University of Sydney; Honolulu: University of Hawai'i Press.

———. 2001. "Marriage by Abduction in Twentieth-Century China." *Modern Asian Studies* 35 (4): 953–84.

Miller, Lucien. 1994. *South of the Clouds: Tales from Yunnan*. Translated by G. Xu, L. Miller, and X. Kun. Seattle: University of Washington Press.

Monschein, Ylva. 1988. *Der Zauber der Fuchsfee: Entstehung und Wandel eines "Femme Fatale"—Motivs in der chinesischen Literatur*. Frankfurt: Haag + Herchen.

Moseley, George. 1973. *The Consolidation of the South China Frontier*. Berkeley: University of California Press.

Mueggler, Erik. 1991. "Money, the Mountain, and the State: Power in a Naxi Village." *Modern China* 17 (2): 188–226.

———. 2001. *The Age of Wild Ghosts*. Berkeley: University of California Press.

Naquin, Susan, and Evelyn Rawski. 1987. *Chinese Society in the Eighteenth Century*. New Haven, CT: Yale University Press.

Nosco, Peter. 1984. "Introduction: Neo-Confucianism and Tokugawa Discourse." In *Confucianism and Tokugawa Culture*, 3–26. Princeton, NJ: Princeton University Press.

Notar, Beth. 2006. *Displacing Desire: Travel and Popular Culture in China*. Honolulu: University of Hawai'i Press.

Oakes, Tim. 2007. "Welcome to Paradise! A Sino-American Joint Venture Project." In *China's Transformations: The Stories beyond the Headlines*, edited by L. Jensen and T. Weston, 240–64. Lanham, MD: Rowman & Littlefield.

Ocko, Jonathan. 1991. "Women, Property, and Law in the People's Republic of China." In *Marriage and Inequality in Chinese Society*, edited by R. Watson and P. Ebrey, 313–46. Berkeley: University of California Press.

Ooms, Herman. 1984. "Neo-Confucianism and the Formation of Early Tokugawa Ideology: Contours of a Problem." In *Confucianism and Tokugawa Culture*, edited by P. Nosco, 27–61. Princeton, NJ: Princeton University Press.

Ortner, Sherry. 1995. "Resistance and the Problem of Ethnographic Refusal." *Comparative Studies in Society and History* 37 (1): 173–93.

———. 1996. *Making Gender: The Politics and Erotics of Culture*. Boston: Beacon Press.

———. 2011. "Neoliberalism." *Anthropology of This Century* 1 (May).

Ortner, Sherry, and Harriet Whitehead. (1981) 1984. "Introduction: Accounting for Sexual Meanings." In *Sexual Meanings*, 1–27. Cambridge, U.K.: Cambridge University Press.

Osgood, Cornelius. 1963. *Village Life in Old China*. New York: The Ronald Press Company.

Overmyer, Daniel. 1985. "Values in Chinese Sectarian Literature: Ming and Ch'ing Pao-chuan." In *Popular Culture in Late Imperial China*, edited by D. Johnson, A. Nathan, and E. Rawski, 219–54. Berkeley: University of California Press.

Perdue, P. 2005. *China Marches West: The Qing Conquest of Central Eurasia*. Cambridge, MA: Harvard University Press.

Perry, Elizabeth. 1985. "Rural Collective Violence: The Fruits of Recent Reforms." In *The Political Economy of Reform in Post-Mao China*, edited by E. Perry and C. Wong, 175–92. Cambridge, MA: Harvard University Press.

Pierterse, Jan Nederveen. 1996. "Varieties of Ethnic Politics and Ethnicity Discourse." In *The Politics of Difference*, edited by E. Wilmsen and P. McAllister, 25–44. Chicago: University of Chicago Press.

Pomeranz, Kenneth. 1997. "The Cult of the Goddess of Taishan." In *Culture and State in Chinese History: Conventions, Accommodations, and Critiques*, edited by T. Huters, R. Bin Wong, and P. Yu. Stanford, CA: Stanford University Press.

Potter, Sulamith, and Jack Potter. 1990. *China's Peasants: The Anthropology of a Revolution*. Cambridge, U.K.: Cambridge University Press.

Pun Ngai. 2003. "Subsumption or Consumption? The Phantom of Consumer Revolution in 'Globalizing' China." *Cultural Anthropology* 18 (4): 469–92.

Rapp, Rayna. 1987. "The Gender Politics of Euro-American Kinship Analysis." In *Gender and Kinship: Essays toward a Unified Analysis*, edited by J. Collier and S. Yanagisako, 119–31. Stanford, CA: Stanford University Press.

Rawski, Evelyn. 1988. "A Historian's Approach to Chinese Death Ritual." In *Death Ritual in Late Imperial China*, edited by J. Watson and E. Rawski, 20–34. Berkeley: University of California Press.

———. 1996. "Re-envisioning the Qing: The Significance of the Qing Period in Chinese History." *Journal of Asian Studies* 55 (4): 829–50.

Rees, Helen. 2000. *Echoes of History: Naxi Music in Modern China*. Oxford, U.K.: Oxford University Press.

Rock, Joseph. 1937. "Studies in Na-Khi Literature: The Birth and Origin of Dto-mba Shi-lo and The Na-khi Hazhipi." *Bulletin de l'Ecole Française d'Extrême-Orient* 37 (1): 1–119.

———. 1939. "The Romance of K'a-mä-gyu-mi-gyki." *Bulletin de l'Ecole Française d'Extrême-Orient* 39 (1): 1–152.

———. 1947. *The Ancient Kingdom of the Southwest*. Cambridge, MA: Harvard University Press.

———. 1959. "Contributions to the Shamanism of the Tibetan-Chinese Borderland." *Anthropos* 54 (5): 796–818.

———. 1963a. *The Life and Culture of the Nakhi Tribe of the China-Tibet Borderland*. Wiesbaden, Germany: Verzeifchnis der Orientalischen Handschriften in Deutschland, Supplementband 2.

———. 1963b. *Na-Khi Manuscripts*. Edited by K. Janert. Wiesbaden, Germany: Franz Steiner Verlag.

———. 1972. *A Na-khi-English Encyclopedic Dictionary*. Rome: Istituto Italiano per il Medio ed Estremo Oriente, Serie Orientale Roma.

Rofel, Lisa. 1999. *Other Modernities: Gendered Yearnings in China after Socialism*. Berkeley: University of California Press.

———. 2007. *Desiring China: Experiments in Neoliberalism, Sexuality, and Public Culture*. Durham, NC: Duke University Press.

Rohter, Larry. 1994. "China Becomes Theme Park, but Cultural Debate Remains Real." *New York Times*, January 9.

Rowe, William T. 1989. "Education and Empire in Southwest China: Ch'en Hung-mou in Yunnan, 1733–38." Paper presented at the Conference on Education and Society in Late Imperial China, June 8–14.

———. 1992. "Women and the Family in Mid-Ch'ing Social Thought: The Case of Ch'en Hung-mou." In *Family and Process and Political Process in Modern Chinese History*. Institute of Modern History. Taipei, Taiwan: Academica Sinica.

Samuel, Geoffrey. 1993. *Civilized Shamans: Buddhism in Tibetan Societies*. Washington, DC: Smithsonian Institution Press.

Sangren, P. Steven. 1987. *History and Magical Power in a Chinese Community*. Stanford, CA: Stanford University Press.

Schein, Louisa. 2000. *Minority Rules*. Durham, NC: Duke University Press.

Scott, David. 1994. *Formations of Ritual: Colonial and Anthropological Discourses on the Sinhala Yaktovil*. Minneapolis: University of Minnesota Press.

Shao, Jing. 2006. "Fluid Labor and Blood Money: Economy of HIV/AIDS in Rural Central China." *Cultural Anthropology* 21 (4): 535–69.

Shih, Chuan-kang. 1993. "The Yongning Moso: Sexual Union, Household Organization, Gender and Ethnicity in a Matrilineal Duo local Society in Southwest China." PhD diss., Stanford University.

Siu, Helen. 1989. "Recycling Rituals." In *Unofficial China*, edited by P. Link, R. Madsen, and P. Pickowicz, 121–37. Boulder, CO: Westview Press.

———. 1990. "Where Were the Women? Rethinking Marriage Resistance and Regional Culture in South China." *Late Imperial China* 11 (2): 32–62.

———. 1993. "Cultural Identity and the Politics of Difference in South China." *Daedalus* 122 (2): 19–43.

Smith, Kent C. 1968. "O-erh-T'ai and the Yung-Cheng Emperor." *Ch'ing-Shih Wen-ti* 1 (8): 10–15.

———. 1970. "Ch'ing Policy and the Development of Southwest China: Aspects of Ortai's Governor-Generalship, 1726–31." PhD diss., Yale University.

Spence, Jonathan. 1978. *The Death of Woman Wang*. New York: The Viking Press.

———. 1987. *The Gate of Heavenly Peace*. New York: Penguin.

———. 1990. *The Search for Modern China*. New York: W. W. Norton.

Spiegel, Mickey. 1992. *Freedom of Religion in China*. New York: Asia Watch.

Spivak, Gayatri. 1988. "Subaltern Studies: Deconstructing Historiography." In *Selected Subaltern Studies*, edited by R. Guha and G. Spivak, 3–32. New York: Oxford University Press.

Stacey, Judith. 1983. *Patriarchy and Socialist Revolution in China*. Berkeley: University of California Press.

Stockard, Janice. 1989. *Daughters of the Canton Delta: Marriage Patterns and Economic Strategies in South China 1860–1930*. Stanford, CA: Stanford University Press.

Stoler, Ann. 1995. *Race and the Education of Desire*. Durham, NC: Duke University Press.

Strathern, Marilyn. (1981) 1984. "Self-interest and the Social Good: Some Implications of Hagen Gender Imagery." In *Sexual Meanings*, edited by S. Ortner and H. Whitehead, 166–91. Cambridge, U.K.: Cambridge University Press.

———. 1988. *The Gender of the Gift*. Berkeley: University of California Press.

Stross, Brian. 1974. "Tzeltal Marriage by Capture." *Anthropological Quarterly* 47 (3): 328–46.

Su, Xiaobo, and Peggy Teo. 2008. "Tourism Politics in Lijiang, China: An Analysis of State and Local Interactions in Tourism Development." In *Tourism Geographies* 10 (2): 150–68.

———. 2009. *The Politics of Heritage Tourism in China: A View from Lijiang.* London: Routledge.

Sutton, Barbara. 1974. *In China's Border Provinces: The Turbulent Career of Joseph Rock, Botanist Explorer.* New York: Hastings House Publishers.

Swain, Margaret. 1990. "Commoditizing Ethnicity in Southwest China." *Cultural Survival Quarterly* 14 (1): 26–29.

Tang, Zhilu, and Jin Zhuotong. 1988. *Lijiang.* Beijing: New World Press.

Taussig, Michael. 1980. *The Devil and Commodity Fetishism in South America.* Chapel Hill: University of North Carolina Press.

Terill, Ross. 1984. *The White-Boned Demon: A Biography of Madame Mao Zedong.* New York: Morrow.

T'ien Ju-K'ang. 1988. *Male Anxiety and Female Chastity: A Comparative Study of Chinese Ethical Values in the Ming-Ching Times.* Leiden: E. J. Brill.

Topley, Marjorie. 1975. "Marriage Resistance in Rural Kwangtung." In *Women in Chinese Society,* edited by M. Wolf and R. Witke, 67–88. Stanford, CA: Stanford University Press.

Tsing, Anna. 1993. *In the Realm of the Diamond Queen: Marginality in an Out-of-the-Way Place.* Princeton, NJ: Princeton University Press.

———. 2000. "The Global Situation." *Cultural Anthropology* 15 (3): 327–60.

Turner, Bryan. 1987. *Medical Power and Social Knowledge.* London: Sage Publications.

Unschuld, Paul. 1985. *Medicine in China: History of Ideas.* Berkeley: University of California Press.

Upton, Janet. 1995. "Home on the Grasslands? Tradition, Modernity and the Negotiation of Identity by Tibetan Intellectuals in the PRC." In *Negotiating Ethnicities in China and Taiwan,* edited by M. Brown. Berkeley: University of California Press.

Wai, Ter. 2001. "Report on the Implementation of the Action Plan of Lijiang, China." August 6.

Waley, Arthur. 1960. "Mu-lien Rescues His Mother." In *Ballads and Stories from Tun-huang.* London: Unwin Brothers.

Walsh, Eileen. 2005. "From Nü Guo to Nü'er Guo: Negotiating Desire in the Land of the Mosuo." *Modern China* 31 (4): 448–86.

Wang, Hui. 2004. "The Year 1989 and the Historical Roots of Neoliberalism in China." *Positions* 12 (1): 9–69.

Watson, James. 1985. "Standardizing the Gods: The Promotion of T'ien Hou ("Empress of Heaven") Along the South China Coast 960–1960." In *Popular Culture in Late Imperial China,* edited by D. Johnson, A. Nathan, and E. Rawski, 292–324. Berkeley: University of California Press.

———. 1988. *Death Ritual in Late Imperial and Modern China.* Berkeley: University of California Press.

Watson, Ruby. 1991. "Afterword: Marriage and Gender Inequality." In *Marriage and Inequality in Chinese Society,* edited by R. Watson and P. Ebrey, 347–68. Berkeley: University of California Press.

Watson, Ruby, and Patricia Ebrey, eds. 1991. *Marriage and Inequality in Chinese Society.* Berkeley: University of California Press.

Watts, Michael. 1992. "Space for Everything (a Commentary)." *Cultural Anthropology* 7 (1): 115–29.

Wellens, Koen. 2010. *Religious Revival in the Tibetan Borderlands: The Premi of Southwest China.* Seattle: University of Washington Press.

Weller, Robert. 1995. "Matricidal Magistrates and Gambling Gods: Weak States and Strong Spirits in China." *Australian Journal of Chinese Affairs* 33: 107–24.

Werner, Cynthia. 2009. "Bride Abduction in Post-Soviet Central Asia." *Journal of the Royal Anthropological Association* 15: 314–31.

White, Sydney. 1993. "Medical Discourses, Naxi Identities and the State: Transformations in Socialist China." PhD diss., University of California, Berkeley.

———. 1997. "Fame and Sacrifice: The Gendered Construction of Naxi Identities." *Modern China* 23 (3).

White, Tyrene. 2003. "Domination, Resistance, and Accommodation in China's One-Child Campaign." In *Chinese Society*, edited by E. Perry and M. Selden,102–19. London: Routledge.

Wiens, Herold J. 1954. *China's March towards the Tropics.* Hamden, CT: Shoestring Press.

Williams, Raymond. 1977. *Marxism and Literature.* Oxford, U.K.: Oxford University Press.

Wilmsen, E. 1996. "Introduction" In *The Politics of Difference: Ethnic Premises in a World of Power*, edited by E. Wilmsen and P. McAllister, 1–23. Chicago: University of Chicago Press.

Wolf, Arthur. 1978. "God's Ghosts and Ancestors." In *Studies in Chinese Society.* Stanford, CA: Stanford University Press.

Wolf, A., and C. Huang. 1980. *Marriage and Adoption in China, 1985–1995.* Stanford, CA: Stanford University Press.

Wolf, Margery. 1990. "The Woman Who Didn't Become a Shaman." *American Ethnologist* 17 (3): 419–48.

Wong, Isabel. 1984. "Geming Gequ: Songs for the Education of the Masses." In *Popular Chinese Literature and Performing Arts in the People's Republic of China*, edited by B. McDougall, 112–43. Berkeley: University of California Press.

Wright, Arthur. 1968. "Comment by Arthur Wright." In *China in Crisis*, edited by P. Ho and T. Tsou, 38–41. Chicago: University of Chicago Press.

Wu, David. 1990. "Chinese Minority Policy and the Meaning of Minority Culture: The Example of the Bai of Yunnan China." *Human Organization* 49 (1): 1–13.

———. 1991. "The Construction of Chinese and Non-Chinese Identities." *Daedalus* 120 (1): 159–79.

———. 1993. "Chinese Dance and the Invented Subjects of the Chinese People and the Shaoshu Minzu." Paper presented at the Conference on the Subject of China, January 21–23.

Yan, Hairong. 2003. "The Spectralization of the Rural: Reinterpreting the Labor Mobility of Rural Young Women in Post-Mao China." *American Ethnologist* 30 (4): 578–96.

Yan Ruxian. 1982. "A Living Fossil of a Family: A Study of the Family Structure of the Naxi Nationality of the Lugu Lake Region." *Social Sciences in China* (4): 60–83.

Yan Yunxiang. 2003. *Private Life under Socialism.* Stanford, CA: Stanford University Press.

Yang, C. K. 1961. *Religion in Chinese Society.* Berkeley: University of California Press.

Yang, Fuquan. 2003. "Mentorship of Indigenous Cultural Specialists: A Case Study of Training Dongba, Naxi Priests." In *Landscapes of Diversity: Indigenous Knowledge, Sustainable Livelihoods and Resource Governance in Montane Mainland Southeast Asia.* Kunming, China: Yunnan Science and Technology Press.

———. 2004. "The 'Ancient Tea and Horse Caravan Road,' the 'Silk Road' of Southwest China." *The Silk Road* 2 (1): 29–32.

Yang, Mayfair. 1989. "The Gift Economy and State Power in China." *Comparative Studies in Society and History* 31 (1): 25–54.

Ye, S. 2006. "Consuming Habits: On the Flood of Fakes." In *China Candid,* 137–44. Berkeley: University of California Press.

Young, N., and J. Yang. 2005. "A Provincial Profile and Situation Analysis: Yunnan Situation Analysis." China Development Brief.

Zhang, Hong. 2004. "The Sustainable Development of Tourism in Lijiang." Yunnan University of Finance and Economics.

Zhang, Li. 2001. "Migration and Privatization of Space and Power in Late Socialist China." *American Ethnologist* 28 (1): 179–205.

Zhang, Li, and Aihwa Ong, eds. 2008. *Privatizing China: Socialism from Afar.* Ithaca, NY: Cornell University Press.

Zhen, Zhang. 2000. "Mediating Time: The 'Rice Bowl of Youth' in Fin de Siècle Urban China." *Public Culture* 12 (1): 93–113.

Zweig, D. 2009. "To the Courts or to the Barricades?" In *Chinese Society: Change, Conflict, and Resistance,* edited by E. Perry and M. Selden. London: Routledge.

CHINESE-LANGUAGE SOURCES

Bai Hua. 1980. *Zhong Guo min ger xuan* (A selection of the songs of the Chinese people). Beijing: Renmin yinyue chubanshe.

———. 1988. *Yuanfang you ge nü er guo.* Beijing: Renmin wenxue chubanshe, 1988.

Bian Xie. *Naxizu zizhuxian gaishuo* (General introduction to the Lijiang Naxi Nationality's Autonomous County). Kunming, China: Yunnan minzu chubanshe, 1986.

Chen Yinke. (1937) 1980. *Huchou yu huchou.* In *Han liu tang ju,* 140–42. 1937; Shanghai: Shanghai guji chubanshe.

Cheng, Lie. 2001. *Dongba jitian wenhua* (The cult to heaven among the *dongba*). Kunming, China: Yunnan People's Press.

Guan Xuexuan. 1743. *Lijiang fuzhilue* (The records of Lijiang Prefecture). Reprinted as part of the *Lijiang Naxizu zizhixian shizhi congshu* (Lijiang Naxi Autonomous Prefecture historical series). Lijiang: Lijiang Naxizu Xian xian shi zhi bian wei hui ban gong shi.

Guo Dalie. 1983. "Dongba wenhua yanjiu gaikuang" (A survey of research on *dongba* culture). *Yunnan Minzu Xueyuan Xuebao* (Journal of Yunnan Nationalities Institute).

Fang Guoyu. 1944. "Moxie minzu kao" (Studies on the Mosuo). *Minzuxue Yanjiu Jikan* (Journal of Ethnological Studies).

Fang Guoyu and He Zhiwu. 1982. *Naxi xiangxing wenzipu* (Naxi pictographic dictionary). Kunming, China: Yunnan renmin chubanshe.

He Duanqi, ed. 1993. *Lijiang Natural Scennery and Ethnic Customs.* Kunming, China:Yunnan Technology Press.

He Rugong. 1988. "Jiefang Qian Naxizu de Hunli" (Pre-1949 marriage ritual of the Naxi). In *Naxizu Shehui Lishi Diaocha* (Investigations of Naxi Society and History) 3: 102.

He Zhonghua and Yang Shiguang, eds. 1992. *Naxizu wenxue shi* (The history of Naxi literature). Chengdu: Sichuan minzu chubanshe.

Lijiang Naxizu Zizhuxian Gaikuang (General introduction to the Lijiang Naxi Nationality's Autonomous County). 1986. Kunming, China: Yunnan minzu chubanshe.

Luo Zhufeng. 1987. *Hanyu da cidian* (Encyclopedic Chinese dictionary). Vol. 5. Hong Kong: Sanlian shudian.

Mu Licun. 1995. *Yulong di san guo* (The third kingdom of Yulong).

Wang Wenshao. 1894 *Yunnan tong zhi gao* (Yunnan provincial records). Yunnan: Yunnan tong zhi ju.

Wu Xueyuan. 2003 "Naxi guyue shi shenme dongxi? (What is this thing called Naxi archaic music). Yishu pinglun (Arts Criticism), October (1): 21–26.

Yang Fuquan and Bai Gengsheng. 1993. *Guoji wenhua yanjiu jicui* (Collection of the best international studies on dongba culture). Kunming, China: Yunnan People's Press.

Yang Fuquan. 1993. *Shenqi de Xunqing* (Mysterious love suicide). Hong Kong: San lian shudian.

Zhang Qiyun, Lin Yin, and Gao Ming, eds. 1967. *Zhongwen da cidian* (The encyclopedic dictionary of the Chinese language). Vol. 12. Taipei: Zhongguo wenhua yanjiusuo.

Zhao Xinghua (Emily Chao). 1993. *Xunqing: Yishi*. In *Guoji dongba wenhua yanjiu jicui* (Collected papers of international *dongba* culture studies), edited by F. Yang and G. Bai. Kunming, China: Yunnan minzu chubanshe.

Zhao Yintang. 1984a. "Jiu shehu de Lijiang Naxizu funü: Lamo, zibu" (Lijiang's Naxi women in the old society: Pulling the grinder, sewing with thread, making liquor, and weaving fabric). Yulongshan (Jade Dragon Mountain Journal) 2: 80–85.

———. 1984b. "Jiu shehui de Lijiang Naxizu funü: Paoxiang, paoji, paochengshi"" (Lijiang's Naxi women in the old society: Market routes in the countryside, outside the area, and within the city). Yulongshan (Jade Dragon Mountain Journal) 4: 53–55.

———. 1985a. "Jiu shehui de Lijiang Naxizu funü: Hunyin, lianai, jiating" (Lijiang's Naxi women in the old society: Marriage, love, household). Yulongshan (Jade Dragon Mountain Journal) 3: 50–53.

———. 1985b. "Jiu shehui de Lijiang Naxizu funü: Huocuo" (Lijiang's Naxi women in the old society: Huocuo). Yulongshan (Jade Dragon Mountain Journal) 2: 44–45.

———. 1985c. "Jiu shehui de Lijiang Naxizu funü: Lijiang funü canjia kangzhan" (Lijiang's Naxi women in the old society: Lijiang women participate in the war effort). Yulongshan (Jade Dragon Mountain Journal) 1: 66–67.

———. 1985d. "Jiu shehui de Lijiang Naxizu funü: Wei lai sheng xiu fu" (Lijiang's Naxi women in the old society: For happiness in the next life). Yulongshan (Jade Dragon Mountain Journal) 4: 76–77.

———. 1986. "Jiu shehui de Lijiang Naxizu funü: Kai ban nüxue tang" (Lijiang Naxi women in the old society: Opening a school for women). Yulongshan (Jade Dragon Mountain Journal) 1: 59–61.

INDEX

Page numbers in italic type refer to illustrations.

biopolitics (cont.)
    discourse and bodily difference,
    141–46; semiotics of smell, 138; spatial
    difference and, 77; taxi driver stories
    and, 121–23, 132–34, 140–41, 150–51,
    155; unforeseen consequences of,
    198; Western women and, 133–34;
    witchcraft accusations and, 135–37;
    yinyangren and sexual ambiguity,
    133–34. *See also* pollution vs. purity;
    quality (*suzhi*) discourses
biopower and self-discipline, 29
Bixia Yuanjun, 139
body odor. *See* fox stench (*huchou*)
body politics. *See* biopolitics
boundary construction: culinary practices
    and, 167; dog meat and, 173; ethnic
    classification and, 72, 76–77, 78; fox
    stench and, 123, 142–43, 146; pure
    vs. polluted bodies, 142–43; race,
    pollution, and, 142; religious practices
    and, 74. *See also* ethnic difference
boundary crossing: bodily difference and,
    122; cuisine and, 169; elopement, bride
    abduction, and, 113; fox spirits and,
    139, 140; fox stench and, 142–43, 150;
    in spatial transgression, witchcraft
    poison, and marriage, 132–37; taxi
    drivers and, 149–50; transformation
    of public space and, 128; witchcraft
    accusations and, 136, 149
brick factory in East Wind Village, 188, 190,
    191, 218n11
bride abduction: accounts of, 87–88,
    92–93; arranged marriage and,
    88; compared to other parts of the
    world, 95–96, 113; continuum of,
    84; Coqbbersa myth and, 82–84,
    93–94, 96, 116–18; criticism of, 84;
    as economic strategy, 86–87, 91–92,
    97–98, 118; elopement conflated with,
    210n28; ethnicization of, 119; gender
    and, 90–91, 208n13; go-betweens,
    bride-wealth, and, 89–90, 93–94; Han
    practices, prestige system, and, 85–86;
    imperial expansion and, 84–86; in

mountain communities, 94; origins
    of, 95–97; other ethnicities and, 113;
    regional variation in, 97–98, 118; role
    in social reproduction, 117; trauma of,
    89; water pouring in, 88–89, 208n14;
    wedding celebrations, 90; of widows,
    92, 209n21, 210n24
bridewealth: bride abduction and, 89–90;
    defined, 208n8; elopement and, 104;
    "private money," 209n19; returned as
    dowry, 92
Bridgehead Strategy Plan, 196–97
Brukman, Jan, 95
Buddhism, 31, 138
Bulag, Uradyn, 206n35, 218n14

cadres (*ganbu*), 21–22
Campaign to Open Up the West (Xibu
    Dakaifa), 12, 162, 174, 175, 180, 196
capitalist transformation of Lijiang Town:
    consumer goods and services, 126–27;
    earthquake as boost to, 123; ethnicized
    consumption, minority women, and,
    155; gender and, 146–51; outside
    workers and entrepreneurs, 126;
    private entrepreneurship and gender,
    130–32; sexualization of space and
    power and, 128; tourism and image
    transformation, 124–26. *See also* market
    economy; tourism, development, and
    promotion
carnival troupe advertisement, 143–44, 145
Ceiheeqbbubbeqmil, 82–83, 116–17, 119
Centre of World Heritage Studies (YASS),
    217n7
Chamagudao (Ancient Tea Horse Road),
    193–98, 194
Chen Kaige, 207n43
Chen Yinke, 142–43, 214n19
China Central Television, 178
China Daily, 58–59, 68
China National Tourism Administration,
    158
Christianity, 176
civilization discourse and civilizing project:
    gender associated with, 63–64; Han

family structure and, 85; marriage practices and, 85, 86, 96, 112, 119; spatialization of, 77–78; witchcraft accusations and, 136; written language associated with, 55. See also *wenhua* (culture or civilization)

Civilized Village Campaign, 109, 212nn42–43

class: bride abduction and elopement as strategies, 114–15; decollectivization and, 27–28; in Maoist era, 22, 149; political rituals of, 34; in post-Mao era, 46; ritual and, 36; village dynamics and, 38–43. See also economic inequality

Cloud Summit Grassland, 125–26

cohabitation, 112

collectivized farming, 21–22, 200n3. See also decollectivization

Comaroff, Jean, 162, 165, 216n12

Comaroff, John, 162, 165, 216n12

Committee of World Heritage Management and Conservation of Lijiang Ancient Town (CWHMC), 217n3

commodification: *dongba* culture and, 67–72, 79, 80; ethnicity as commodity, 158, 162–64, 192–93; Red Culture in stores, 4, 199n4; of sex, 128; tourist marketing and, 159. See also market economy; tourism, development, and promotion

Communist Party, 43–44, 180, 202n21

Confucius, 32–33

conscription, avoidance of, 30

consumer goods and services, new availability of, 126–27

Coqbbersa myth, 82–84, 87, 93–94, 96, 116–18

corporate family organization, 209n22

corruption, 188–92

court case. See litigation

cremation, 203n3

Crossley, Pamela K., 85

Crouching Tiger, Hidden Dragon (film; Lee), 214n16

cuisine and food: ethnic mixing of, 169; pollution vs. purity and, 167; restaurants and ethnic difference in Lijiang Town, 168–73. See also dog meat discourse

Cultural Revolution, 4, 23–24; *dongba* religion and, 50–51, 203n1; fiction from, 140, 214n17; and Lei Feng, 23–24; political rituals during, 34; tourism and images from, 4

culture or civilization (*wenhua*), 55, 203n6. See also civilization discourse and civilizing project

Daoism, 205n27

Da Tiao dancers, 163, 216n9

Davis, Sara, 211n41

Dayanzhen. See Old Town (Dayanzhen), Lijiang

death escorts (*peisha*), 201n11

decollectivization: and Communist Party officials, 202n21; defined, 22–23, 200n3; identity failure and, 46; marriage and, 106

deities. See gods or deities

demons: illness and, 26, 29; in "Knife Marching Song," 23, 28; Republican purging of demonology, 141–42

Deng Xiaoping: deification of, 26, 27, 29, 45; postsocialism and, 10; shamanic evocation of, 19, 23, 44–45; taxi amulets and, 202n17

development in minority regions, 192

Diamond, Norma, 105, 136

difference, economic. See economic inequality

difference, ethnic. See ethnic difference

disaster capitalism, 10–11, 182, 199n10

disease, body spectacles of, 143. See also madness and illness

dog meat discourse: defamation lawsuit and, 157–58, 164–65, 166–67; *dongba* culture and, 171; ethnic boundary construction and, 166–67, 171–73; Han as dog eaters, 166–67, 168–69; multiple meanings, 157; restaurants and, 171–73, 172

dogs, in Naxi society, 166

elopement (*paohun*): Bai and Naxi, compared, 211n39; bride abduction conflated with, 210n28; continuum of, 84; criticism of, 84; economic inequality and, 106–9, 112–15; end of craze, 115–16; ethnicization of, 110–16, 119–20; gender and, 107–9; go-betweens and, 100–101, 102; intravillage and intralineage, 105, 211n37; long-distance, 107; meaning of term, 98–99; modern romance and, 104; other ethnicities and, 113; parental preference against, 104; spectrum of, 102–6; state discourse, village perception, and, 109–10; types of, 99–102

entrepreneurship. *See* capitalist transformation of Lijiang Town

essentialization: authenticized marginality of space and gender and, 74–78; bodily abnormality and, 122–23; Coqbbersa myth and, 83–84; *dongba* culture as Naxi focal point, 72; ethnic absolutism and, 114; failed ritual, failed theory, and, 47–48; and Han kidnapping practices, 119; invention of tradition and, 163–64; and local history, 149; market economy and, 178; marriage and, 119–20; "quality" discourse and, 8–10; Tibetans and, 204n19

ethnic absolutism, 113–14

ethnic categorization and construction: biopolitics of, 8–10; as contemporary invention, 114; discreteness, presumption of, 72–74; dog meat metaphor and, 166–67; imperial constructions and, 77; marriage law exceptions and, 116, 212n49; marriage practices and, 84; national identity and discursive creation of difference, 6–8; primordialist, constructivist, and instrumentalist understandings, 161–62. *See also* multiethnic identification

ethnic difference: barbarian classification of, 85; cultivation of, 72–74, 205n33; denunciation of He for ethnic nationalism, 35; dog meat and, 168–69;

dongba culture and, 51–53; elopement as ethnic, 110–16; folk tale translation and, 66; Han prestige and, 76–77; imperial expansion and, 63–64; Maoist suppression of, 52; migration and ethnic tensions, 159–60; minority women representing, 61–63; mountain people and, 75–76; multiethnic identification, 6–8, 9, 51–53; and religion reframed as culture, 34–35; representation of, vs. autonomy, 52; in Republican era, 78, 159, 207n45; restaurants and, 170–73; shift from homogeneity ideal to ethnic diversity ideal, 35–36; tension in and historical context, 158–60; in theme parks, 52–53; tourism and, 11–12; in TV and film, 76

ethnic essentialization. *See* essentialization

ethnicity as commodity: globalization, reinvention of cultural practices, and, 162–64; market economy and, 158; subsidies for production of ethnic goods, 192–93. *See also* capitalist transformation of Lijiang Town; tourism, development, and promotion

ethnic nationalism, 35

ethnic ownership, 165, 174, 216n11

"ethno-commodities," 165, 173, 216n12

ethno-preneurialism, 165

eugenics, 143. *See also* quality (*suzhi*) discourses

evolutionary epistemology, 65, 146, 207n3

factories: closures of, 170, 216n18; in East Wind Village, 188, 190, 191, 218n11

family organization, corporate, 209n22

Fang Guoyu, 204n17

Farquhar, Judith, 8–9

femininity: Bixia Yuanju and behavior standards, 139; body image and, 134; fox-stench surgery and, 155; in Maoist vs. reform era, 132; taxi drivers and, 128; women assessed for labor potential vs., 130. *See also* beauty; gender

litigation (cont.)
216n13; Xuan's action against Liang,
180
"living fossil" category, 125, 146, 161
Longwang, 32
love, romantic, 95, 104, 211nn34–35
love suicides, 86, 125–26, 213n3
Lulu people, 72, 205n32

Mackerras, Colin, 199n5
madman, the: shamanic ritual for, 19,
23–29; later years and death of, 185–88,
187. See also madness and illness
madness and illness: demons and, 26,
29; fox spirits and, 138; kinship
and, 40, 42–43, 202n20; the moral
community and, 29, 186–91; shaman's
desocialization of, 27–29; si and, 42;
social order and, 41; two madmen,
contrast between, 40–41; in Western vs.
Chinese medicine, 202n19
magic: deification of national figures and,
29; historical figures and, 33; Mao
and, 37, 202n17; prohibition on, 34;
witchcraft, 135–37, 214n13. See also
ritual; shamanism and sanba shamans
Makley, Charlene, 204n19
Mann, Susan, 96
Maoism: and ethnic difference, 52; identity
failure and, 45–47; perceptions of,
in "East Wind Village," 21–23, 45;
religious suppression and, 33–34;
renkou suzhi (population quality) and,
143; shamanic evocation of, 23–27;
women's identity under, 132. See also
Cultural Revolution
Maorabilia (Mao memorabilia),
202n17
Mao Zedong: deification of, 26, 27, 29,
34, 45; Quotations from Chairman Mao
Tse-tung, 23–24; second cult of ("Mao
fever"), 37, 199n2, 201n16; shamanic
evocation of, 19, 23, 44–45; statue of,
in Lijiang Town, 3–4, 17
marginality: imperial constructions
of, 77; shamanism and, 44; of women

and mountain people, 74–78. See also
economic inequality; poverty
market economy: exploitation and
resignation under, 188–92; factory
closures and shift to, 174; income gap
and, 183, 184–85; market principle
underlying the state, 162; neoliberal
philosophy and, 158; quota for
local-owned businesses (proposed),
184; rural effects of, 185; shift from
academic representation to, 177; and
social subjectivity, 186–92; value shift
and, 177–78; wealthy investors and,
183. See also capitalist transformation of
Lijiang Town; commodification
marriage, and marriage practices: age and,
209n20, 210n32; bridewealth, 89–90,
92, 104, 208n8, 209n19; capitalist
development, blurring hierarchy, and,
129; child betrothal and arranged, 85–
86, 88, 89, 209n18, 209n20; courtship
in mountain villages, 111–13; courtship
and parental disapproval in the basin,
212n46; disabled sons and, 210n30;
dowries, 38, 89–90, 91–92, 209n17,
209n19, 209n22; costly ceremonies
for, 111; engagement, cancellation of,
91–92; Han, intermarriage with, 169;
hazing of newlyweds, 105, 211n38;
hypergamy, 104, 136, 214n13; imperial
expansion and, 84–86; kidnapping and
sale of women, 107, 119–20; laws, 110,
116, 208n16, 212n49, 212n52, 213n53;
"leading a girl home" (ling guniang hui
jia), 99; in Maoist era, 212n52; in Naxi
communities, 117–18; prestige and
economic status gauged by, 112–15;
romantic courtship as modern, 104,
211nn34–35; rural-urban migration
and, 115–16; siku ritual, 36, 42, 105,
210n25; suicide as resistance to, 86;
syncretic, 105–6; uxorilocal (shangmen),
40, 202n20, 214n13. See also bride
abduction; elopement (paohun)
masculinity, 91, 98, 215n20. See also gender
matriarchal society, exoticized image of, 125

private economy, 147–51; perception of men in, 213n8; shift to Household Responsibility System, 22–23, 46, 106, 200n3, 202n21; "teacher" as term of respect in, 213n5

statues, in Lijiang Town, 3–4

"The Story of the White Snake," 214n17

Strathern, Marilyn, 61

Su, Xiaobo, 217n8

subsidies for production of ethnic goods, 192–93

subsistence agriculture in villages, 21

Suhe village, 195

suicide: fox stench and, 153; for love, 86, 125–26, 213n3; as resistance to marriage practices, 86, 208n10; as tourist point of interest, 125–26

superstition, "feudal," 53, 201n12

Su Xiaokang, 76, 199n9

suzhi (body quality). *See* quality (*suzhi*) discourses

Taoism (Daoism), 205n27

taxi amulets, 37, 202n17

taxi drivers, 152; bodily difference and danger to others, 121, 123, 133–34; and feminine ideal, 155; fox spirits and, 140–41; fox-stench advertisements and, 155; proliferation of taxis, 121–22; stories of danger to, 121–22, 132–33, 150–51

"teacher" as term of respect, 213n5

Tea Horse Road (Chamagudao), 193–98, 194

Temple to the Dragon King (Longwang Miao), 32

Temple to Three Gods (San Shen Miao), 32

Teo, Peggy, 217n8

tertiary economy, 49. *See also* tourism, development, and promotion

theme parks, 52–53

Tian Qing, 165

Tian Zhuangzhuang, 193–95, 207n43

Tibetans, gendered essentialism of, 204n19

toilets, Western-style, 124, 170

tourism, development, and promotion: Ancient Naxi Music and, 160–61; Ancient Tea Horse Road and, 193–98, 194; and backpackers, 168; cuisine, restaurants, and ethnic difference and, 168–69, 170–73; Cultural Revolution images and, 4; *dongba* culture and, 67–72, 79, 201n12, 203n2; earthquake as boost to, 123; ethnic commodification and, 159; ethnic difference and, 11–12; ethnicized consumption, minority women, and, 155; global vs. ethnic ownership and, 164–65; invented traditions and, 162–64; modern identity vs. ancient appearance and, 124, 148; number and origins of tourists, 124–25, 174–75; placemaking and, 168; planning for, 174–76; postsocialism and, 11; restaurants and, 170–73; rural-urban migration of youth and, 115–16; social hierarchies reshaped by, 178–79; state policies and, 158; tertiary economy and, 49; town transformation for, 124, 169–70, 174, 215n5; weddings at Naxi culture yard, 73. *See also* capitalist transformation of Lijiang Town; UNESCO

tradition, invention of. *See* invention of tradition

translation, textual, 58, 66

trickery elopement, 99–100

tusi system, 31–32, 85

tzoguze (a woman with a man's heart), 130

UNESCO: authenticity and, 215n5; Intangible Cultural Heritage list, 160–61, 164, 175–76; Memory of the World Program, 164, 184, 217n6; philosophy of global ownership, 164–65; World Heritage Site designation, 11, 164, 174, 196, 197

unfilial sons, 39

Unschuld, Paul, 214n19

Upton, Janet, 206n35

uxorilocal marriage (*shangmen*), 40, 202n20, 214n13